DISCOVERING PAST BEHAVIOR

LIBRARY OF ANTHROPOLOGY

Editor: Anthony L. LaRuffa

Editorial Assistants: Patricia Kaufman and Phyllis Rafti

Advisory Board: Edward Bendix, Robert DiBennardo,
May Ebihara, Paul Grebinger, Bert Salwen, Joel Savishinsky

SAN CIPRIANO   Life in a Puerto Rican Community
Anthony L. LaRuffa
THE TRAIL OF THE HARE   Life and Stress in an
Arctic Community
Joel S. Savishinsky
LANGUAGE IN AFRICA   An Introductory Survey
Edgar A. Gregersen
OUTCASTE   Jewish Life in Southern Iran
Laurence D. Loeb
DISCOVERING PAST BEHAVIOR   Experiments in the Archaeology of the American
Southwest

Other volumes in preparation

DISCOVERING PAST BEHAVIOR

Experiments in the Archaeology of the American Southwest

EDITED BY

Paul Grebinger

Department of Anthropology, Eisenhower College
Seneca Falls, New York

GORDON AND BREACH
New York   London   Paris

Copyright © 1978 by Gordon and Breach Science Publishers, Inc.

Gordon and Breach Science Publishers, Inc.
One Park Avenue
New York, NY 10016

Gordon and Breach Science Publishers Ltd.
42 William IV Street
London WC2N 4DE

Gordon & Breach
7-9 rue Emile Dubois
Paris 75014

Printed in Great Britain.

Introduction to the Series

One of the notable objectives of the *Library of Anthropology* is to provide a vehicle for the expression in print of new, controversial and seemingly "unorthodox" theoretical, methodological, and philosophical approaches to anthropological data. Another objective follows from the multidimensional or holistic approach in anthropology which is the discipline's unique contribution toward understanding human behavior. The books in the series will deal with such fields as archaeology, physical anthropology, linguistics, ethnology and social anthropology. Since no restrictions will be placed on the types of cultures included, a New York or New Delhi setting will be considered as relevant to anthropological theory and methods as the highlands of New Guinea.

The *Library* is designed for a wide audience and, whenever possible, technical terminology will be kept to the minimum required. In some instances, however, a book may be unavoidably somewhat esoteric and consequently will appeal only to a small sector of the reading population—advanced undergraduate students and graduate students in addition to professional social scientists.

My hopes for the readers are two fold: first, that they will enjoy learning about people; second, and perhaps more important, that the readers will come to experience a feeling of oneness with humankind.

New York City   *Anthony L. LaRuffa*

Preface

The purpose in calling for contributions to this volume was to provide a comprehensive look at Southwestern archaeology through a collection of contemporary essays. As it was originally conceived, broad geographic and temporal coverage would be given to the area through substantive work in an attempt to display both the promise and reward of archaeological research in the Southwestern laboratory. As limitation of space and frequently intractable archaeological data would have it, the present volume falls somewhat short of the original goal. I regret that some whose work I had solicited were unable to contribute.

Contributors were all selected from among Southwesternists who were just emerging from formal academic training. This choice was deliberate as these young scholars stand an academic generation removed from the clash of new and old approaches in anthropological archaeology that has made the 1960's and early 1970's a most exciting time in the development of our subdiscipline. I hoped that this choice might result in some papers not in the mold of *New Perspectives in Archeology* (Binford and Binford, 1968). There is a need for frequent reexamination of the "paradigm" developed by Binford, and possibly his intellectual grandchildren stand the best chance of maintaining their perspective on the heated issues that have led to the radical transformation of archaeology. Several, although not all, of the papers do point to new directions.

The study of Southwestern prehistory has attracted and continues to attract the interest of leading theorists and methodologists in the field of anthropological archaeology. The Southwest has been and continues to be the laboratory in which archaeological theory and method are given their most exacting tests. Archaeologists are attracted by the quality of the preservation of material culture, by the chronological control afforded by dendrochronology and by the economy of scale—small local and regional populations insure that an archaeological experiment can be brought to full completion within the lifetime of individual archaeologists. The Southwest is also a land in which Indian ancestors are still recalled in the lives and minds of their own people. And, too, there is the allure of the postcard Southwest. The charm of improbable land forms juxtaposed against azure sky, and of harsh wastelands relieved by naturally landscaped gardens, has seduced many graduate students into careers as South-westernists.

The students have not been alone. There has been a surge of activity in Southwestern archaeology that is directly attributable to the sudden leap in population growth, especially in Arizona and Colorado during the post World War II era. Much archaeological research over the past two decades has been designed to mitigate the impact of road construction, water conservation and power projects developed to meet the needs of ever greater numbers of people. This population has become a source of revenue from which support for expanded university facilities could be drawn. The role of a growing regional population in making both necessary and possible present levels of archaeological activity is of great interest.

Political developments on the national level also have been important in bringing about present levels of activity in Southwestern archaeology. The fact that the national economy had been pumped up by government spending in support of military activity in Southeast Asia had multifarious ramifications for higher education in general. Monies were available to support the education of graduate students in unprecedented numbers. Teachers with graduate degrees were in demand to meet swelling university enrollments as children of the post World War II baby boom reached their late teens. Anthropology departments in the Southwest, as elsewhere, grew in size to meet the demand for trained professionals. The contributors to this volume were among those graduate students who found in the South-western laboratory the challenging research that was required for their advanced degrees.

In short, through the 1960's and early 1970's archaeological research in unprecedented variety, quantity and scale has been conducted in the Southwest. This period might be referred to as the "Golden Age" of Southwestern archaeology. That such efflorescence in research activity should also coincide with important theoretical transformations in anthropological archaeology is fortuitous. The result is an unusual, if not unique, opportunity to illustrate aspects of new approaches in archaeology from research within a single region. The *Southwest Issue* of the *American Anthropologist* (1954) notwithstanding, *Discovering Past Behavior: Experiments in the Archaeology of the American Southwest* is a first attempt to bring together recent research representative of the region. We may hope that there will be future opportunities to bring together contemporary studies that might serve as a chart of the course that archaeologists followed in their investigation into cultural development in the Southwest.

It is difficult in a work such as this to properly acknowledge everyone who has had a hand in one aspect of it or another. I would like to thank Tony LaRuffa for making it possible. Several people were consulted for suggestions about content and promising sources of papers. I would like to thank Bill Robinson, Mike Schiffer and Jamie Lytle-Webb for their helpful suggestions, some of which I did follow. The contributors have been most patient in what has been admittedly a long time between the first call for papers and their final publication. However, these papers are substantial contributions of current as well as future interest. Judy Zimmerman typed the final manuscript, and never once complained about turgid prose! Ellen Grebinger helped to keep things in perspective, and provided assistance in preparing the index. Only I had control over preparation of the final manuscript and, consequently, accept full responsibility for any persistent imperfections.

Table of Contents

xi

Contents

List of Figures

List of Tables

INTRODUCTION

Southwestern archaeologists are engaged in a rebuilding process. After little more than cursory examination of a regional synthesis of Southwestern archaeology (e.g., Willey, 1966, or Martin and Plog, 1973) one becomes aware that solidly based archaeological knowledge of the past lifeways and processes of cultural development in the Southwest is not at all well-developed. This may come as a surprise to those familiar with the fact that serious archaeological research has been going on in the area for almost 100 years.

Southwestern archaeologists have compiled a vast body of knowledge about the material culture produced by the prehistoric Indians. Also, they do know about the society and culture of contemporary Southwestern Indians. Unfortunately, this has led to the substitution of analogies from present behavior and its material products for archaeologically derived description and explanation of past behavior. Where analogy is accepted as established fact, rather than hypothesis, it is tantamount to creating a history instead of seeking to answer questions about the past. As a result we don't know very much about the actual behavior of the ancestors, or predecessors, of the present inhabitants. Consequently, for the past decade and a half archaeologists have been trying to develop a new understanding of the native peoples of the Southwest. Various aspects of the new understanding, and the fresh approach in archaeological theory and method on which it is based, are well illustrated in this volume.

CONTEMPORARY ARCHAEOLOGICAL SYNTHESIS

There is a useful perspective from which we can view developments in archaeological theory and method over the past 15 years. Arthur Koestler, (as discussed by J. Kestin, 1970: 251) has coined a word, "bisociation," which describes the union of "two independent matrices of perception or reasoning . . . with each other to produce a collision" or frequently a synthesis. This, according to Kestin, is the stuff of discovery. One matrix of reasoning is characterized by the efforts of many to solve problems in terms of its structure all of which lead to blockage (failures in problem solving). Eventually there is a sudden movement out of the blocked matrix of reasoning into a second, differently structured matrix, with a resultant bisociation of the two leading to a new understanding. As Kestin (1970: 255) notes,

1

a bisociation is unexpected because it imaginatively unites skills or modes of thought that have previously and happily led separate and disjoint existence in many minds. Being unexpected . . . it is not, however, random, but comes to a peculiarly predisposed, conditioned mind.

Prior to 1962 archaeological methods of inference were locked into a blocked matrix. The discussion of "theory" by Gordon Willey and Philip Phillips (1958) formally defined the predicament. In retrospect, this work reads like a road sign advising the unsuspecting traveler of a dead end ahead. There were noteworthy efforts to find alternative routes. Walter W. Taylor (1948) had already clearly perceived the predicament. And Raymond H. Thompson's (1958) essay epitomizes the desire to develop new directions, but the inability to discover an epistemology and a logic of inquiry to free archaeology from its impasse.

After 1962 there was a sudden movement out of the blocked matrix into a second, differently structured matrix. This shift is marked by James Deetz's study of Arikara ceramics (1965), and by Lewis Binford's main theoretical contributions (1962, 1964, 1965, 1967, 1968a,b). Theory and method adapted from other fields was adopted. Systems theory and a hypothetico-deductive (H-D) methodology provided a different theoretical and methodological structure for data analysis and new directions for inference. Additional techniques such as multivariate statistics were employed to deal with data now clearly perceived as the products of behavior. Traditional or normative "theory" was discarded, while basic techniques of chronological control and field research, and terminologies that describe time and space dimensions were retained. This was bisociation, a new synthesis.

As I see it (cf. Martin, 1971; Watson, LeBlanc and Redman, 1971; Leone, 1972) there has been a synthesis of five key elements in the so-called "new archaeology," or more accurately, modern synthetic theory of archaeology. Some of these were totally unfamiliar to traditional archaeologists. Others were familiar, but were transformed by their integration with new elements. First, Binford and others embraced (even though they did not fully understand all its ramifications) an entirely new framework for developing knowledge about the past, general systems theory. As a consequence we now view human behavior as a multi-dimensional phenomenon. That is elements of a particular system, for example subsistence, may well cross-cut the traditional categories of culture such as technology, economy, society, and ideology that had so rigidly structured the archaeologist's thinking about past lifeways and cultural development. Also, it has now become possible to think about specific episodes and particular processes of behavior as instances of more general principles that govern the operation of a wide variety of physical, biological and cultural systems.

Second, there is the ecological framework. The environment is viewed as a system that is quite naturally linked with sociocultural systems. Social systems and environmental systems interact in dynamic ways that promote stability or bring about change. Environmental factors are frequently viewed as determiners of the state of a system, that is, whether it will be static, dynamically stable or undergoing major transformations.

A third mode of thought in the new synthesis is the aim of discovering the general processes of stability and change in the development of cultural systems. Contemporary archaeology will make its most important contributions to general anthropology through research designed to generate and test hypotheses about cultural processes. In the use of the term "processual archaeology" to describe the post 1962 period, we frequently confuse this element with the entire synthetic theory of which it is only part.

Fourth, items of material culture are viewed as the material correlates of human behavior. They are the main link between the archaeologist and the behavior of people, interpreted in terms of the systems, ecological and processual frameworks outlined above. This is currently the least explored element in the synthetic theory.

Fifth, and finally, all of the above are integrated by a formal logic of inquiry. We have all been extraordinarily self-conscious about developing a scientific archaeology. The issue of how one does science has centered on the role of deductive vs. inductive reasoning in formulating and testing hypotheses. Following some basic misunderstanding (Fritz and Plog, 1970) this issue seems to have fizzled. The diplomats among archaeologists, and interested bystanders in the philosophy of science, have put us on the course of a normal scientific methodology (Hill, 1972; Levin, 1973; Salmon, 1975).

Most of the fundamental assumptions and theory that underlie the new synthesis will hold their ground. But all of the ramifications of the new understanding were not obvious, even to those who brought it about. Much on-going archaeological research is an effort to strengthen original tenets, to question weak assumptions, to formalize methods and to clarify the potential for the use of archaeological remains in understanding past behavior, especially the creation of a theory of material culture. In short, we continue to attempt to define the limits of a new approach to archaeological inference. All of the papers in this volume contribute toward this end. They also make substantial contributions to our understanding of cultural development in the Southwest.

INTERPRETATIVE SYNOPSIS OF THE ESSAYS

This volume begins with an important cautionary tale, Jamie Lytle-Webb's "Pollen Analysis in Southwestern Archaeology." Southwestern archaeologists have often found simple causation an easy device to explain away large-scale population movement and major cultural developments. Most recently, processual archaeologists have found a convenient *deus ex machina* in climatic change. They rely on reconstructions of past environments and environmental changes based on studies of pollen samples from archaeological contexts. Climatic change, in particular, is inferred where weed pollen shows increases over time relative to declines in tree pollen. As Lytle-Webb points out, however, in samples from archaeological context, such changes may reflect the cultural activities of man. In constructing and living in their villages, people create optimum conditions for the growth of weeds. She has marshalled strong support for this alternative hypothesis from her work at Whiptail and Ushklish ruins in southern and central Arizona, and from her studies of a contemporary Papago village in Arizona, and modern Pueblo fields in New Mexico.

Palynology is a relatively new science in the Southwest. There are still many basic assumptions that will have to be tested. There are important methodological problems that have not yet been resolved. Southwestern archaeologists can take heart in knowing that improvements are on the way. However, they also should pause in any haste to embrace environmental determinism (cf. Reid, this volume; Grebinger, this volume).

Dendrochronology is another of the geosciences that has a venerable association with archaeological studies in the Southwest. Tree-rings have given Southwestern archaeologists (especially those working within the Mogollon and Anasazi areas) control over site, local and regional chronologies that is the envy of archaeologists everywhere. Tree-rings may also be used in the interpretation of past climate. Meade Kemrer's article, "Maximizing the Interpretative Potential of Archaeological Tree-Ring Dates," deals with the problem of fine-tuning tree-ring dates. Much of his discussion is addressed to other dendrochronologists. At the same time, however, he develops interesting cultural interpretations from the condition and distribution of wood specimens collected from historic Navajo sites. For years now dendrochronologists have been urging archaeologists to be as systematic in their collection of tree-ring specimens as in their collection of the other material products of past behavior. Kemrer's work illustrates the potential for discovering significant aspects of extinct behavior from wood samples alone.

Early Man studies are represented in this volume by Larry Agenbroad's investigations at a Chiricahua stage Cochise site in his paper "Cultural Implications from the Distributional Analysis of a Lithic Site, San Pedro Valley, Arizona." The Cochise culture is one manifestation of a widespread Desert tradition that occurs throughout the Southwest and the Great Basin. The Desert tradition succeeds the Big-Game Hunting tradition, and represents a readaptation to increasingly arid post-pluvial conditions. In spite of its importance as a transitional period between the nomadic Big-Game hunters and the development of sedentary life, there has been a lack of scientific interest in the Desert culture (Irwin-Williams, n.d.). In this simple, but well designed distributional analysis, Agenbroad has been able to define aspects of the activity structure and social organization at the Lone Hill site. With the exception of Norman Whalen's San Pedro Valley survey (1971, 1975), there have been no comparable studies of the Cochise, or of the Desert culture, anywhere in the Southwest.

There are no papers in this volume that treat cultural developments between the Archaic or Desert cultures *c.* 500 B.C. and A.D. 1000. This is another of those time periods about which Southwesternists know relatively little, in part a consequence of sparse, unspectacular remains and correspondingly low levels of scientific interest. By comparison, the period after A.D. 1000, one of abundant, often large and spectacular sites, has been the focus of intensive research. The remainder of the papers presented here reflect this research orientation. The three major regional cultural traditions (Anasazi, Mogollon and Hohokam) are represented in that order.

The Chaco phenomenon is the subject of Paul Grebinger's "Prehistoric Social Organization in Chaco Canyon, New Mexico: An Evolutionary Perspective." The Canyon and the archaeological manifestation that is centered on it has received more attention from archaeologists than almost any other in the Southwest. Numerous sites have been excavated, and numerous monographs and papers that describe the material remains have been published. There have been relatively few attempts to synthesize the results of this vast research effort or to construct a general model of cultural development in the Canyon. Two notable exceptions to the paucity of systematic thinking about the Chaco phenomenon include Gordon Vivian's excellent summary of Chaco research, published in conjunction with both a report on excavations at Kin Kletso (with Tom Mathews) and a summary evaluation of tree-ring dates from archaeological sites in the canyon and its vicinity by Bryant Bannister (Vivian and Mathews, 1965). This work is a key that has unlocked the tremendous potential of the Chaco data. The other exception has been Gwinn Vivian's model of social organization that developed out of his early investigation into Chaco water control systems (Vivian, 1970a, 1970b). Grebinger's model was formulated as an alternative to Gwinn Vivian's "An Inquiry into Prehistoric Social Organization in Chaco Canyon, New Mexico" (1970a). Vivian's model of social organization is static, and Grebinger's alternative is dynamic. The development of a pristine rank society is postulated. An attempt is made to account for the rise, and then decline, of this form of social organization. Continuing interest in the archaeology of Chaco Canyon is evident in the development by the National Park Service of a coordinated multi-disciplinary research program and by presentation of a symposium on the "Chaco Phenomenon" (organized by Cynthia Irwin-Williams) at the 49th Pecos Conference. Concerted efforts to produce alternatives such as Vivian and Grebinger have proposed, and research designed to test them, will be necessary in order to achieve new understanding of the behavior of the pre-historic inhabitants of the Chaco.

As archaeologists ask new questions of data, they find old methods in-adequate for developing appropriate answers. One response to the dilemma involves reassessment and refinement of existing methodologies. For example, both Lytle-Webb and Kemrer have shown that it is possible to increase the power of geoscientific techniques that traditionally have been important adjuncts of archaeological research in the Southwest.

Dorothy Washburn's paper "A Symmetry Classification of Pueblo Ceramic Design" illustrates another response to the stress of inadequate methodology, cross-fertilization from other fields of science. As Wash-burn's review of earlier work indicates, ceramic studies hold a venerable position in the history of Southwestern archaeology. In spite of the fact that ceramic analysis has been a consuming passion of many Southwesternists, there have been few significant improvements in the traditional typological method and no innovations that break from it. Washburn has developed a promising new approach to the study of ceramic design. Symmetry analysis is based in principles of geometry and crystallography. Be-sides a clear explication of the new technique, Washburn provides tests of its utility in estimating the nature of interaction between regional popu-lations. Samples of ceramics from the Upper Gila Drainage, El Morro Valley and Salmon ruin are used in the study.

An objective method of stylistic analysis that would allow the South-western archaeologist to investigate the interaction of local and regional populations should prove an invaluable tool. Since the early 1960's South-westernists have been working within an ecological framework, and have been asking and attempting to answer questions about responses of human populations to environmental stress. Usually, where there is evidence of stress we anticipate population movement (e.g., Grebinger, Grebinger and Adam, and Reid, this volume). It should be possible with the assistance of Washburn's symmetry analysis to detect population shifts as perturbations in ceramic design.

Among the most important major archaeological investigations in the

American Southwest have been the Field Museum of Natural History Southwestern Expedition to the Pine Lawn Valley, New Mexico and to east central Arizona, and The University of Arizona Archaeological Field Schools at Point of Pines and Grasshopper ruins in east central Arizona. Present knowledge of the Mogollon cultural tradition is in large part a product of these research efforts. The papers in this volume by Michael Schiffer, "Chipped Stone and Human Behavior at the Joint Site," and Frederick Gorman, "Inventory Operations Research in Southwestern Prehistory: An Example from East Central Arizona," are based on data collected by the Field Museum's Southwestern Expedition. Jeff Reid's paper, "Response to Stress at Grasshopper Pueblo, Arizona," derives from data collected at Grasshopper pueblo. In their papers Schiffer, Gorman and Reid have identified and boldly confronted a crucial issue in archaeological inference.

The theoretical synthesis that has powered archaeological investigation since the early 1960's incorporated a new "sense" of the relationships between behavior and the material products of that behavior. In his early statements (1962, 1965) Binford presented a model of behavior that treats individuals and groups as actors in the context of on-going social systems. System is the important word here. In effect, Binford was attempting to introduce a mode of thinking about the past that was gaining wide acceptance among social scientists. American archaeologists at the time were still operating within a nineteenth century natural scientific framework.

Binford then further introduced the ideotechnic, sociotechnic and technomic classification of material things as a device for linking material products of behavior to the ideological, social and technological subsystems that broadly define all societies. In effect archaeologists could begin to think about the behavioral content of archaeological data in multiple, simultaneous dimensions. The same object can have different import depending upon its systemic contexts. Although most archaeologists no longer bother to acknowledge it, this is a fundamental postulate in the theory of material culture, fundamental to all inferences in contemporary archaeology. It has been one of Binford's most enduring contributions.

But Binford's insight has not been sufficiently powerful to avert an impending crisis of inference in archaeology. The crux of the problem is one that a traditional archaeologist would not find unfamiliar. There is an all too familiar subjective element associated with the generation of test implications from propositions about past behavior, and the inference of patterns of action from patterns of material culture distribution. We each generate expectations of the archaeological record, or read it with a knowledge that has been learned piecemeal. In spite of concerted efforts to force archaeology into the mold of a science, it continues to be unscientific.

Schiffer and Reid have recognized this problem and have attempted similar solutions. Objectivity is achieved by carefully identifying the various law-like propositions that archaeologists assume in the inferencing process, but hardly ever formally acknowledge. These statements are classified into four groups by Schiffer: *correlates* tie material objects to behavior; *c-transforms* are statements about the material culture output of the cultural system; *n-transforms* have to do with changes that affect archaeological sites and material culture remains after occupation of the locality has ceased; and, finally, *stipulations* are statements that may be required in the justification of a specific inference. They provide information about conditions that existed in the past and may have a bearing on the application of the other types of statements described above.

Schiffer's solution is of considerable interest as he succeeds in identifying the weakest members in the inference structure of contemporary archaeology. By formalizing the structure of inference, he hopes to reduce the element of epistemological uncertainty that has characterized archaeological reconstruction of extinct societies and cultural processes up to the present time. The application of the framework to the problem of extracting behavioral information from chipped stone at the Joint site indicates the promise and limitations of the approach. On the one hand, we find that it may now be possible for the archaeologist to probe previously unimagined behavioral potential in the material remains of the past. On the other hand, the requirements for the justification of a single inference have become so cumbersome that archaeology, on the scale that we know it at the present time, cannot be sustained. Research designs with regional focus, and contract archaeology involving mitigation of the impact of construction projects affecting large sites, many sites, and extensive areas of considerable archaeological complexity have become the norm. If archaeologists accept Schiffer's epistemological synthesis, and the rigor it implies, they will have to lower their expectations of the scope of archaeological reports. Or, they will have to find scientifically acceptable means for ordering priorities concerning what it is necessary to discover about the past in any particular archaeological investigation.

One logical choice is to develop and test hypotheses about cultural process in which selected sets of data are employed, as in Reid's study of stress and strain at Grasshopper pueblo. The methodology of this inquiry focuses on identifying strain in the subsistence system during the periods of aggregation and abandonment between A.D. 1275–1400. Among its key features is the use of an explanatory law, "diversity promotes stability," to generate test implications about the response of Grasshopper pueblo people to subsistence stress. Relevant issues concerning chronological control, the relationship between systemic and archaeological contexts, and important assumptions are each treated. Reid has succeeded in incorporating within an explicitly processual analysis the concerns for inference justification that characterize Schiffer's work.

Another alternative is represented in this volume by Frederick Gorman's application of information theory to groundstone and bone tools from the Joint site. Gorman has chosen to illustrate his approach through the analysis of a small portion of the total material culture inventory. He is clearly concerned with certain aspects of the archaeological formation process, primarily the *c-* and *n-transforms* of Schiffer's metalanguage. With respect to the question of "correlates" that relate material remains to past behavior, there is a marked difference. Where Schiffer calls for the formulation of archaeological laws to assist inference, Gorman applies an already established set of propositions from inventory operations research. This ready-made theory allows him to proceed directly to inferences concerning processes of change at the Joint site as these are reflected in changes in the artifact inventory array.

Gorman's paper is an example of recent efforts to explore the potential of general systems theory in the interpretation of still another realm of phenomena, the material remains of past human behavior. When the systems framework was introduced as one of the elements of the modern synthetic theory of archaeology it is doubtful that this outcome was clearly perceived. Nonetheless, archaeologists may yet find general systems theory a fruitful source of statements of relationship between material culture and behavior. If so, then the element of the modern synthetic theory of archaeology that has received least attention, a theory of material culture, will undergo rapid development over the next decade.

Today, as has been the case throughout the history of Southwestern archaeology, research interest in the Hohokam tradition has lagged behind interest in the Mogollon and Anasazi traditions. Until recently, archaeological investigations into the Hohokam have lacked regional focus. Research designs have been developed to deal with site specific problems, and attempts to generalize from single sites to the larger area have not been satisfactory.

Paul Grebinger and David Adam in their paper, "Santa Cruz Valley Hohokam: Cultural Development in the Classic Period," attempt to fill this need with a processual model of cultural development for the Classic period in the Santa Cruz Valley, located in southeastern Arizona. The model derives from the evaluation of some old, and some recently collected data. Multivariate statistical techniques are used in order to discover patterns of intra- and intersite variability in the data. These patterns are interpreted in terms of relationships among Classic period communities through time. A model of cultural development is derived from these observations and interpretations. The utility of the model will depend upon how well it stands up under research designed to check it. Test implications have been generated that may be checked in the normal course of any archaeological work that is carried out in the Santa Cruz Valley, especially contract archaeology and projects of limited scope.

Another new direction in Hohokam archaeology is presented here in William Doelle's "Hohokam Use of Non-Riverine Resources." Archaeological remains that are found scattered in areas between archaeological sites have patterned distributions and significant contextual relationships with features of the environment, both natural and cultural. Southwestern archaeologists have long been aware of these remains, but have paid little attention to them. An appreciation of the information potential of such resources has only emerged with increased attention to questions about cultural process that have a regional focus. Concurrently, efforts to mitigate the impact of the exploitation of the Southwest by business and government have led to the investigation of nonsite remains through contract archaeological projects such as Doelle's for Continental Oil Company at Florence (cf. Goodyear, 1975; Raab, 1976). Doelle's full report (1976) of the CONOCO Project is in many respects a model that others might follow in developing inferences about the past from nearly invisible archaeological remains. He and Frank Bayham, a contributor to the report, use ethnographic observation of contemporary Papago subsistence activities, and imitative experiment in the productive sense of analogy as hypothesis. In the paper that Doelle has contributed to this volume, the reader will find evidence of the careful reasoning that characterizes the larger report. Also, the potential significance of contract archaeology in the future development of Southwestern archaeology is clearly illustrated.

CONCLUSION

The chief aim of this project, which was to bring together original, data based studies that would be representative of the diverse opportunities for, and achievements of, archaeological research in the Southwest, has been attained by the various authors. Among the essays presented here one finds evidence of the metamorphosis of current archaeological theory and method. There are studies designed to test hypotheses about culture process, as well as studies to discover patterns of behavior that might lead to testable hypotheses about processes of cultural development. There are reconstructions of prehistoric social organization and activity structures.

The raw data upon which the studies are based derive from a variety of sources, including field schools where specific research objectives guide excavation, already extant museum and laboratory collections, and published sources.

As in past years, the techniques and methods of archaeological inquiry that are being developed and tested in the Southwest have been adopted widely in the practice of archaeology elsewhere. In addition, the Southwestern laboratory continues to produce data from which archaeologists learn about Southwestern Indian ancestors. But, and perhaps most importantly, what archaeologists are learning about cultural development in the Southwest has applications in the past and present far beyond the geographical boundaries of the region. This is both the promise fulfilled and the exciting prospect for continuing research in the Southwest.

REFERENCES

Binford, L. R. (1962) Archaeology as anthropology. *American Antiquity* **28**, 217–25.
Binford, L. R. (1964) A consideration of archaeological research design. *American Antiquity* **29**, 425–41.
Binford, L. R. (1965) Archaeological systematics and the study of culture process. *American Antiquity* **31**, 1–12.
Binford, L. R. (1967) Smudge pits and hide smoking: the use of analogy in archaeological reasoning. *American Antiquity* **32**, 1–12.
Binford, L. R. (1968a) Archeological perspectives. In *New Perspectives in Archeology*, edited by S. R. and L. R. Binford, pp. 5–32. Aldine, Chicago.
Binford, L. R. (1968b) Some comments on historical versus processual archaeology. *Southwestern Journal of Anthropology* **24**, 267–75.
Binford, S. R. and L. R. Binford (1968) *New Perspectives in Archeology*. Aldine, Chicago.
Deetz, J. (1965) The dynamics of stylistic change in Arikara ceramics. *Illinois Studies in Anthropology* **4**.
Doelle, W. H. (1976) Desert resources and Hohokam subsistence: the Conoco Florence project. *Arizona State Museum Archaeological Series* **103**.
Fritz, J. M. and F. T. Plog (1970) The nature of archaeological explanation. *American Antiquity* **35**, 405–12.
Goodyear, A. C. (1975) Hecla II and III, an interpretative study of archaeological remains from the Lakeshore project, Papago reservation, south central Arizona. *Arizona State University Anthropological Paper* **9**.
Haury, E. W. (editor) (1954) Southwest issue. *American Anthropologist* **36** (4).
Hill, J. N. (1972) The methodological debate in contemporary archaeology: a model. In *Models in Archaeology*, edited by D. L. Clarke, pp. 61–108. Methuen, London.
Irwin-Williams, C. (n.d.) Paleo-Indian and Archaic cultural systems in the Southwestern United States. In *Handbook of North American Indians* (in press).
Kestin, J. (1970) Creativity in teaching and learning. *American Scientist* **58**, 250–7.
Leone, M. P. (1972) Issues in anthropological archaeology. In *Contemporary Archaeology: A Guide to Theory and Contributions*, edited by M. P. Leone, pp. 14–27. Southern Illinois University Press, Carbondale.

Levin, M. E. (1973) On explanation in archaeology: a rebuttal to Fritz and Plog. *American Antiquity* **38**, 387–95.

Martin, P. S. (1971) The revolution in archaeology. *American Antiquity* **36**, 1–8.

Martin, P. S. and F. Plog (1973) *The Archaeology of Arizona—A Study of the Southwest Region*. Natural History Press, Garden City.

Raab, L. M. (1976) The structure of prehistoric community organization at Santa Rosa Wash, southern Arizona. Ph.D. dissertation, Arizona State University, Tempe.

Salmon, M. H. (1975) Confirmation and explanation in archaeology. *American Antiquity* **40**, 459–64.

Taylor, W. W. (1948) A study of archeology. *American Anthropological Association, Memoir* 69.

Thompson, R. H. (1958) Modern Yucatecan Maya pottery making. *Society for American Archaeology, Memoir* 15.

Vivian, G. and T. M. Mathews (1965) Kin Kletso: a Pueblo III community in Chaco Canyon, New Mexico. *Southwestern Monuments Association, Technical Series* **6** (1).

Vivian, R. G. (1970a) An inquiry into prehistoric social organization in Chaco Canyon, New Mexico. In *Reconstructing Prehistoric Pueblo Societies*, edited by W. A. Longacre, pp. 59–83. University of New Mexico Press, Albuquerque.

Vivian, R. G. (1970b) Aspects of prehistoric society in Chaco Canyon, New Mexico. Ph.D. dissertation, The University of Arizona, Tucson.

Watson, P. J., S. A. LeBlanc and C. L. Redman (1971) *Explanation in Archeology: An Explicitly Scientific Approach*. Columbia University Press, New York.

Whalen, N. M. (1971) Cochise culture sites in the central San Pedro drainage, Arizona. Ph.D. dissertation, The University of Arizona, Tucson.

Whalen, N. M. (1975) Cochise site distribution in the San Pedro Valley. *The Kiva* **40**, 203–11.

Willey, G. R. (1966) *An introduction to American archaeology*, Vol. 1, *North and Middle America*. Prentice-Hall, Englewood Cliffs.

Willey, G. R. and P. Phillips (1958) *Method and Theory in American Archaeology*. The University of Chicago Press, Chicago.

Pollen Analysis in Southwestern Archaeology

JAMIE LYTLE-WEBB

California State University at Dominguez Hills

Pollen analysis has been employed in the interpretation of archaeological sites in the Southwest for over 20 years. Increasingly it is being utilized for the reconstruction of environments of sites occupied by prehistoric man. Pollen data from two archaeological sites and one contemporary Indian village in Arizona and several modern pueblo fields in New Mexico indicate the need for a reevaluation and testing of sampling methods in structures and of assumptions concerning the origin of pollen in archaeological sites.

Palynology has been used as an archaeological tool in the Southwest for over twenty years. With the development of processual archaeology in the early 1960's, archaeologists have tended to rely ever more heavily upon the palynologist for assistance in reconstructing past environment. Increasingly, climatic change has been used as a key causal factor in the explanation of processes of culture change (e.g., Hill, 1970). Nonetheless, there are still a number of unresolved problems inherent in the use of pollen analysis in palaeoenvironmental reconstruction.

In this paper I have three main objectives. First, I shall point out the most important problems that palynologists who work in the Southwest encounter in analyzing and interpreting their samples. Second, I present a review of the history and present state of palynology in the Southwest. And, third, I present the results of four recent studies that raise questions concerning the kinds of interpretation about past environments that can be made from pollen collected in archaeological context. This paper is a reexamination of some basic assumptions about the use of archaeological pollen in the interpretation of past environments. It is also a cautionary tale and calls for further attempts to reevaluate the uses of palynology in archaeological interpretation.

ASSUMPTIONS AND BASIC PROBLEMS

The palynologist assumes that when he examines the pollen present in sediment he is viewing the pollen rain in that area at a past time. If he

13

knows what types of pollen are present in the sample he can define or at least describe the wind-pollinated vegetation in the area from which the sample was taken. The size of that area is limited by the topography of the site sampled; a pond would give a more localized picture than a lake. From the vegetation present in the environment it is possible for the palynologist to reconstruct aspects of the climate of the area. The relationship may be expressed as follows:

Pollen sample ⇋ Pollen rain ⇋ Vegetation ⇋ Climate.

Unfortunately, as with many processes, the components of this one have not been fully tested. The palynologist cannot always predict other elements of the equation from knowledge of one element. This problem is being studied (Bryson and Kutzbach, 1974; Davis, Brubaker, and Webb, 1974).

In the arid Southwest some problems arise which do not normally occur in other areas. The most basic of these is the low concentration of pollen in the atmosphere. There are several reasons for low pollen counts. First, a large amount of the desert flora is animal or insect pollinated (zoophilous), while most of the pollen types in the pollen rain are carried by wind (anemophilous). Second, as the Southwest is arid there is a low density of plant cover. This further decreases the amount of pollen in the air. A third factor is the rigorous climatic regime of the area. The combination of high summer temperatures and unreliable precipitation causes many plants to live a marginal existence with minimal resources available for processes such as pollination.

Finally, a fourth factor is laboratory technique. Since Sears (1937) first attempted to extract pollen from desert soils the method has changed drastically. The extraction technique used in the Paleoenvironmental Laboratories at The University of Arizona was formulated by Mehringer (1967). Basically, it consists of a swirl in dilute hydrochloric acid to concentrate the pollen and eliminate carbonates, treatment with concentrated (50 to 70%) hydrofluoric acid to dissolve the silica, washes with concentrated hydrochloric acid and 30% nitric acid to destroy any colloids, followed by a brief wash with 5 to 7% potassium hydroxide or sodium hydroxide to dissolve organic matter. It is possible that the use of caustic acids combined with dilute hydroxides may cause already corroded grains to either become corroded beyond recognition or to disappear. Experimentation with the method continues.

HISTORICAL SKETCH

Sears' (1937) was the first to attempt to extract pollen from alluvial samples collected in the Southwest.[1] Pollen was present in some of his slides but not in quantities sufficient for statistical analysis. The first successful extraction of alluvial pollen from Southwestern samples was performed in conjunction with an archaeological excavation at Ramanote Cave, Santa Cruz County, Arizona, by Anderson (1955).

Since 1955 the use of pollen analysis in archaeological studies has grown in volume and scope. In the late 1950's and early 1960's Martin (1963) analyzed samples from early man sites in southeastern Arizona. Work in this area has been continued by Mehringer and Haynes (1965), Jelinek (1966) and Mehringer, Martin and Haynes (1967).

A new dimension was added by Martin and Sharrock (1964) when they analyzed prehistoric human feces. Kelso (1971) studied human coprolites in relation to floor fill and is presently working with an absolute counting method for pollen in human excrement (Kelso, personal communication). Human coprolites from a rock shelter in southwest Texas analyzed by Bryant (1974) have been used to determine aboriginal diet patterns and seasonality of site occupation. Other palynological research in archaeological sites includes the comparison of archaeological and lacustrine samples (Hevly, 1964), salvage archaeology (Schoenwetter and Eddy, 1964), intra-site comparisons (Hill and Hevly, 1968), and ethnobotanical reconstructions of cultural cycles controlled by the seasons (Bohrer, 1970).

At the present time pollen analysis in Southwestern archaeology may be divided into four nonmutually exclusive areas:

1) interpretation of palaeoenvironment and climate;
2) intra- and inter-site dating;
3) introduction and use of plants by man;
4) extent of man's disturbance of an area.

The interpretation of palaeoenvironment and palaeoclimate is based on the previously mentioned assumption that pollen samples reflect the environment and climate of an area at a certain time. Inter-site dating is in turn based on the palaeoclimatic interpretation. This means that sites yielding samples which show a similar climate or change of climate are

---

[1] By geologic definition "alluvial deposits are formed in stream channels and associated floodplains of individual streams, or as broad alluvial fans or plains where stream braiding dominates an appreciable area." (Krumbein and Sloss, 1963:255). "Alluvial samples" in this chapter refers to those samples which contain a large amount of sand, silt and clay, from which small amounts of pollen must be separated.

contemporaneous or near contemporaneous. Some reports which illustrate this use of palynology include Hevly (1964), Schoenwetter (1962, 1965), Schoenwetter and Eddy (1964). Schoenwetter's chronology is based on the interpretation of effective moisture (Schoenwetter, personal communication).

Analyses concerned with information on man's use of the vegetation in his environment are best exemplified by the previously mentioned human coprolite studies (Martin and Sharrock, 1964; Kelso, 1971; Bryant, 1974). Unfortunately fossil human coprolites are rare or not recognizable in most archaeological sites. However, interpretation of man's use of plants is still possible under the assumption that the pollen rain in a site will include pollen present on vegetal material that man brought into the structures. This is an acceptable assumption since both corn pollen, which is not carried far by the wind (Raynor, Ogden and Hayes, 1972) and squash pollen, which is insect pollinated, have been found in numerous localities in archaeological sites (Schoenwetter, 1962; Bohrer, 1970; Martin and Byers, 1965; Hevly, 1964). Hill and Hevly (1968) employed this assumption in dating and identifying structures within Broken K pueblo, Arizona.

Finally, the use of pollen analysis in order to measure man's disturbance of his immediate physical surroundings is based on the idea that in an area where man is present greater disturbance will occur than in areas untouched by man. This disturbance will favor the growth of certain plants which in turn will increase the amount of that type (or types) of pollen in the pollen rain in the site.

In the Old World the interpretation of pollen diagrams for Mesolithic and younger sites has been based not only on disturbance caused by man but also on major changes in vegetation due to man's cutting and clearing (Godwin, 1944; Keef, Wymer and Dimbleby, 1965; Smith, 1970; Turner, 1970). This aspect has been sadly neglected in pollen interpretations of Southwestern sites. Jelinek (1966) estimates a 35 to 40% increase in pollen from plants favored by disturbance. Martin and Byers (1965) interpret vegetational changes at Wetherill Mesa, Colorado, to be due to man's disturbance.

Pollen analysis in Southwestern archaeological sites has progressed from an initial experimental stage to a time when a reexamination of the basic assumptions is not just desirable, but necessary for further advancement of the science. Controlled studies of archaeological sites as well as modern sites which are based on more primitive life styles would greatly expand our knowledge and enhance our interpretive abilities. My own investigations over the past few years in both types of sites have led me to reconsider some of the basic assumptions that underlie the interpretation of pollen samples from archaeological contexts.

POLLEN IN ARCHAEOLOGICAL CONTEXT:
A REEXAMINATION

POLLEN ANALYSIS AT WHIPTAIL RUIN

Whiptail ruin (Arizona BB:10:3) is a Classic period Hohokam site located about fifteen miles northeast of Tucson in the upper bajada region of the eastern Tucson Basin. The Santa Catalina Mountains are immediately north, Agua Caliente Hill is adjacent on the east, and the Rincon Mountains are south and east of Whiptail ruin. The site, situated on about fifty acres, consists of single and clustered Tanque Verde phase pithouses (Grebinger and Adam, 1974).

The present vegetation of the area is dominated by a creosotebush-bursage (*Larrea tridentata-Franseria dumosa*)[1] association with many saguaros (*Carnegiea gigantea*), various prickly pear and cholla (*Opuntia* spp. and cylindropuntia), and a ground cover of the family types Chenopodiaceae (goosefoot family), Amaranthaceae (pigweed family), and Gramineae (grasses). About a quarter of a mile north of the site is a warm spring which was dammed by man in the early 1900's and now forms a pond. The present vegetation around the pond includes willow (*Salix* sp.), cattail (*Typha* sp.), and other aquatic species of plants. Before the spring was dammed the vegetation was probably typical of both standing water and a cienega-type environment. The effects of the spring might not have been felt farther than a few feet from the mouth due to the high potential evaporation of this climate and the high permeability and porosity of the sediment surrounding the spring.

In the spring of 1969 I was made aware by Paul Grebinger and Bruce Bradley, who were conducting excavations of the site for the Arizona Archaeological and Historical Society, of the possibility of doing a palaeo-environmental study at Whiptail ruin. It was postulated that a palynological analysis of samples from the site might be the best available method for reconstruction of the environment at the time of occupation by the Hohokam. Samples were available, since they had been collected by the archaeologists during the first year of excavation, and interest was keen. No other Hohokam site with enough pollen for 200 grain counts had previously been studied.

Because of the very real possibility that the samples might be sterile (have no pollen or an amount insufficient for analysis) I decided to extract pollen from a variety of locations. Samples from floors, vessels, fill, pits and under artifacts were extracted and analyzed. In addition I took samples from two

---

[1] Scientific and common names are those found in Kearney and Peebles 1960.

stratigraphic columns in two structures, two surface samples and one sample from the dry wash which transects the site. In all, 40 samples were analyzed. Fortunately, all samples contained enough pollen for a 200 grain count, the generally accepted sample number necessary for representative percentages (Martin, 1963).

The results of the counts are shown in Figures 1, 2, and 3. The major

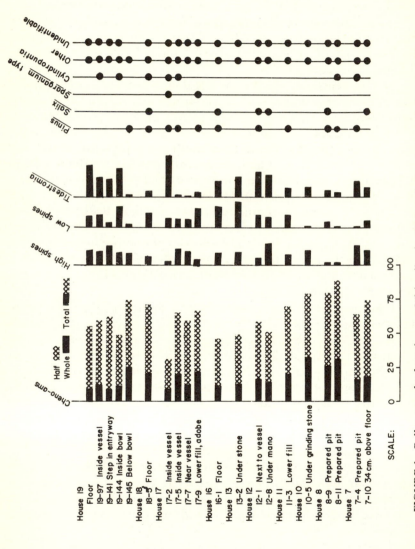

FIGURE 1 Pollen samples from houses, Whiptail ruin, Tucson Basin, Arizona. Pollen types that occur in frequencies of less than 2% are indicated by dots.

pollen types present are cheno-ams, Compositae, and *Tidestromia*. Minor types include pine (*Pinus* sp.), willow (*Salix* sp.), burreed or cattail (*Sparganium* type), and cholla (cylindropuntia).

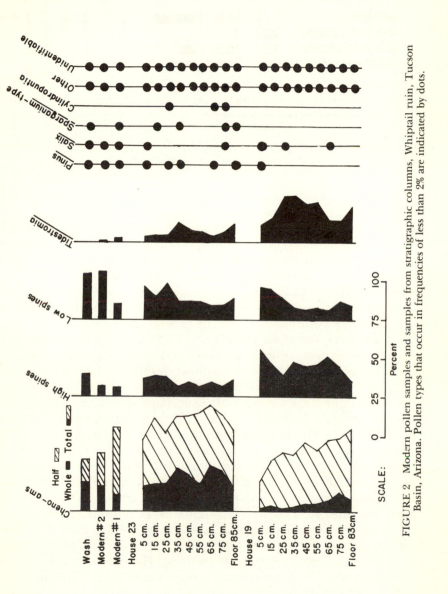

FIGURE 2 Modern pollen samples and samples from stratigraphic columns, Whiptail ruin, Tucson Basin, Arizona. Pollen types that occur in frequencies of less than 2% are indicated by dots.

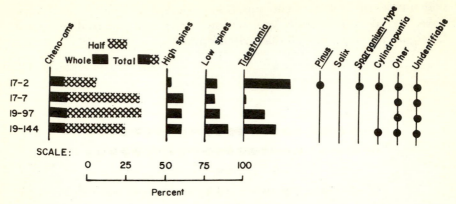

FIGURE 3   Pollen samples from vessels, Whiptail ruin, Tucson Basin, Arizona. Pollen
types that occur in frequencies of less than 2% are indicated by dots.

The group of pollen called cheno-ams is composed of pollen of plants in
the family Chenopodiaceae and the genus *Amaranthus*. Both grow as
weeds in numerous geographical situations in the Southwest, mainly in
disturbed *(Amaranthus)* or saline soils (Chenopodiaceae). The pollen of
the two groups is, with a few exceptions, indistinguishable, so the general
grouping is made. In the site the cheno-ams vary from *c.* 30 to 80% of the
samples (Figures 1 and 3). These percentages are larger than those found in
the modern counts of the Sonoran Desert vegetation at this altitude (Hevly,
Mehringer and Yocum, 1965) and, in general, larger than the modern
surface samples taken at the site (Figure 2). These higher percentages may
be due to two factors, cultural influence and environmental change.

Compositae are members of the sunflower family. In the Southwest they
include the wind pollinated (low spine) false ragweeds and the insect pollinated (high spine) aster, daisy, and thistle. High spines vary from 2 to 14%
in the archaeological samples, from 6 to 23% in the stratigraphic columns,
and from 20 to 30.5% in the surface samples. The wash sample contains 29%
low spines. No trends or clusterings are apparent in the Compositae.

Tidestromia is an insect pollinated annual in the family Amaranthaceae.
Within the site *Tidestromia* varies from 2 to 30% (Figures 1, 2, and 3). The
modern surface samples contain 1 and 2.5% *Tidestromia* and the wash
sample contains no *Tidestromia* (Figure 2). A number of reasons are
possible for the high percentages of *Tidestromia* found in the site samples.
First, the plant may have been used by the Hohokam, though there is no
ethnobotanical evidence to support such use. The species of *Tidestromia*
(T. languginosa) which is presently found around Whiptail ruin occurs in
a variety of habitats, by streams, in sand, in gravel, on mesas, bajadas,

pediments, and in association with numerous plant communities. Many of these environments are associated with disturbed soil. The activities of the human population of the site would have resulted in disturbed soils and, therefore, could have created a favorable environment for the *Tidestromia*.

Two of the pollen types represent standing or running water. *Sparganium* type pollen consists of pollen from a number of plants, all associated with water ("aquatic or semi-aquatic," Kearney and Peebles, 1964:64) including cattail or *Typha* sp. The other riparian type is willow (*Salix* sp.). Willow and *Sparganium* type pollen do not usually occur in sediments in the Sonoran Desert (Hevly and others 1965). They are presently growing around the man-made lake. It is quite possible that they were growing there when the Hohokam occupied Whiptail ruin, especially since remains of reeds used in the roofing of some of the houses were found during the excavation. Willow and cattail type pollen could have been introduced either with the plants or with drinking and cooking water carried from the springs.

Cylindropuntia pollen refers to pollen which is produced by cholla cacti. It is found in low percentages (0 to 2%) but consistently in the samples from the rooms (Figures 1 and 3). The samples of modern pollen from the surface of the site and from the wash contained no cholla pollen (Figure 2). A probable interpretation of the cylindropuntia pollen found in the site is that the people were eating some part of the cholla. This interpretation is supported by the presence of carbonized cholla buds in one structure that has been tentatively interpreted as a storage facility.

Pollen labeled "Unidentifiable" (Figures 1, 2, and 3) refers to those grains which are pollen, but cannot be identified to type as a result of poor preservation (corrosion, crushing).

A few statements can be made about the pollen counts in the houses. First, there are no consistent associations of one or two pollen types with houses of a particular type (Figure 1) or with vessels (Figure 3) or other artifacts. In fact, in a single house the amount of the different types of pollen may vary by as much as 20%. The same is true of pollen in vessels and pollen under artifacts. Some of the floor and vessel samples may be post-occupation since it is not likely that the Indians kept dirt in their jars, and sediment and pollen could have filtered to the floor after abandonment of the site.

Environmental interpretations are often made on the basis of changes in the pollen from stratigraphic columns. A column was taken from House 19 and another from House 23. In the column from House 19 there is no real change until 25 cm below the surface. This lack of change is interpreted to be the result of one single period of continuous deposition. In general the samples below 25 cm in the column agree well with the modern surface samples from the site, especially with the sample collected next to the site. The major difference between the stratigraphic samples and the surface samples is that *Tidestromia* is represented by very low amounts in the modern surface samples (1 to 2.5%) (Figure 1), but found in higher percentages (3.5 to 30%) in most of the samples in the stratigraphic column (Figure 2). The reason for this difference is not readily apparent.

There is a major difference between the stratigraphic column from House 19 and that from House 23. In House 23 there is a rise in the Compositae, especially the low spines, and a decline in the cheno-ams and *Tidestromia* from 35 to 25 cm below the surface. From 25 to 15 cm the low spines decline and the cheno-ams rise. Then there is another reversal from 15 to 5 cm when the cheno-ams drop lower than before and the low spines climb to their previous high. The column in House 19 has one change at 25 cm below the surface. The differences in the two columns are probably a local phenomenon. Such localized variations in the pollen rain are supported by the modern surface samples from the site. The second surface sample contains over 20% more low spines than the first sample and 30% fewer cheno-ams. These differences may be due to drainage patterns, topography, or to the high local variability that characterizes arid land surface and alluvial samples.

While the analysis at Whiptail ruin did not fulfil the original intent, that of microenvironmental interpretation, it did show that pollen analysis was possible in desert sites. Since 1971 I have completed three more pollen studies at Hohokam sites. As material becomes available comparison of the pollen diagrams from many sites may shed new light on the man-plant relationship in the desert.

The palynological study at Whiptail ruin and those at other sites raise the question of the reliability of making palaeoenvironmental interpretations from pollen analyses of archaeological sites. This problem can be considered in two parts. First, what does a single pollen sample from a floor represent? Does it reflect the whole floor or only that part of the floor which is sampled? Second, what is the immediate source of the pollen in the samples taken from an archaeological site? Is it the environment or the cultural activity of the occupants?

How well do floor samples reflect the general pollen rain in a structure? In previous studies a single sample from a room, indeed in some cases from a site, has been used for palynological interpretations (Schoenwetter, 1962, 1967; Hevly, 1964). Bohrer (1968) in the Hay Hollow Valley, Arizona, used more than one sample per structure and noted large discrepancies in pollen percentages between them. Further evaluation of this problem was desirable.

POLLEN ANALYSIS AT USHKLISH RUIN

In 1972 I conducted a pollen study at Ushklish ruin, a Hohokam site in the Tonto Basin, Arizona (Webb, 1973). The hypothesis of the analysis was that one sample per archaeological structure does not reflect the average pollen rain in that structure or in the site and is not sufficient, therefore, for accurate interpretation of the environment, either cultural or natural. To test the hypothesis two or more samples from areas of the same floor were analyzed and evaluated using a chi-square test[1]:

$$\chi^2 = \frac{\sum (\text{observed} - \text{expected})^2}{\text{expected}}$$

The statistic was applied to the Compositae, cheno-ams, and "all other types" in the samples of each structure (Figure 4). Nine houses, 2, 3, 5, 7, 8, 9, 10, 11, and 12, were included in the study. Houses 1 and 6 were excluded because one of the samples from each structure was collected from under an artifact and was, therefore, inherently biased. Table 1 gives the chi-square value for the samples in each house. The sets of samples from Houses 5, 9, 10, and 12 were significantly different at the .05 level of significance. Houses 9 and 10 were especially notable in that one sample from each house was high in Compositae pollen and low in cheno-am pollen and the other sample was high in cheno-am pollen and low in Compositae. In either case different interpretations could have been made if only one sample had been analyzed.

Table 1

Chi-square values of pollen samples from floor context in houses at Ushklish ruin, Tonto Basin, Arizona

House	X^2
2	2.313
3	1.440
5	19.064
7	4.451
8	4.145
9	16.901
10	33.572
11	0.067
12	11.219

[1] The "expected" in this study is the average of the observations.

It is obvious from this study that a single sample from a floor is not sufficient for interpretation. How many samples are necessary is not known. At the present time some experimentation is needed. Theoretically, however, a composite sample which includes pollen from many places should be acceptable as reflecting the pollen rain over the whole floor.

The study at Ushklish ruin still does not answer the question of the source of the pollen rain in an area inhabited by man. In considering the pollen rain in an archaeological site it is apparent that the rain can be divided into three major components: (1) the pollen from those plants which would be there regardless of man's presence; (2) the pollen from natural plants which are affected either adversely or positively by man's presence; and, (3) the pollen from cultigens and other plants which are introduced into the site by man. Which of these components is the major contributor to the pollen rain in a site? In order to approach the solution of this problem in 1973 I sampled a modern situation which would be analogous to an archaeological site.

POLLEN ANALYSES OF CONTEMPORARY INDIAN VILLAGES AND FIELDS

With the help of Dr. Bernard Fontana (Department of Anthropology, The University of Arizona) samples were taken from structures in the Papago villages surrounding San Xavier Mission, on the floodplain of the Santa Cruz River southwest of Tucson. The native vegetation is a typical lower Sonoran creosotebush-bursage community. Near the roads and villages saltbush (*Atriplex* sp.), careless weed (*Amaranthus palmeri*) and Russian thistle (*Salsola kali*) are common. Dense mesquite thickets (*Prosopis juliflora*) grow close to the river bed. Introduced plants in and around the villages include salt cedar (*Tamarix pentandra*) and Aleppo pine (*Pinus halepensis*).

For the pollen study three samples were collected from occupied houses (two from the same house), one each from two abandoned houses, one from a storage room, four from areas around a house, one from a nearby cotton field, and one from beneath a ramada. Floor samples were taken by sweeping large parts of the rooms with wisk brooms in order to obtain enough material for analysis and to produce composite samples. Samples outside of houses were also composite samples, collected by combining trowel tips of dirt taken in a circle as described by Hevly, Mehringer and Yocum (1965).

The general locality of the mission is becoming urbanized; a freeway transects the reservation and the mission is bordered by residential subdivisions on three sides. It was therefore not possible to take a control sample which would reflect an undisturbed environment. The control sample used is from "Modern Pollen Rain in the Sonoran Desert" (Hevly and others, 1965). The sample consists of two pollen spectra (19 and 20) from a floodplain in Avra Valley *c.* ten miles northwest of San Xavier. There is possibility for error in comparing this control with the village samples, but the results of the comparison are so dramatic that the implications are inescapable.

In all but one area the samples from San Xavier had over 30% more cheno-ams than did the control sample (Figure 5). Around Tucson plants which contribute cheno-am pollen to the pollen rain are those which are favored by disturbance. They include careless weed and saltbush which, as previously mentioned, are found near roads and houses on the mission.

Four other types also show distinct differences in relation to the control sample. Both low and high spine Compositae are under-represented in all of the mission samples when compared with the Avra Valley sample. Gramineae percentages are lower in all but one sample. These differences in percentages may not reflect actual quantitative differences. If there is an increase in numbers of one type of pollen, such as cheno-ams, this could cause a decrease in percent of all other pollen types even though there is no numerical decrease. Conversely, a decrease of one or two pollen types would cause a relative increase of other types. The interpretation of relative pollen counts (i.e., diagrams based on percentages) is complex and often ambiguous. Presently various methods which give quantitative results are being studied.

One sample from San Xavier was quite different from both the control sample and other village samples. The sample from beneath the ramada contained 59% salt cedar pollen, far more than any other sample. Salt cedar is insect pollinated, but the flowers are small and numerous and the pollen could easily be carried by the wind. Fontana (personal communication) does not know of any use of salt cedar in the ramada. It is assumed, therefore, that the surrounding trees contributed the high percent of *Tamarix* pollen. Since salt cedar is introduced this is another example of the effect of man on the pollen rain in his environment.

Another study which supports an increase in pollen from disturbance plants which grow near inhabited areas involves a comparison of field samples from two New Mexico pueblos with control samples collected away from the fields. In the spring of 1974 Dr. Allen Solomon, Mr. Gerald Kelso, and I analyzed samples from nineteenth and twentieth century fields near Tesuque and Nambe Pueblos, north of Santa Fe, New Mexico (Webb and Solomon, 1974). In almost all cases the percentage of nonarboreal (disturbance) pollen is much greater in the field samples than in the control samples (up to 47% at both Nambe and Tesuque Pueblos). In no instance is the ratio of arboreal pollen to nonarboreal pollen greater in the field samples than in the control samples for either pueblo.

The above studies indicate that great caution should be used in attempting to make climatic interpretations of culturally related pollen samples. It is obvious that modern man affects, both intentionally and unintentionally, the surrounding soil and vegetation. This effect is reflected in the pollen rain. Palaeoman also produced changes in vegetation and soil which caused variation of the pollen rain. The total extent of these changes is not known and probably varies with location and site size. This problem deserves attention. Until our understanding is increased, palaeoclimatic interpretations based on archaeological samples and the resulting chronologic interpretations should be accepted as tentative and used with great care.

THE FUTURE

Palynology in Southwestern archaeology is still young, but it has come a long way since Sears first attempted pollen extraction in the 1930's. In subsequent years the discipline has been used in diverse ways, to interpret the palaeoclimate of sites, to develop chronologies, to study man's use of plants, to define man's effect on his environment. Areas of real worth have become apparent, but it has also become apparent that there are still problems and previously accepted assumptions which must be tested and retested.

Pollen studies which test collecting methods in archaeological sites are necessary to ensure that a maximum of unambiguous information is received for the time and money invested. Further investigation into the source of the pollen found in archaeological sites is also of high priority. Such studies will allow for better, more comprehensive interpretations of many aspects of site analysis.

When properly used palynology is a valuable archaeological tool. With testing, its value to the archaeologist for palaeoenvironmental or man-related interpretations will grow. One of the primary factors in this growth is an increase in communication between palynologists and archaeologists.

An archaeologist who plans to collect pollen samples from a site should contact a palynologist before excavation begins. By discussing hypotheses, collecting methods, and hopes prior to excavation, results which are satisfactory to both the archaeologists and the palynologist can be achieved.

ACKNOWLEDGMENTS

I am indebted to the following people and institutions for their aid in the collection and analysis of the data in this chapter. Drs. Paul Grebinger and Bruce Bradley initiated and directed pollen sampling at Whiptail ruin, Arizona. Excavation and analysis at Ushklish ruin were financially supported by the Arizona State Highway Department (University of Arizona Fund cA5020-8790-18). Statistical analysis of the Ushklish pollen data was guided by Dr. James Gebert. Pollen sampling at San Xavier Mission would not have been possible without the help of Dr. Bernard Fontana. The Bureau of Indian Affairs was responsible for the collection and financed the analysis (Fund cAFU4M00-010814) of the pollen samples from the pueblo fields. Facilities for pollen extraction and analysis were provided by the Paleoenvironmental Laboratory, Tumamoc Hill, The University of Arizona. In addition I would like to express my warm thanks to Dr. Allen Solomon, Prof. Terah Smiley, Messrs. David Doyel, Laurens Hammack, and John P. Webb for their comments, criticisms, advice and support.

REFERENCES

Anderson, R. Y. (1955) Pollen analysis, a research tool for the study of cave deposits. *American Antiquity* 21, 84-5.
Bohrer, V. L. (1968) Paleoecology of an archaeological site near Snowflake Arizona. Ph.D. dissertation, The University of Arizona, Tucson.
Bohrer, V. L. (1970) Ethnobotanical aspects of Snaketown, a Hohokam village in southern Arizona. *American Antiquity* 35, 413-30.
Bryant, V. M., Jr. (1974) Prehistoric diet in southwest Texas: the coprolite evidence. *American Antiquity* 39, 408-20.
Bryson, R. A. and J. E. Kutzbach (1974) On the analysis of pollen-climate canonical transfer functions. *Quaternary Research* 4, 128-35.
Davis, M. B., L. B. Brubaker and T. Webb III (1974) Calibration of absolute pollen influx. In *Quaternary Plant Ecology*, edited by H. J. B. Birks and R. G. West, pp. 9-26. John Wiley, New York.
Godwin, H. (1944) Age and origin of the "Breckland" heaths of East Anglia. *Nature* 154, 6.
Grebinger, P. and D. P. Adam (1974) Hard times?: Classic period Hohokam cultural development in the Tucson Basin, Arizona. *World Archaeology* 6, 226-41.
Hevly, R. H. (1964) Pollen analysis of Quaternary archaeological and lacustrine sediments from the Colorado Plateau. Ph.D. dissertation, The University of Arizona, Tucson.
Hevly, R., P. J. Mehringer, Jr. and H. G. Yocum (1965) Modern pollen rain in the Sonoran Desert. *Journal of the Arizona Academy of Science* 3, 123-35.
Hill, J. N. (1970) Broken K pueblo: prehistoric social organization in the American Southwest. *Anthropological Papers of The University of Arizona* 18.
Hill, J. N. and R. H. Hevly (1968) Pollen at Broken K pueblo: some new interpretations. *American Antiquity* 33, 200-10.
Jelinek, A. J. (1966) Correlation of archaeological and palynological interpretations. *Science* 152, 1507-9.
Kearney, T. H. and R. H. Peebles (1960) *Arizona Flora*. University of California Press, Los Angeles.
Keef, P. A. M., J. J. Wymer and G. W. Dimbleby (1965) A Mesolithic site on Iping Common, Sussex, England. *Proceedings of the Prehistoric Society* 31, 85-92.
Kelso, G. K. (1971) Hogup Cave, Utah: comparative pollen analysis of human coprolites and cave fill. In Hogup Cave, C. M. Aikens and others, pp. 251-62. *University of Utah Anthropological Papers* 93.

Krumbein, W. C. and L. L. Sloss (1963) *Stratigraphy and Sedimentation* (2nd ed.). W. H. Freeman, San Francisco.

Martin P. S. (1963) *The Last 10,000 Years*. The University of Arizona Press, Tucson.

Martin, P. S. and F. W. Sharrock (1964) Pollen analysis of prehistoric human feces: a new approach to ethnobotany. *American Antiquity* 30, 168–80.

Martin, P. S. and W. B. Byers (1965) Pollen and archaeology at Wetherill Mesa. In Contributions of the Wetherill Mesa Archeological Project, assembled by D. Osborne, pp. 122–35. *Society for American Archaeology, Memoir* 19.

Mehringer, P. J., Jr. (1967) Pollen analysis of the Tule Springs area, Nevada. *Nevada State Museum Anthropological Papers* 3, 130–200.

Mehringer, P. J., Jr. and C. V. Haynes, Jr. (1965) Pollen evidence for the environment of early man and extinct mammals of the Lehner Mammoth site, southeastern Arizona. *American Antiquity* 31, 17–23.

Mehringer, P. J., P. S. Martin, and C. V. Haynes, Jr. (1967) Murray Springs, a mid-postglacial pollen record from southern Arizona. *American Journal of Science* 265, 786–97.

Raynor, G. S., E. C. Ogden and J. V. Hayes (1972) Dispersion and deposition of corn pollen from experimental sources. *Agronomy Journal* 64, 420–7.

Schoenwetter, J. (1962) The pollen analysis of eighteen archaeological sites in Arizona and New Mexico. In Chapters in the prehistory of eastern Arizona, I., P. S. Martin, J. D. Rinaldo, W. A. Longacre, C. Cronin, L. G. Freeman, Jr. and J. Schoenwetter. *Fieldiana: Anthropology* 53, 168–209.

Schoenwetter, J. (1965) A reevaluation of the Navajo reservoir pollen chronology, *El Palacio* 73, 19–26.

Schoenwetter, J. and F. W. Eddy (1964) Alluvial and palynological reconstruction of environments, Navajo reservoir district. *Museum of New Mexico Papers in Anthropology* 13.

Sears, P. B. (1937) Pollen analysis as an aid in dating cultural deposits in the United States. In *Early Man*, edited by G. G. MacCurdy, pp. 61–6. J. B. Lippincott, London.

Smith, A. G. (1970) The influence of Mesolithic and Neolithic man on British vegetation. In *Studies in the Vegetational History of the British Isles,* edited by D. Walker and R. G. West, pp. 81–96. Cambridge University Press.

Steel, R. G. D. and J. H. Torrie (1960) *Principles and Problems of Statistics*. McGraw-Hill, New York.

Turner, J. (1970) Post Neolithic disturbance of British vegetation. In *Studies in the vegetational history of the British Isles,* edited by D. Walker and R. G. West, pp. 97–116. Cambridge University Press.

Webb, J. L. (1973) Pollen analysis of Ushklish ruin. *Arizona Academy of Science, Abstracts* 8, 5.

Webb, J. L. and A. M. Solomon (1974) Human disturbance in arid lands: pollen evidence of prehistoric land use. *Bulletin of the Ecological Society* 55, 28.

Maximizing the Interpretive Potential of Archaeological Tree-ring Dates

MEADE KEMRER

Wilkes College

Tree-ring dates can provide refined dating controls for microtemporal analyses if: (1) it is known how the wood was used; (2) it is known how tree growth and wood preservation is affected by the environment; and, (3) the number of tree-ring samples is large enough for statistical analyses. Tree-ring data collected from Navajo architecture in northeastern Arizona are analyzed. A number of exterior ring characteristics on the wood samples are shown to be related to Navajo wood use activities. Relations between other tree-ring characteristics and the environment of the study area are identified. For a portion of the tree-ring dates, these relationships are then used to quantitatively determine the degree to which the calendrical year assigned by the dendrochronologist to the outermost ring of a sample approximates the year in which the tree segment actually died.

Tree-ring dates from archaeological sites require interpretation to assign meaning to them. The researcher must show how the dates relate to the context in which the wood was found. The number of relationships between tree-ring dates and other kinds of information available to the archaeologist approaches infinity. However, the degree to which the interpretive process is fully realized is structured by the nature of the problems undergoing investigation and is constrained by the availability of research time and funds.

The archaeological, dendrochronological, and informant data used in this study were collected during the course of the Navajo Land Claim survey (Correll, 1961) of abandoned Navajo sites in northeastern Arizona (Figure 1). My research problems dictated maximum use of time controls. I sought to discover: (1) how Navajo local group organization could be characterized within the study area between A.D. 1750 to 1900; (2) what locational strategies were utilized by the Navajo during this period; and (3) how Navajo economic systems operated and changed from A.D. 1750 to 1900.

Arguments substantiating my resolution of these problems will not be the subject of this paper. Instead, I shall discuss how I have attempted to make the greatest possible use of the tree-ring information for application to these problems. This information was developed in the process of

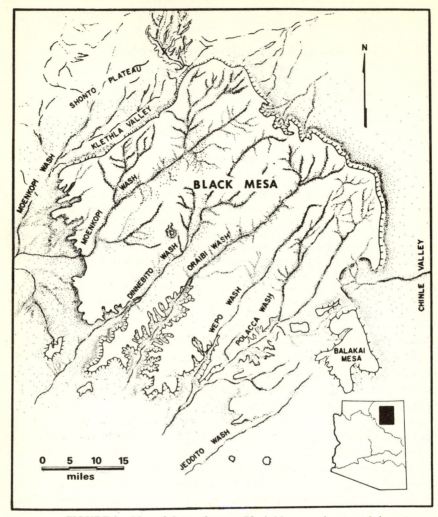

FIGURE 1   Map of the study area, Black Mesa, northeastern Arizona.

answering the following questions. First, to what degree does the calendrical year assigned by the dendrochronologist to the outermost ring of the wood sample approximate the year the tree trunk or limb segment actually died? And second, what aspects of Navajo behavior are specified by the death date of the tree-ring sample? To answer these questions, the dendrochronological methods employed by the Land Claim staff and the properties of the dated tree-ring sample population were examined in detail.

DESCRIPTION OF THE SAMPLE

A total of 1,045 wood samples were removed from architectural features located within 277 Navajo sites. The number of samples collected from each site varied from 1 to 23. The site sample frequencies, therefore, constituted a minimal representation of the hundreds, and for some sites, thousands of tree segments used in architecture. The sample was sufficient for the Land Claim purpose of demonstrating Navajo use and occupancy of the study area through time. And, in terms of the broader technical and methodological implications of this paper, the number of tree-ring samples from each site is no less representative than wood collections recovered from most prehistoric excavations.

All of the dated samples were pinyon pine (*Pinus edulis*). Although the Navajo made use of several species of juniper, the dating potential of these species was regarded to be significantly lower than pinyon (Stokes and Smiley, 1964a). Consequently features and communities constructed of juniper were not sampled.

Consistent with dendrochronological procedure, several local chronologies were established within the study area. Sets of core samples were removed from mature living pinyon trees. The trees selected were greater in age and diameter than those generally used by the Navajo for construction purposes. The modern cores, therefore, represent longer time spans of tree growth than most of the archaeological samples. The ring width values of the modern samples were averaged into subareal chronologies four or five centuries in length (Stokes and Smiley, 1963, 1964b, 1966, 1969). Local chronologies reflect variations in ring width patterns that are unique to an area. Therefore, the odds are increased that each archaeological sample can be dated by comparing it with the appropriate local chronology (cross-dating).

A total of 316 or approximately 30% of the tree-ring samples were dated. The number of tree-ring dates per site ranged from one to nine. However, 233 or 74% of these dates were derived from sites where the number of dates per site ranged from one to three. Based upon this array it became apparent that estimates of tree death dates and regularities in Navajo wood related behaviors would have to be derived from analyzing large populations of dates rather than small sets of dates from each site.

The observations that are of particular interest in evaluating tree-ring dates from archaeological contexts are those made on the exterior of the dated sample. A transverse cross section of each timber was made, ranging from ½ to 2 cm in thickness. This subsample constituted the observational universe for all datable or partially crossdated samples. A series of symbols are used to describe each published tree-ring date. Essentially the smybols are informal probability statements made by the dendrochronologist to signify the degree to which the exterior date represents the exact year of death for the sample.

The symbols employed by Stokes and Smiley (1963, 1964b, 1966, 1969) to describe the exterior of a dated or partially crossdated sample may be viewed as a sequence of interchangeable elements within each subset of the exterior ring condition set:

$$(+,\phi1) \quad (\mathrm{inc,c},\phi2) \quad (\mathrm{C},\phi3) \quad (\mathrm{G},\phi4) \quad (\mathrm{B},\phi5).$$
$$\quad\ 1 \qquad\qquad 2 \qquad\quad\ 3 \qquad\quad 4 \qquad\quad 5$$

The five subsets and their elements are defined below.

Subset 1: *Datability of the sample toward the exterior.*
+ The outermost rings are either very small and/or complacent, and the sequence of ring width variation in the outer part of the sample cannot be crossdated with the known ring chronology for that period. Therefore, a ring count was made to the outside. Or, the outermost rings fall into a period in which one or more very small rings are known to occur, but the sample does not possess enough additional rings to permit the presence or absence of these rings to be verified.
$\phi1$ (= blank) The sample is datable through the final ring.

Subset 2: *Growth condition of the sample.*
inc The outermost ring is incomplete in growth.
c   The outermost ring is complete in growth.
$\phi2$ (= blank) The condition of growth is not determinable.

Subset 3: *Relative position of the terminal ring of the sample to the true exterior of the tree stem (I).*
C The outermost ring is continuous around the circumference of the sample. Hence erosional activity has been minimal, implying that the assigned date is close to, if not that of tree stem death.
$\phi3$ (= blank) The outermost ring is not continuous. Or, this observation is not recorded in view of more conclusive information.

Subset 4: *Relative position of the terminal ring of sample to the true exterior of the tree stem (II).*
G Beetle galleries are present on the exterior of the sample. Since these organisms thrive on the phloem layer located between the bark and the woody portion of the stem, the assigned date is close to, if not the true death date of the stem.
$\phi4$ (= blank) Galleries are not present on the sample.

Subset 5: *Presence or absence of the true exterior on the sample.*
B Bark is present on the sample. Hence the outermost ring is the true exterior of the sample.
φ5 (= blank) Bark is absent from the sample.

The various kinds of element combinations within the ring condition set represent a considerable array of probability assignments as to the exact death date of the sample. Statements of set content stand as informal estimates and cannot be transformed into formal probability statements until they can be quantitatively related to the behavioral and physical environmental contexts in which they were found. One of the goals of this study is to demonstrate that these transformations are both possible and warranted in evaluating tree-ring dates in archaeological analyses.

A complete listing of all exterior ring condition set outcomes is presented in Table 1.

TABLE 1

Consistency of element combinations with independent dating evidence

Ring condition set outcome	Consistent	%	In-consistent	%	Unknown	%	Total
(+) (φ2) (φ3) (φ4) (φ5)	21	30	27	40	21	30	69
(+) (inc) (φ3) (φ4) (φ5)	14	61	5	22	4	17	23
(+) (c) (φ3) (φ4) (φ5)	1	50	0	0	1	50	2
(+) (φ2) (φ3) (G) (φ5)	27	71	7	18	4	11	38
(+) (inc) (φ3) (G) (φ5)	24	80	1	3	5	17	30
(+) (c) (φ3) (G) (φ5)	2	67	1	33	0	0	3
(+) (φ2) (φ3) (φ4) (B)	1	100	0	0	0	0	1
(φ1) (inc) (φ3) (φ4) (φ5)	25	58	7	16	11	26	43
(φ1) (c) (φ3) (φ4) (φ5)	1	50	1	50	0	0	2
(φ1) (φ2) (C) (G) (φ5)	1	100	0	0	0	0	1
(φ1) (φ2) (φ3) (G) (φ5)	23	92	1	4	1	4	25
(φ1) (inc) (φ3) (G) (φ5)	51	88	3	5	4	7	58
(φ1) (c) (φ3) (G) (φ5)	11	85	0	0	2	15	13
(φ1) (inc) (φ3) (G) (B)	2	100	0	0	0	0	2
(φ1) (c) (φ3) (G) (B)	1	100	0	0	0	0	1
(φ1) (inc) (φ3) (φ4) (B)	1	100	0	0	0	0	1
(φ1) (c) (φ3) (φ4) (B)	2	100	0	0	0	0	2
(φ1) (φ2) (φ3) (φ4) (B)	2	100	0	0	0	0	2
All outcomes	210	66	53	17	53	17	316

The information is cross-classified in terms of the degree to which independent evidence is consistent with the thesis that a given sample was initially harvested from a live tree. The dates considered to be consistent were characterized by one or more of the following three criteria:

1) *Temporal clustering of tree-ring dates within a site.* Outside dates that fall within a decade were considered to represent wood harvesting activity from living trees. If dead wood was collected for construction purposes, the disparity between the dates would probably be greater than ten years, for the decay rate of wood is low in this semiarid environment, and usable dead wood can persist as long as 300 years (Dean, 1969: 144, 190).

2) *Informant estimates of site occupancy.* Statements from local Navajo informants were collected during the survey. These persons often possessed direct or indirect knowledge concerning the former inhabitants of the individual sites. Tree-ring dates falling within ten years of an informant's estimate of occupancy were considered to be consistent with this estimate.

3) *Dated historic artifacts.* Samples of historic artifacts were collected from sites by the Land Claim survey crews. Tree-ring dates falling within ten years of dates assigned to historic goods (Caywood 1961) were considered to be consistent with the tree-ring evidence.

When independent evidence failed to meet these criteria, the dated samples involved were considered to be "inconsistent." Dated tree-ring samples from sites where there was no means of independent evaluation were assigned to the "unknown" category.

The element combinations in Table 1 are listed in terms of increasing likelihood that the assigned outside date represents the actual death date of the limb or trunk segment. Note that the proportional frequencies of "consistent" dates tend to vary directly with increased confidence in the actual death dates of the samples. A quantified estimation of this error, however, required detailed knowledge concerning Navajo wood use behavior patterns.

WOOD USE BEHAVIOR PATTERNS

Haury (1935), Bannister (1962, 1965: 123-6) and Robinson (1967) demonstrated the presence of elements describing the basic behavioral options for a general architectural wood procurement–use activity system. The behavioral elements in the sequential subsets of the architectural wood procurement–use activity set may be viewed as follows:

Subset 1: *Wood procurement.*
1a) Wood is removed from live trees.
1b) Wood is removed from dead trees.
1c) Wood is removed from previously constructed features.

Subset 2: *Wood storage.*

2a) The procured wood is stockpiled for some period prior to use.

2b) The procured wood is used immediately for construction purposes.

Subset 3: *Wood use.*

3a) The wood is used to construct a feature *de novo.*

3b) The wood is used to repair a portion of a previously constructed feature.

3c) The wood is used to completely repair or rebuild a previously constructed feature.

Strictly speaking, the outcomes of the subsets are applicable independently to each wood sample. A considerable body of evidence must be presented to decide which element combinations characterize the wood in a given structure, community, or a population of communities.

WOOD HARVESTING

At least 66% of the tree-ring dates shown in Table 1 were consistent with independent dating evidence. This would indicate that a dominant pattern was to harvest wood from living trees. Moreover, the fact that a large portion of the dated samples (157) exhibit the incomplete growth condition suggests a pattern as to the scheduling of Navajo wood havesting activity.

In the southern Colorado plateau, the annual growth event in pinyon begins in mid-June and continues into July and early August (Fritts, Smith, and Stokes, 1965: 102–6). Based upon the assumptions that the (inc) and the (c) samples were harvested from live trees, and the (inc) condition is observable in pinyon tree-ring samples that died within the months of June through August, or one-quarter of the year, the following hypotheses can be initially tested:

$H\phi$: Tree cutting activity occurred randomly throughout the year.

H_1: Tree cutting activity was significantly restricted to the summer months.

A comparison of the observed and the expected outcomes of the growth condition is shown in Table 2. The chi-square analysis, using Yates' correction factor (since $df = 1$) indicates that the observed population is significantly nonrandomly distributed ($p < .001$), and supports the H_1 hypothesis.

A comparison of the consistency of (inc) and (c) tree-ring samples with independent dating evidence from early through late Navajo settlements showed no significant differences that would suggest any departures from the general practice of harvesting wood from living pinyon trees. Most of the wood, moreover, was procured during the summer months.

TABLE 2

Observed and expected growth condition outcomes

Growth condition	Observed outcomes	Expected outcomes	Totals
Incomplete (inc)	157	45	202
Complete (c)	23	135	158
Totals	180	180	360

There is evidence that the season for harvesting wood coincides with the season for constructing dwellings. One observation recorded for most domestic structures by the Land Claim survey was the orientation of the doorway. The practice of locating the entry towards the rising sun has been noted for many American Indian societies, including the Navajo (Mindeleff, 1898). The location of the sunrise point on the horizon is not constant, but shifts across the eastern hemisphere as the earth tilts on its axis every year. The extreme northerly and southerly sunrise points, the solstices, occur every June 22 and December 22 respectively. If the doorways of Navajo domestic structures were accurately oriented toward the sunrise point at the time of construction, then seasonal preferences for building dwellings are determinable.

Information concerning the location of dwelling entries was not uniformly available. Entry orientation observations were precluded where the structures had completely collapsed or the wood had been removed. Other recorded information was not accompanied by an actual compass reading and thus was not utilized in the analyses. There were only four cases out of several thousand in which two dwellings were contiguous. On the basis of this fact, it is assumed that the direction that each doorway faces is the product of a behaviorally independent construction episode, and thus independent of any other entrance orientation outcome.

The distributional array of entry orientations in Figure 2 in the total sample shows more doorways located within the spring–summer range (64%) than the fall–winter range (5%). Moreover, 78% of the entries fall within the solstices.

In the process of collecting entry orientation data, it became apparent that in some cases, environmental conditions existing prior to the construction of the dwelling had constraining effects on the location of the doorway. The physical restrictions were as follows:

1) The structure was incorporated into a geological feature in such a manner as to restrict the range of entry orientations. Examples are dwellings incorporated into bedrock forms such as ledges or caves, and derivative geological forms such as boulders or talus slopes.

2) The doorway architecture was constructed from fixed natural features which served to eliminate doorway orientation options. For example, an entry was occasionally located between two boulders, or between two living trees, or a tree-boulder combination.

3) A domestic structure built contiguous to another served to restrict entry orientations.

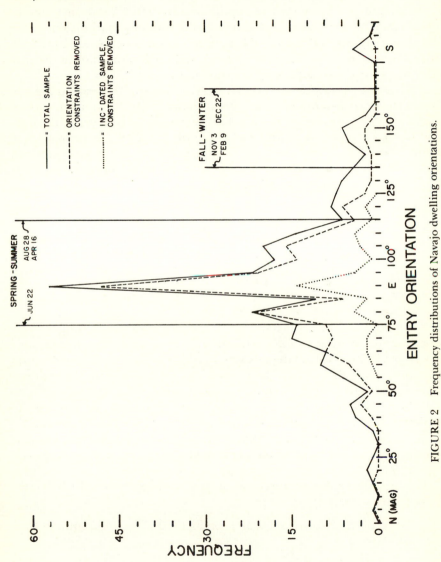

FIGURE 2   Frequency distributions of Navajo dwelling orientations.

Domestic structures that met one or more of the above criteria were removed from the sample. The frequency distribution of the non-constrained entry orientations is shown in Figure 2. In this sample 79% fall on or between the solstices. The proportion of doorways oriented within the spring–summer range increases to 76% and those within the fall–winter range decrease slightly to 3%.

A visual inspection of the two populations in Figure 2 indicates that the elimination of entry "error" produces a reduction in variation. Therefore, the spring–summer period was the preferred season for constructing dwellings. Formal analyses of central tendency and dispersion characteristics of the two populations support this contention.

The means ($\overline{X}$) of the two populations are within 3° of each other and bisect the spring–summer range (total sample = 92.4°, nonconstrained sample = 89.7°). However, the standard deviation (s) is lower in the non-constrained sample of entries (total sample = ±27.8°, nonconstrained sample = ±20.1°). The ratio of variances (s^2) of the nonconstrained population (s^2) is significantly smaller than the total sample population (s^1). Given the hypothetical relationship

$$\frac{(s_{e2})^2}{(s_{e1})^2} = \frac{(s_{02})^2}{(s_{01})^2}$$

where the expected ratio of variances (se) would be 1.00. However, the observed (so) ratio is .52 which is smaller beyond the .001 level of significance (Croxton, 1953: 288–95, 332–3).

A third population, shown in Figure 2, is composed of dwellings having one or more tree-ring samples exhibiting the (inc) condition. In this set of doorways, 88% fall within the solstices. In addition, 83% are oriented within the spring–summer range, and none are found within the extreme fall–winter range. Analyses similar to those presented above indicated no significant difference in the mean, standard deviation, or the ratio of variances between the nonconstrained sample and the (inc) population.

To summarize the findings concerning Navajo wood procurement, the following behavior patterns have emerged:

1) Pinyon wood for architectural purposes was preferentially harvested from living trees.

2) Wood procurement was usually conducted during the months of June through August.

3) The scheduling of wood procurement coincides with the preferred season for building dwellings.

WOOD MODIFICATION

When treated analytically as artifacts, wood from archaeological sites is a potentially rich source of information concerning technological and other activity systems (Robinson, 1967). Architectural features dated by the tree-ring method, informants, or associated artifacts, produced a considerable amount of information concerning regularities in Navajo wood segment-ing techniques. The modes of felling, reducing and shaping wood (often termed "beam condition") were noted by the Land Claim staff for ap-proximately 1,000 datable structures. Over 90% of the architecture fell within the five categories listed in Table 3.

TABLE 3
Beam conditions in five major classes of architecture

Architectural type	Beam condition type								
	Stone axe	%	Burn-ing	%	Break-ing	%	Metal axe	%	Total
A.D. 1750–1800									
Domestic structures	6	12	9	18	27	54	8	16	50
Game traps	1	33	1	33	0	0	1	33	3
Livestock structures	1	7	5	33	7	47	2	13	15
Windbreaks	0	0	0	0	0	0	0	0	0
Sweathouses	0	0	0	0	0	0	0	0	0
Totals	8	12	15	22	34	50	11	16	68
A.D. 1801–1867									
Domestic structures	7	4	29	16	85	46	64	34	185
Game traps	7	29	4	17	7	29	6	25	24
Livestock structures	2	3	15	21	25	35	29	41	71
Windbreaks	0	0	1	17	3	50	2	33	6
Sweathouses	0	0	4	29	5	36	5	36	14
Totals	16	5	53	18	125	42	106	35	300
A.D. 1868–1880									
Domestic structures	0	0	20	9	42	20	149	71	211
Game traps	0	0	0	0	0	0	0	0	0
Livestock structures	1	1	20	18	35	31	56	50	112
Windbreaks	1	3	3	9	11	31	20	57	35
Sweathouses	0	0	0	0	2	6	31	94	33
Totals	2	1	43	11	90	23	256	65	391
A.D. 1881–1900									
Domestic structures	0	0	4	3	8	6	121	91	133
Game traps	0	0	0	0	0	0	0	0	0
Livestock structures	0	0	5	9	12	23	36	68	53
Windbreaks	0	0	0	0	4	19	17	81	21
Seathouses	0	0	0	0	0	0	16	100	16
Totals	0	0	9	4	24	11	190	85	223

The impact of technological change on wood cutting behavior is illustrated in Table 3. As the metal axe became available, Navajo groups used it more frequently and other cutting methods less frequently.

Despite this general trend, variability exists in wood cutting methods within each time period. Wood use varied with architectural type. From A.D. 1868 to 1900, deviations from the total percentage within each beam condition class correspond to stem sizes generally selected for use in the various classes of architecture. Sheep corrals, lamb pens, and windbreaks, for example, are usually constructed from tree branches. Domestic structures and game traps, however, are characteristically built with wood from the main stem. Note in Table 3 that between A.D. 1868–1900 the incidence of burning and breaking methods in livestock and windbreak structures is greater than in dwellings and sweathouses.

A complex but consistent set of behaviors are responsible for these patterns. Additional wood trimming was undoubtedly required in the construction of domestic and sweathouse structures. The length of the beams and chinking material was probably adjusted to maximize structural stability and wood-to-wood contact. Both of these requirements are necessary to carry the weight and to maintain the integrity of the earthen covering that is placed upon Navajo sweathouses and dwellings. In contrast, little or no trimming or stem length adjustment is required in the construction of windbreaks and livestock structures. Consequently, the post-A.D. 1868 beam condition frequencies in habitation and sweathouse structures do not accurately reflect the changing incidence of tree felling techniques alone. Rather, the patterns illustrate the increased availability of the metal axe to perform felling *and* secondary modification behaviors.

WOOD STORAGE

Although the spring–summer season was preferred for wood procurement and building dwellings, these activities may not have been carried out in the same year. Analyses of the tree-ring data within the $(G, \phi 4)$ subset of the exterior ring condition set produced sufficient evidence to make inferences concerning Navajo wood storage activities.

The frequency of tree-ring samples exhibiting beetle galleries is high (G = 171 or 54%) compared with prehistoric tree-ring collections from the area. Data compiled from Table 1 shows that (G) samples are highly consistent with independent dating evidence ("consistent" = 142 = 83%; "inconsistent" = 13 = 8%; "unknown" = 16 = 9%).

Essentially two conditions could be responsible for the high occurrence of galleries; environmental stress on the pinyon trees, or Navajo post-harvesting behaviors. Bark beetles do not attack trees indiscriminately.

Dead or freshly killed trees and stems are most susceptible to infestation (Graham, 1965). However, living trees weakened by environmental stress may also become infested. Entire pinyon groves are reported to have been killed by massive beetle activity during periods of extreme drought in the Southwest (Little, 1944).

Tree-ring characteristics are accurate indicators of changing environmental conditions. In the American Southwest moisture is the primary limiting factor in annual tree growth (Douglass, 1914; Schulmann, 1956; Fritts, Smith, and Stokes, 1965). Therefore, tree-rings smaller than average generally reflect years of increased moisture stress, and tree-rings that are larger than average reflect conditions of decreased moisture stress (Fritts, 1965).

The amount of variability in a ring series is also influenced by the environment. Trees growing under optium conditions with abundant water supply will usually show little interannual ring width variation. Similarly, trees growing under extreme stress frequently produce small rings with little year-to-year variation (Fritts, Smith, Cardis, and Budelsky, 1965; Fritts, 1966).

Both measures of tree growth, annual variation and total variability in ring widths, were compared with beetle gallery incidence. If the high frequency of beetle galleries in the samples is related to environmental stress, then among samples exhibiting galleries (1) the year of tree death should be one in which below normal growth conditions prevailed leading to smaller than average ring widths, and (2) trees living in habitats where annual growth is severly inhibited should be more susceptible to beetle infestation. Thus the incidence of galleries should be highest on samples that reflect these combined sets of conditions.

The first set of conditions is measured by annual deviation from average growth, expressed as tree-ring indices. Modern and archaeological tree-ring samples from the study area were combined into an array of chronologically ordered index series (Stokes and Smiley, 1964b: 24–5). As trees increase in age, the amount of annual growth decreases. This nonclimatically related growth factor is eliminated from each sample in the set by fitting a curve to the plotted ring width measurements. The line of the growth curve essentially corresponds to the mean and is assigned a value of 1.00. Thus annual ring width departures greater or less than 1.00 signifies above and below normal growth respectively. The curve fitting and numerical assignment to the mean renders the index departures comparable between samples for any given time period (Stokes and Smiley, 1968).

No significant relationship was found between below normal terminal ring width and the presence of galleries. The various subsets containing (G) are not associated with tree death in a year when below normal growth

($<$ 1.00) occurred in trees within the study area (G$^1<$1.00 = 81 = 49%; G$<$1.00 = 85 = 51%).

The second set of conditions were measured by comparing those samples that reflect prolonged with those that reflect less inhibition of growth. The symbol (+) of the exterior ring condition set was assigned to partially cross-dated samples, where a ring count was made to the outside of the specimen. Virtually all of the (+) samples from the study area had compacted, smaller than average rings that accompany chronic tree growth inhibition (Stokes and Smiley, 1964a; Fritts, 1966).

No significant relationship can be demonstrated between relatively poor habitat and gallery incidence (ϕ1G$<$1.00 = 46 = 47%; ϕ1G $>$1.00 = 52 = 53%; and +G$<$1.00 = 35 = 52%; +G$\leq$1.00 = 33 = 48%). Therefore, the high occurrence of beetle galleries in the tree-ring sample population is not significantly related to environmental stress.

Galleries indicate wood procurement from living trees that were subsequently attacked by bark beetles. The amount of galleries on the surface of a wood segment increases with the amount of time the beetles have access to the phloem layer beneath the bark (Graham, 1965). In the prehistoric Southwest, wood was often harvested and stockpiled until the beetles had loosened the bark, thus facilitating bark peeling (Graham, 1965; Dean, 1969). Bark removal, however, terminates beetle activity. In view of these facts, two behavioral options were possible: (1) wood was cut primarily from live trees, stockpiled until the beetles had thoroughly burrowed beneath the bark, debarked, and used for construction purposes; or, (2) wood was harvested from live trees, incorporated into structures immediately with the bark remaining on the wood, and extensive beetle galleries produced while the wood was in use.

Evidence from subsequent analyses supports the second alternative. Approximately 70% of the tree-ring samples from each type of architecture exhibit the (G) condition. This fact becomes significant in view of the differential selection of stem sizes. As mentioned above, untrimmed branches were usually used in the construction of windbreaks, corrals, and lamb pens. It is highly unlikely that the bark was peeled from the branches as these are small in diameter and show no evidence of trimming. Similarly game traps were constructed with tree trunks that usually possessed most of the branches (Van Valkenburgh, 1956: 34). Although dwellings and sweathouses were built with wood trimmed of branches, the incidence of galleries does not differ from the other types of architecture.

Wood storage activity patterns changed dramatically after A.D. 1817. Among tree-ring samples from dwellings dating from A.D. 1700–1817, 14 out of 40 (35%) exhibit (G), whereas among samples from domestic structures built within the A.D. 1818–1900 period, 113 out of 150 (75%)

possess (G). The shift in (G) occurrence is not related to sampling error. The pattern also obtains on dated tree-ring samples from Navajo dwellings outside of the study area. Within a zone contiguous to northeastern Arizona, in northwestern New Mexico and southwestern Colorado, the (G) incidence in Navajo dwellings increases and exceeds (ϕ4) only after A.D. 1817.

The increase in galleries accompanied the increasingly widespread use of the metal axe which in turn, eliminated the wood storage phase. As indicated above, stockpiling facilitates bark removal. Bark beetle activity, bark decomposition, and wood shrinkage loosens the bark sufficiently for manual peeling. However, bark removal from freshly cut wood from live trees must be performed with an axe or an adze.

Bark removal is an activity designed to render a dwelling comfortable. If the bark is not peeled, the inhabitants of a Navajo-style structure will be showered constantly by small bits of bark. Hundreds of dwellings where the interior-facing wood was purposely trimmed with a metal axe were noted in the Land Claim survey reports. All of the datable structures fell within the A.D. 1818–1900 period.

Tree-ring dated wood from dwellings where beam condition was noted is plotted as cumulative frequency through time (Figure 3). The initial sharp increase in the use of the metal axe occurs between A.D. 1808–1819, the period when (G) also increases.

There is a limited amount of direct evidence to support the relation between (G) and the use of the metal axe in constructing domestic structures. The Land Claim survey crews reported 31 dwellings where bark remained on the wood. All were built after A.D. 1817, and all of the wood exhibited metal axe marks.

To summarize, prior to A.D. 1817, wood to be used in Navajo dwellings was stockpiled. The length of the storage period was probably short, with sufficient time allotted for the wood to shrink and bark beetle activity to commence. The bark was then peeled, probably manually, terminating beetle activity. Wood storage and peeling were activities performed by Navajo groups that lacked the metal axe.

By A.D. 1818 a significant proportion of the Navajo in the study area possessed metal axes. Wood storage was no longer required to facilitate bark removal. Bark was often trimmed from the interior-facing side of each freshly cut timber with the metal axe. The wood was then used immediately in construction. The bark remaining on the wood was attacked by bark beetles while the timbers were in use, producing extensive galleries.

Throughout the period A.D. 1750–1900, however, wood to be used for windbreaks, livestock structures, and game traps was not debarked and, judging by the high incidence of (G) through time, probably not stockpiled prior to use.

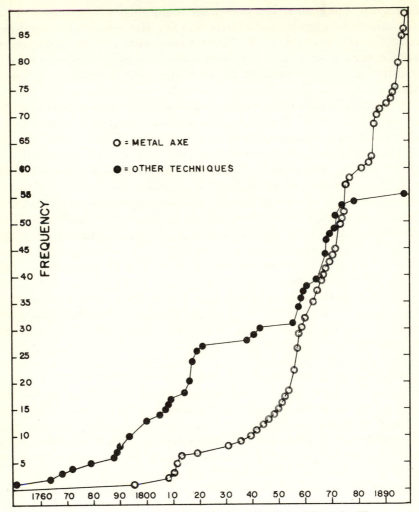

FIGURE 3   Graphs of cutting methods on dated wood from dwellings.

WOOD REUSE AND REPAIR

Tree-ring dated wood serves as an index of rebuilding and repair activities in dwellings (Table 4). The distribution was generated on a case-by-case basis. For example, each dwelling with two or more identical dates is considered a single case of the "O" category. A structure with three samples that date to three different years yields three unique chronological differences, and so on.

TABLE 4
Chronological differences between cutting dates

No. years difference	No. cases	No. years difference	No. cases	No. years difference	No. cases
0	20	10	1	51	2
1	4	11	1	70	1
2	2	14	2	94	1
3	1	15	1	100	1
4	2	18	4	141	1
5	1	20	1	155	1
7	2	25	3	159	1
8	1	28	1	166	1
9	2	31	1	182	1

The most populous class, "O," probably represents the initial construction event. The remaining differences, particularly the cluster between 1–31 years, probably records repairs made by the inhabitants. The 20 year gap between 31–51 years probably separates rebuilding and repair activities from the use of dead wood or the use of wood from older dwellings.

There is additional evidence for the use of old wood in the construction of dwellings. There are two structures that informants dated 50 years later than the tree-ring dates. Dated historic artifacts associated with both dwellings support informant estimates.

Wood reuse probably exceeded the use of dead trees in construction. Within sites where beam condition was noted, the Land Claim crews reported 12 dwellings in which more than one cutting technique was employed. In four of these cases, individual timbers exhibited more than one cutting method, indicating reuse. Additional information available for six of the domestic structures supported the notion of wood reuse. For example, timbers cut by the older methods such as the stone axe or burning were more severely weathered or cracked than those bearing metal axe marks. In other instances, trade items associated with the structure were consistent with the condition of the metal axe cut timbers.

All of the cases mentioned above are confined to regions where Navajo occupation was longest. In areas of short-term occupation, virtually all of the dates from a structure are consistent. Wood reuse increases with the increased availability of abandoned structures. In 37 sites where the dates derived from two or more dating methods are inconsistent, or where more than one cutting technique was used on the wood in a given structure, there are one or more dismantled dwellings.

Wood harvesting may have exceeded tree replacement, particularly in zones of long-term occupation. As discussed above, tree growth is limited by water stress throughout the study area. Consequently a long time is required for trees to reach sufficient diameter for use in dwellings. The average age of beams from habitation structures is 180 years, with a range of 60–400 years.

The amount of dead wood used in architecture is minimal. On the basis of independent dating evidence alone, the proportion of "inconsistent" samples having one or more of the elements (inc), (c), (G), or (B) does not exceed 12% (Table 1). Since a portion of the inconsistencies is attributable to repair or reuse activities, the amount of dead pinyon wood used in construction is probably lower than the 12% estimate. In terms of the wood use behavior patterns obtained in these analyses, it can be stated with approximately 90% confidence that an isolated tree-ring date from a Navajo structure in the study area possessing one or more of the exterior ring condition elements (inc), (c), (G), or (B), represents the date of a wood harvesting event.

CUTTING DATE ESTIMATION

Dating controls can be refined if it can be stated with measurable confidence that: (1) a tree-ring sample crossdated to the outermost ring, and exhibiting a particular set of exterior ring characteristics, died in the year specified by the outside date; or, (2) the death date of a sample crossdated to the exterior, but missing one or more outside rings, can be estimated within a specified range of error; or, (3) the death date of a sample that was not crossdated to the exterior, where the sample exhibits a particular set of ring characteristics, can be estimated within a specified range of error.

A number of previous studies in dendrochronology have approached the problem of estimating the cutting date of a wood sample. Exterior ring characteristics such as complete or incomplete growth combined with the presence of bark or phloem on the sample have been demonstrated on a *de facto* basis to be useful indicators of the final growth event prior to cutting (Bannister, 1962: 511).

Quantitative methods have been devised to estimate the cutting date of wood samples that lacked exterior ring characteristics. Douglass (1939) found that the heartwood–sapwood ratio in ponderosa pine (*Pinus ponderosa*) and Douglas-fir (*Pseudotsuga menziesii*) was highly uniform. The number of years from the exterior boundary of the darker tissue in the central stem (heartwood) through the lighter tissue (sapwood) to the outside of crossdated samples exhibiting true exteriors, was found to be relatively constant for each species. The heartwood–sapwood method was tested further by Smiley, Stubbs and Bannister (1953). They discovered that the ratio varied considerably by species and environmental setting. Thus the ratio must be empirically established in living datable trees growing within each study area. In their archaeological study, they found that their estimated cutting dates in wood samples with exterior rings eroded or exfoliated from them correlated well with historical information concerning the dates of construction.

The techniques used to estimate death dates should not be confused with crossdating. Crossdating and the associated verification methods are designed to answer the question "What exact span of calendrical years is represented in the sequential ring series in this sample?" The methods used to estimate cutting dates, however, are designed to answer the question "In what calendrical year did this tree segment die?"

Methods for estimating cutting dates can be coupled with probability statistics to formally measure the strength of quantitative relationships, given the provisions that; (1) it is known how the wood was used; (2) it is known how tree growth and wood preservation is affected by the environment; and (3) the number of tree-ring samples is sufficiently large for statistical analyses.

Dendrochronology and Navajo wood use behaviors are closely related. In previous sections of this paper, I have established that an outside tree-ring date followed by one or more of the observations (inc) (c), (G), and (B), is likely to represent the actual cutting date of the sample. However, Table 1 shows that when all details concerning growth, galleries, and bark are not observable on wood samples, the tree-ring dates are less likely to be consistent with other kinds of dating information. This pattern is predictable, given erosion and decay processes operating on the surface of the timbers that could, in time, remove one or more outside rings and eradicate all traces of the exterior ring condition.

The dating properties of samples are significantly associated with the wood stem sizes selected for use in the various classes of architecture. Thick mainstem wood from game traps and dwellings was more likely to survive corrosive forces than the smaller branches used in the construction of livestock, windbreak, and sweathouse structures. During the period covered in this analysis (A.D. 1700–1900), dated branchwood was much more likely to lack evidence of a true exterior than dated mainstem timbers (43% as compared with 18%).

The environment of the study area is also significantly related to problems the dendrochronologists encountered when crossdating tree-ring samples from Navajo structures. Out of the 316 dated samples, 166 (52%) were assigned the (+) symbol, indicating that the specimens were either partially crossdated, with a ring count made to the exterior, or the outermost rings fell within a period when small rings are known to occur and thus may be locally absent from the samples. A locally absent ring is the failure of the annual growth event to be expressed in the particular tree stem cross section undergoing analysis. The growth ring, however, may have been produced elsewhere on the tree from which the sample was taken.

Most of the (+) samples from the study area are characterized by narrow compact rings that exhibit little ring width variation (Stokes and Smiley, 1964a). Previous studies have shown that datable tree species showing these growth characteristics are likely to have a high incidence of locally absent rings (Fritts, Smith, Cardis and Budelsky, 1965: 7–14; Fritts, Smith, Budelsky and Cardis, 1965: 396–9; Fritts, 1966: 973–4).

Tree-ring samples from the area rarely possess "double" rings which result when a tree initiates growth more than once a year. The dendrochronological work notes do not list any occurrence of double rings for any dated sample from the region. Therefore, if a (+) sample was partially crossdated with a ring count made to the exterior, it is highly unlikely that the outside date would be an overestimate of the true cutting date due to double rings. Rather, the expectably high incidence of locally absent rings that would not be tabulated in a ring count could produce an underestimate of the death date.

Dated (+) samples lacking any evidence of the true exterior were not considered for cutting date estimation in the absence of data concerning wood erosion rates. A total of 69 (22%) of the tree-ring dates were in this category and were excluded from further analyses. The (+) samples with one or more of the elements (inc), (c), or (B) were used in cutting date estimation.

Tree-ring dates from multiple dated architecture, having a mixture of (+) and fully crossdated samples, were examined to see if (+) dates were consistently earlier or later than the true cutting dates. Only dwellings were used in this analysis. Game traps were not included, for it was apparent that they were repaired more frequently than domestic structures. Comparable data were insufficient from the other architectural types. A larger number of cases was obtained by including multiple dated dwellings located immediately adjacent to the study area.

In terms of the relationships discussed above, two kinds of error patterns could occur. First, (+) dates could be earlier than the true cutting dates from each dwelling due to untabulated locally absent rings within the ring count period. Second, if part of the wood was reused, or a series of repairs were made over a sufficiently long period of time, the underestimated (+) dates from the youngest wood might well date later than the fully crossdated samples derived from reused or initial construction timbers.

Table 5 illustrates that the first type of error pattern ("N (+) Early") occurs with a significantly higher frequency than error of the second type ("N (+) Late"). If the ratios in Table 5 are viewed as crude measures of rate, then the number of wood cutting events fell within a short period of time, and the "rate" of short-term wood cutting and error associated with locally absent rings is consistently twice as high as wood reuse or extended periods of dwelling repair in all sample areas.

TABLE 5

Comparison of (+) with fully crossdated samples from dwellings

Sample area	(1) N (+) early	(2) N dwellings	Ratio (1) : (2)	(3) N (+) late	(4) N dwellings	Ratio (3) : (4)
Study area	25	6	4.17	11	5	2.20
Circumstudy area	47	7	6.71	10	3	3.33
Total region	72	13	5.54	21	8	2.62

Another class of (+) dates was omitted from cutting date estimation. The (+) symbol is also assigned when the outermost rings fall within a period when one or more narrow rings are known to occur, but the sample does not possess enough additional rings to determine whether or not any rings are locally absent.

The evidence from Table 5 would indicate that the primary source of error in the class of (+) dates where ring counts were made can be attributed to locally absent rings. If so, cutting dates can be approximated where the number of missing rings can be estimated.

The odds that a ring will be locally absent from a tree-ring sample are not equally distributed through time. As dendrochronologists have discovered, relatively narrow rings are more likely to be missing from a sample than relatively wide rings. Since ring width sizes tend to be randomly distributed through time, the amount of error in a (+) date is not a function of the length of the ring count period, but is related to the number of years in a particular ring count period where locally absent rings are known to occur. The problem, therefore, is to discover the ring width size range in which locally absent rings are most likely to occur in tree-ring samples from the study area.

On the assumption that the interpretation of Table 5 is correct, a Pearson's *r* correlation coefficient was obtained from two sets of variables: (1) the number of years difference between fully crossdated samples and (+) dated specimens from the same dwelling; and, (2) within the ring count period of the (+) date, the number of rings falling within a particular range of ring width values. The ring width values (indices) were obtained from the regional chronology (Stokes and Smiley, 1964b). Index values < 1.00 signify the years of below average growth (narrow rings) and values of > 1.00 specify above average tree growth (wide rings). Only those cases were included in which the (+) samples were earlier than the fully crossdated specimens. Several (+) dates were omitted where no information as to the length of the ring count period was available. A total of 22 cases were suitable for correlational analysis.

It was to be expected that the smaller the ring width index values, the greater the likelihood that the rings corresponding to these values would be locally absent (Fritts, 1966). In order to determine the value range where most locally absent rings occurred, therefore, an *r* correlation was made with each of a series of increasingly wider tree-ring index values.

The results of the correlation analyses are presented in Table 6. All of the *r* coefficients are significant within the 95% confidence limits for a sample population of 22 (Young and Veldman, 1965: 420). The threshold for maximum covariation is the 0–.59 ring width index range.

TABLE 6

Date differences and ring index correlations (r)

Ring width index range	Correlation coefficient
0–0.09	0.616
0–0.19	0.510
0–0.29	0.673
0–0.39	0.578
0–0.49	0.464
0–0.59	0.847
0–0.69	0.750
0–0.79	0.689
0–0.89	0.630
0–0.99	0.578

The erratic fluctuations of the *r* coefficients up to the 0–.59 range are empirically justifiable. Ring width index values vary on a year-to-year basis in the regional chronology and the range of these values also vary through time. For example, the A.D. 1700–1750 period may contain narrow rings varying only from 0–.29, but the smallest index values in the A.D. 1751–1800 period may range only from .19–.49. However, each dwelling was usually constructed during a unique year within the A.D. 1700–1900 period and, moreover, the length of the ring count for each (+) sample was unique. Therefore, until the ring width index range is reached where most of the locally absent rings can be accounted for, regardless of construction date and length of the ring count, the r coefficients could, and did, vary considerably.

After the 0–.59 threshold is reached, however, increasing the range of index values does not increase covariation. Instead, error accumulates in the form of fewer locally absent rings in the higher index ranges, and the r coefficients drop smoothly in the .60–.99 range.

Cutting date estimation is warranted based upon the findings given in Table 6. The acceptable ring width index range in which the annual tree growth events are most likely to be locally absent from (+) dated samples is 0–.59, and is specified by the r correlation coefficient of .847. The characteristics of this presumably straight-line relationship are given by

$$Y_c = a + bX$$

Where Y_c = the computed Y value, a = the Y intercept, and b = the slope of the line. In this case Y_c = 2.30 + 0.8666X. A visual inspection of the data plotted against the line of this equation indicates that the relationship between the X and Y variables was indeed linear. The error of the estimating equation is given by

$$S_{y \cdot x} = \sqrt{\frac{Y^2 - (aY + bXY)}{N}} = \pm 2.39 \text{ years.}$$

The dispersion characteristics of the data around the axis of the estimating equation show that 95% of the cases ($\frac{2}{3}S_{y \cdot x}$) will fall within ± 4.78 years of the true death date of the (+) tree-ring samples (Croxton, 1953: 115–20).

Cutting date estimates were made for those (+) samples exhibiting (inc), (c), (G), or (B) not included in the correlation analyses. For each sample where the length of the ring count period was recorded, the number of rings within the 0–0.59 index range was accepted as the ring width index variable in the equation presented above. The mean number of years error specified by the X,Y intercept on the line of the equation was then added to each (+) date.

This death date estimation method enhanced dating controls. There is evidence to show that the estimated cutting dates are reasonably accurate. In eight out of 14 sites uncorrected (+) dates seemed to be inconsistent with independent dating evidence, but, were shown to be consistent through death date estimates. Moreover, there was no change in the status of those (+) specimens that were previously assessed to be consistent with other kinds of dating information.

Out of 69 (+) dates exhibiting evidence of a true exterior, ring count information was available for 51. In all, 16% more cutting dates were added to those that were fully crossdated, raising the total percentage of tree-ring dates useful for microtemporal analyses from 48 to 64%.

The equation derived here probably does not apply outside of the study region. An analysis was performed using tree-ring samples from Navajo structures in the Chinle Wash area, located immediately east of the study area. The range of ring width index values in which locally absent rings will most likely occur for the Chinle samples is 0–0.79, as compared with 0–0.59 for the study area. Similarly the values of the Chinle estimating equation differ.

In zones where considerable environmental variation exists, several equations will probably be required to accurately estimate cutting dates. Earlier studies have shown that growth characteristics are usually correlated within the same tree, and among trees growing in the same environment (Fritts, Smith and Stokes, 1965; Fritts, 1966). However, as the Chinle study illustrates, death date estimating equations must be independently derived. Dendrochronologists have devised a series of quantitative methods that are routinely applied to dated tree-ring samples to measure growth characteristics and to evaluate tree growth coherence in populations of tree-ring samples. Consequently, collaboration with fully qualified dendrochronologists is a prerequisite for the effective use of this cutting date estimation method or to evaluate its feasibility for a particular project.

ACKNOWLEDGMENTS

This paper represents a segment of my doctoral dissertation (Kemrer, 1974) submitted to the Department of Anthropology, The University of Arizona. I am greatly indebted to a number of individuals who made this study possible, particularly J. Lee Correll, Navajo Parks and Recreation Service, and several members of the Laboratory of Tree-Ring Research, including Bryant Bannister and Marvin A. Stokes. I am also grateful for the encouragement provided by my dissertation committee, R. Gwinn Vivian, Jeffrey S. Dean, and William J. Robinson.

REFERENCES

Bannister, B. (1962) The interpretation of tree-ring dates. *American Antiquity* **27**, 508–14.
Bannister, B. (1965) Tree-ring dating of archaeological sites in the Chaco region, New Mexico. *Southwestern Monuments Association, Technical Series* **6**, 115–214.
Caywood, L. R. (1961) Trade materials from Navajo sites identified and dated by L. R. Caywood. Manuscript, Navajo Land Claim files, Window Rock, Arizona, Typewritten.
Correll, J. L. (1961) Site reports. Navajo exhibit 520, Vols. 18–23, Dockett 229. Indian Claims Commission, Washington, D.C.
Croxton, F. E. (1953) *Elementary Statistics.* Dover, New York.
Dean, J. S. (1969) Chronological analysis of Tsegi phase sites in northeastern Arizona. *Papers of the Laboratory of Tree-Ring Research* **3**. The University of Arizona, Tucson.
Douglass, A. E. (1914) A method of estimating rainfall by the growth of trees. In The climatic factor, edited by E. Huntington, pp. 101–22. *Carnegie Institution of Washington, Publication* 192.

Douglass, A. E. (1939) Notes on beam dating by sap-heart contact. *Tree-Ring Bulletin* 6, 3–6.

Fritts, H. C. (1965) Tree-ring evidence for climatic changes in western North America. *Monthly Weather Review* 93, 421–43.

Fritts, H. C. (1966) Growth-rings of trees: their correlation with climate. *Science* 154, 973–9.

Fritts, H. C., D. G. Smith, C. A. Budelsky, and J. W. Cardis (1965) The variability of ring characteristics within trees as shown by a reanalysis of four ponderosa pine. *Tree-Ring Bulletin* 27, 3–18.

Fritts, H. C., D. G. Smith, J. W. Cardis and C. A. Budelsky (1965) Tree-ring characteristics along a vegetation gradient in northern Arizona. *Ecology* 46, 393–401.

Fritts, H. C., D. G. Smith and M. A. Stokes (1965) The biological model for paleoclimatic interpretation of Mesa Verde tree-ring series. In Contributions of the Wetherill Mesa Archeological Project, assembled by D. Osborne, pp. 101–21. *Society for American Archaeology, Memoir* 19.

Graham, S. A. (1965) Entomology: an aid in archaeological studies. In Contributions of the Wetherill Mesa Archeological Project, assembled by D. Osborne, pp. 167–74. *Society for American Archaeology, Memoir* 19.

Haury, E. W. (1935) Tree-rings: the archaeologist's time-piece. *American Antiquity* 1, 98–108.

Kemrer, M. (1974) The dynamics of western Navajo settlement: an archaeological and dendrochronological analysis. Ph.D. dissertation, The University of Arizona, Tucson.

Little, E. L., Jr. (1944) Destructive insects on pinyon pine (*Pinus edulis*). *Southwestern Forest and Range Experiment Station, Research Notes* 110, 1–4.

Mindeleff, C. (1898) Navajo houses. *Annual Report of the Bureau of American Ethnology* 17.

Robinson, W. J. (1967) Tree-ring materials as a basis for cultural interpretation. Ph.D. dissertation, The University of Arizona, Tucson.

Schulman, E. (1956) *Dendroclimatic Changes in Semiarid America*. The University of Arizona Press, Tucson.

Smiley, T. L. (1949) Pithouse number 1, Mesa Verde National Park. *American Antiquity* 14, 167–71.

Smiley, T. L., S. A. Stubbs and B. Bannister (1953) A foundation for the dating of some late archaeological sites in the Rio Grande area, New Mexico. *The University of Arizona Bulletin* 24.

Stallings, W. A., Jr. (1933) A tree-ring chronology for the Rio Grande drainage in northern New Mexico. *National Academy of Sciences, Proceedings* 19, 803–6.

Stokes, M. A. and T. L. Smiley (1963) Tree-ring dates from the Navajo land claim I: the northern sector. *Tree-Ring Bulletin* 25, 8–18.

Stokes, M. A. and T. L. Smiley (1964a) Dating of Navajo land claim specimens. Paper presented at 1964 Southwestern and Rocky Mountain Division, American Association for the Advancement of Science meeting, Lubbock.

Stokes, M. A. and T. L. Smiley (1964b) Tree-ring dates from the Navajo land claim II: the western sector. *Tree-Ring Bulletin* 26, 13–27.

Stokes, M. A. and T. L. Smiley (1966) Tree-ring dates from the Navajo land claim III: the southern sector. *Tree-Ring Bulletin* 27, 2–11.

Stokes, M. A. and T. L. Smiley (1968) *An Introduction to Tree-Ring Dating*. University of Chicago Press, Chicago.

Stokes, M. A. and T. L. Smiley (1969) Tree-ring dates from the Navajo land claim IV: the eastern sector. *Tree-Ring Bulletin* 29, 2–14.

Van Valkenburgh, R. F. (1956) Report of archaeological survey of the Navajo-Hopi contact area. Manuscript, Navajo Tribal Museum, Window Rock, Arizona. Typewritten.

Young, R. K. and D. J. Veldman (1965) *Introductory Statistics for the Behavioral Sciences*. Holt, Rinehart and Winston, New York.

Cultural Implications from the Distributional Analysis of a Lithic Site, San Pedro Valley, Arizona

LARRY D. AGENBROAD

Chadron State College

The Lone Hill site is located on the western periphery of the San Pedro Valley, southeastern Arizona. The site is assigned to the Chiricahua stage of the Cochise culture variant of the pre-ceramic Desert culture. It is a large surface site with an abundance of lithic debris, flaked stone tools, milling stones and hearths indicating either a large occupation or a long period of seasonal use.

The quantity of material and the surface exposure prompted a method of analysis which would have been impossible, or at least infeasible, in most excavated sites because of the difficulty in obtaining material such as retouch debris. Statistically valid techniques were used to sample surface debris and artifacts and to correlate their concentrations with milling equipment and hearth areas. The analysis shows that there is a nonrandom distribution of male-produced versus female-produced items on the site, indicating sexual division of labor as well as sexual division of site occupancy.

INTRODUCTION

The Lone Hill site, Arizona BB:10:17, is a pre-ceramic site of the Chiricahua stage of the Cochise culture variant of the Desert culture. It is located approximately 20 airline miles northeast of Tucson, Arizona, on the eastern flank of the Santa Catalina Mountains (Figure 1 upper), and lies on the west side of the San Pedro River Valley. This large surface site is somewhat unique in that it lies several miles from the river.

Previous work in sites of this period has been concentrated within the alluvium of the valley floor where material has been exposed in arroyo walls as a result of erosion. Other sites have been located near the mouths of canyons which emerge from mountain masses onto valley floors. The Lone Hill site does not fall into either of these categories, as it lies in the foothill-transition zone between the Santa Catalina Mountains and the Cenozoic valley fill of the San Pedro structural trough.

Early work on the Cochise culture centered in the San Pedro and Sulphur Spring Valleys of southern Arizona. It was within this core area that the cultural manifestation was first defined (Sayles and Antevs, 1941). The size of the culture area has been expanded with further investigation. The

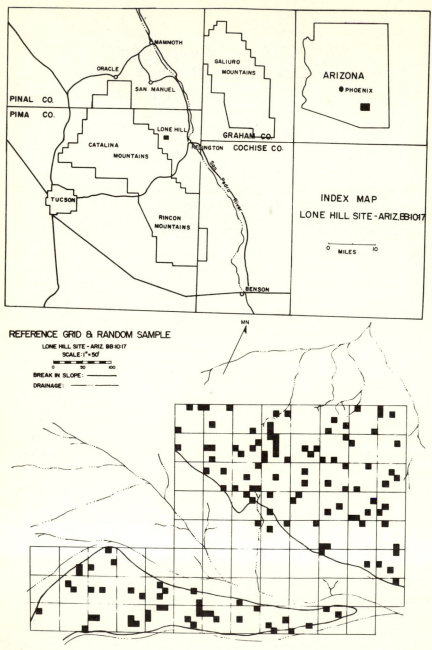

FIGURE 1 Location of the Lone Hill site, Arizona BB:10:17 (upper); reference grid and random sample (lower).

western extension lies at least as far as Ventana Cave (Haury, 1950); the eastern, as far as Tularosa Cave (Martin and others, 1952), Bat Cave (Dick, 1952), and the Rio Grande Valley (Campbell and Ellis, 1952). To the north and the northeast were the similar Concho complex (Wendorf and Thomas, 1951) and the San Jose culture (Bryan and Toulouse, 1943; Bryan and McCann, 1943). The Cochise culture undoubtedly extends into Mexico (Fay, 1955, 1956). Farther to the west, the cultural affinity to the Pinto Basin and Amargosa was early recognized (Campbell and Campbell, 1935). More recent work (Whalen, 1971, 1975; Huckell, 1973; Windmiller, 1973; Windmiller and Huckell, 1973) has done much to increase our knowledge of the Cochise culture in Arizona.

Cochise culture remains are associated with a series of lake beds, usually buried by later deposits and exposed by modern arroyo formation. Sayles and Antevs (1941) named the culture after investigations of a series of sites in Cochise County, southeastern Arizona. The artifact assemblages are somewhat meager since only the lithic material could survive in open locations over such a period of time. Sayles presents the Cochise culture in three stages, based on cultural evolution and a geologic chronology from stratigraphic analysis and associated fossils. The three stages are, in decreasing age: Sulphur Spring (*c*. 7,000 B.C. and earlier); Chiricahua (*c*. 7,000 –2,000 B.C.); and San Pedro (*c*. 2,000–200 B.C.).

The Sulphur Spring stage, named for the valley in which the principal sites occur, is reported to be associated with extinct fauna (dire wolf, native horse, mammoth) as well as modern bison, coyote, and antelope. Many of the bones appeared to have been burned and split. Cummings in 1926 (Haury, 1959) removed articulated bones and a mammoth skull from a stratigraphically higher horizon than that at which the artifacts occur at the type site of Double Adobe. The material culture included a great many grinding tools consisting of thin flat milling stones and small handstones. There were few percussion flaked, plano-convex implements for cutting, chopping and scraping. No projectile points were found in the original work, but later investigations produced points of leaf shape as well as stemmed and barbed types from the Sulphur Spring horizon (Willey and Phillips, 1958: 90–3). The preponderance of grinding tools suggests an economy based primarily on food gathering, with subsidiary hunting activity.

The Chiricahua stage, named for the Chiricahua Mountains, was initially found as midden and hearth sites along the eastern slopes of the mountains. Examples are the type site at the mouth of Cave Creek and sites in erosion channels of later age than the Sulphur Spring stage (Sayles and Antevs, 1941). The Chiricahua material culture showed a change from the earlier period involving shallow basin metates with accompanying handstones, bifacial percussion flaked tools, bone awls, and miscellaneous bone and antler material. Evidence from Bat Cave and Tularosa Cave adds substantially to our knowledge of the material culture inventory of the Chiricahua stage. But more important, they produce evidence of corn agriculture as early as 3,500 B.C. associated with stone tool assemblages differing from Chiricahua Cochise (Willey and Phillips, 1958). In the Tularosa Cave area of New Mexico, there is no evidence of the later San Pedro stage of the Cochise culture; the Chiricahua is transitional with the later pottery producing, agricultural Mogollon culture (Martin and others, 1952).

The terminal stage of the Cochise culture is the San Pedro, named for the river on which the type site occurs (Sayles and Antevs, 1941). The material culture is characterized by pressure flaked stone tools, mortars and pestles, and metates with deep basins and large manos. At the type site, large pits dug in the valley fill possibly served as storage facilities. The extent of the site and its long occupation suggested the presence of some type of housing. Several depressions were noted at the site, none of which were excavated; these may have been shallow houses. Later work on San Pedro stage sites exposed shallow, oval house floors with poorly defined fire areas and without definite evidence of roof supports. Some had a side entry with a wall step. Storage pits took up a large portion of the floor area. At the Cave Creek and San Simon villages (Sayles, 1945), a sequence of house types was revealed, with the addition of a developed ceramic technology which was acquired by late Cochise people from an unknown source. This evidence records the transition to the pottery-making Mogollon culture.

METHODOLOGY

The Lone Hill site consists of two ridges which lie to the northeast of the topographic high known as Lone Hill. The ridges are separated by an actively eroding gully, which may have dissected the original site. Encroachment by erosion of the headward migration of the drainage is evident. Also, the presence of tools and lithic debris in the channels of drainage patterns in these areas indicates dissection by erosion.

Since it is a surface site, with little or no stratigraphy, it lends itself to analytical methods which would be impossible, or at least infeasible, in most excavated sites because of the difficulty in obtaining the finer material such as retouch debris. Some observable features are present at the site, but many are noted only with difficulty after one has become familiar with the area. I decided to adopt a method of random sampling which would enable the analysis of portions of the site which had no observable features.

The entire site was referenced to a single grid. On the ground grid squares that were 50 feet on a side were laid out. Smaller ten foot grid squares were recorded on the map (Figure 1 lower). The decision to sample the two portions of the site independently was based on the knowledge that there was a natural separation of the north and south portions of the site, and that a statistical population of fewer than 1,000 is easier to handle than a population larger than 1,000. Plane table and alidade were used in order to plot the spatial relationship of the obvious features, such as the hearths; the milling tools, projectile points, and other artifacts, were mapped as they were encountered. The entire grid area was assigned numbered ten foot squares (900 on the northern portion and 450 on the southern portion), and a 10% sample of these populations was obtained from a table of random numbers.

All modified or unmodified stone that was either uncommon to the area or was obviously used by man was picked up from each sample area of 100 square feet. Some errors in sampling were inevitable: vegetation or erosional detritus covered the sample square and obscured or covered artifacts; erosion enriched or depleted artifact inventories; the experience and judgment of the samplers varied. It was especially difficult to decide whether quartz flakes, which are local in the area, were modified or natural. Any sampling bias as to stone type is definitely in the favor of quartz. Abundance of quartz tools collected on the site indicates that quartz was used extensively. All other tool-making material had to be imported.

All material collected from each sample square was bagged with appropriate square designation and returned to The University of Arizona for laboratory analysis. Manos, metates, and projectile points were mapped in position, assigned field numbers, and removed to the laboratory for description and analysis. Hearth areas were also mapped and tested. The chronological placement of the site which is based on attempts to date hearth contents is discussed in a later portion of this paper.

LITHIC ANALYSIS

Lithic material from the Lone Hill site was separated into three general categories: flaked stone debris, flaked stone tools, and pecked stone tools.

FLAKED STONE DEBRIS

More than 13,000 pieces of flaked stone debris, or waste flakes, were collected from the 135 squares sampled at the site. The flaked stone debris from each square was classified as decortication flakes (primary and secondary), core flakes (struck from a core), thinning flakes (to shape and thin core flakes), retouch flakes, core renewal flakes (to reshape a more desirable core), and shatter (irregular material as a consequence of flint knapping activity). The percentage of flaked stone debris recovered in each category is shown in Table 1.

TABLE 1

Relative proportions of flaked stone debris types from the Lone Hill site

Type of debris	Number of fragments	Percentage
Decortication flakes	121	0.9
Core flakes	5,080	39.0
Thinning flakes	5,015	39.0
Retouch flakes	1,870	14.0
Core renewal	243	2.0
Shatter	677	5.0
Totals	13,006	99.9

Classification of material as to type shows a preponderance of quartz, which as mentioned earlier, may result from sampling error. Other materials include jasper, agate, basalt, chert, rhyolite, quartzite, andesite, and obsidian in that order of frequency.

From the abundance of quartz in all categories of lithic material from the site, plus the occurrence of this variety of quartz in outcrop on the flanks of Lone Hill, it is most probable that one function of the site was that of a material source or quarry. The agate obtained in the sampling is of the variety which occurs in outcrop in the Palaeozoic limestones in the area (Agenbroad, 1967), such as the Black Hills to the northeast of the site. Obsidian occurs in low grade outcrops near the west front of the Galiuro Mountains, near the head of Redfield Canyon. The nearest known source of high quality obsidian is near Superior, Arizona. Jasper, basalt, andesite, and rhyolite are available in the adjacent San Pedro Valley.

FLAKED STONE TOOLS

An inventory of flaked stone tools includes 52 scrapers and 156 projectile points; 147 from the northern portion of the site and nine from the southern portion. Of all the projectile points collected on the site, 73% lie within the 100 equal density contour, following the trend of lithic debris, indicating a nonrandom location of projectile points relative to areas of lithic debris concentration, and reaffirming the presence of functionally specific areas within the site.

Projectile points (complete)

Projectile points have been grouped according to their stylistic attributes into five types (Haury, 1950; Sayles, 1945). Strong affinities are noted with San Jose (Bryan and Toulouse, 1943), Pinto (Campbell and Campbell, 1935), and Amargosa (Rogers, 1939; Haury, 1950) types. There is also a strong resemblance to the Gypsum Cave points (Harrington, 1933) of Nevada and the El Riego and Coxcatlán phases on the Tehuacan Valley in the states of Puebla and Oaxaca in Mexico (MacNeish, Nelken-Terner, and Johnson, 1967).

The projectile points were classified according to a modification of the method employed by Haury (1950) at Ventana Cave. Points were initially separated on the presence or absence of stems. Those without stems were then subdivided by overall shape and basal characteristics; those with stems, by basal characteristics only.

Five major projectile point types with subtypes resulted from this classificatory scheme (Figure 2).

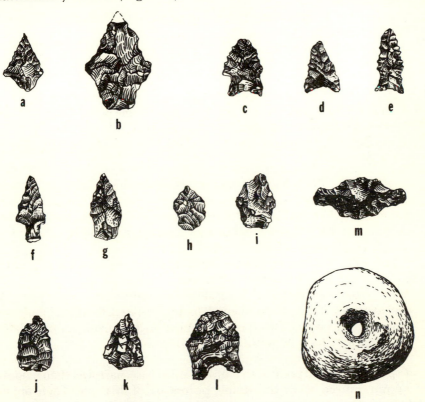

FIGURE 2   Projectile points from the Lone Hill site: *a,b*, Type A; *c-e*, Type B; *f,g*, Type C; *h,i*, Type D; *j-l*, Type E. Possible spokeshave, *m*. Perforated schist disk, *n*.

The major projectile point types and their subtypes from the Lone Hill site are:

Type A. Stemmed point with tapered base, narrower than the blade of the point. Thirty-four of the classifiable points fall within this type. Stylistically, there is a strong resemblance to the Gypsum Cave point (Harrington, 1933), and the El Riego point of Central Mexico (MacNeish and others, 1967) and Type D (Diamond) points of Ventana Cave (Haury, 1950). Only three of the 34 points do not have the bulb of percussion at the basal portion. Four subtypes are recognized within Type A.

Subtype A-1: Convex, tapering base; 17 specimens: 7 manufactured from quartz, 3 from andesite, 2 from agate, 2 from jasper, 1 each from basalt and chert. This group contains the three exceptions to a basal bulb of percussion.

Subtype A-2: Straight base; 4 specimens: 3 manufactured from quartz, 1 from obsidian.

Subtype A-3: Pointed base; 10 specimens: 4 quartz, 2 obsidian, 2 agate, 1 basalt, 1 jasper.

Subtype A-4: Square, tapered base; 3 specimens: 1 rhyolite, 1 jasper, 1 andesite.

Type B. Stemmed point with concave base, either narrower or wider than blade of the point. Twenty-six of the classifiable points from the Lone Hill site fall within this category. They are recognizable as within the range of Pinto Basin–Amargosa II–San Jose types. There are four subdivisions of Type B.

Subtype B-1: "Pinto Basin"; concave base wider than blade; 5 specimens: 3 obsidian, 1 basalt, 1 rhyolite.

Subtype B-2: "Winged" points; concave base with flaring "wing" caused by rudimentary side notching; lack of seration; 6 specimens: 2 jasper, 1 basalt, 1 andesite, 1 agate, 1 chert.

Subtype B-3: Stemmed with concave base narrower than blade of point, 6 specimens: 3 basalt, 2 agate, 1 obsidian.

Subtype B-4: "Rectangular" base; stemmed point with concave base and concave sides of stem; 9 specimens: 2 basalt, 2 agate, 2 rhyolite, 1 andesite, 1 obsidian, 1 jasper. Two specimens have such narrow pointed blades that they may have been utilized as drills.

Type C. Stemmed point with parallel-sided base, narrower than blade of the point. Fifteen of the classifiable points are of this type. There are no subtypes: 3 basalt, 5 jasper, 3 quartz, 2 agate, 2 rhyolite.

Type D. Stemmed point with blunt (stub) base, unmodified striking platform. The fifteen specimens of this group have been subdivided based on the possibility that two of the points might be burins or gravers rather than projectile points.

Subtype D-1: Straight to irregular "stub" base; usually with more or less pronounced stem which is generally short and tapering; 13 specimens: 5 quartz, 3 agate, 2 basalt, 2 rhyolite, 1 andesite.

Subtype D-2: Possible burins or gravers which are asymmetrically pointed and of less than average size; 2 specimens of quartz.

Type E. Points without stems. Six specimens of this type fall into three subgroups. It is within this type that two points reminiscent of Palaeo-Indian tool traditions occur.

Subtype E-1: Triangular with concave bases; 2 jasper specimens.

Subtype E-2: Lanceolate leaf-shaped points that may have been used as knives; 2 specimens: 1 basalt, 1 andesite.

Subtype E-3: Concave base "Palaeo" points. Each point is basically ground and lacks distinctive fluting, or would be classed in Llano and Folsom complexes. The basal portion of a large rhyolite point is strongly suggestive of Clovis projectile points from farther south in the San Pedro Valley. One variegated agate point lacks the characteristic flute and would be classed as a Folsom point. It may be a Midland variant of the Folsom type.

Of the 96 classifiable points from the site, 90 are stemmed. Of these, 38% are Type A, 28% are Type B, 17% are Type C, and 17% are Type D.

Projectile points (fragmentary)

Sixty unclassified projectile points were collected. Of these broken projectile points, 49% were tips, 20% were bases, and 30% were midsections. This distribution suggests that approximately 80% of the fragmentary non-classifiable projectile points from the site were the result of accidental breakage during manufacture, rather than of retipping projectiles broken in the hunt, as a high percentage of bases might have suggested. Rhyolite, jasper, agate, quartz, and basalt are the dominant materials among these fragmentary points. The difficulty of working rhyolite and quartz may in fact account for the abundance of fragmentary remains.

Drills

Bases of two broken drills were collected. Both are flaked and are of the long, straight, bifacial type which commonly tapers to a point. Bases differ in size and shape, but the blade portions are similar. One, of agate, has what Haury (1950) terms a straight base. The second, of jasper, has what is termed a large flange base.

Possible spoke shave

The occurrence of a flaked stone object of basalt (Figure 2) with two intentional stems at right angles to bifacial cutting edges has its closest analogy in a modern tool kit to a small draw-knife or "spoke shave." The two projections may have been used to haft the tool, resulting in a cutting edge between and at right angles to the handles. No similar artifacts were noted on the site.

Knives and scrapers

Flaked stone tools, other than projectile points, are classified as bifacial or unifacial. The unifacial material in most cases represents scrapers of one form or another. Most of the bifacial material could be classified loosely as knives.

Twenty-eight unifacial tools were recovered and divided into five types: end scraper (8), end and side scrapers (9), side scrapers (5), 3/4 (end and two sides) scrapers (4), and gravers (2). Twenty-two of the unifacial tools are made from flakes with modified dorsal sides. Five tools are made from cores. Agate, quartz and jasper are the predominant materials used.

Twenty-four bifacial tools were classed as "knives" (19), choppers (2), or scrapers (3), based on stylistic attributes. Most of these tools are fragmentary, usually represented by the base or tip of the original tool. They vary considerably in style and workmanship. Some are possibly "blanks" made for further modification, and used as is or discarded. The low percentage of retouch flakes from the site also indicate that some of these "tools" may be blanks. Agate, quartz, jasper, quartzite, rhyolite, and chert are the predominant materials.

Only 27% of these unifacial and bifacial tools fall within the 100 equal density contour. Most are found in close proximity to hearths or milling equipment.

Perforated schist disk

One of the more atypical items from the Lone Hill Cochise site is a perforated schist disk (Figure 2). The disk is circular in shape with a diameter of 45–49 mm, a thickness of 10 mm, and a central perforation 6 mm in diameter. The edges have been shaped and the object has been perforated by drilling from each side. It is inferred that because of the high sheen of the micaceous minerals, especially in bright sunlight, this object was probably worn as a pendant suspended by the central perforation.

Cores

Cores are the irregular or roughly hemispherical blocks of rock from which flakes were struck for tool manufacture. Fourteen cores were recognized on the Lone Hill site. The abundance of flakes indicates that there should have been more cores. Materials probably were pretrimmed at quarry sites.

All but six of the cores are rounded in shape, with a flat plane serving as a striking platform. Steep angle flakes have been removed from them. Six of the cores are irregular and appear to have been struck at random as long as they would yield suitable flakes. Two of the latter variety appear to have remnant planar surfaces, suggesting former use as metates. Jasper, quartzite, and basalt cores are the most abundant.

Hammerstone

In addition to the cores listed above, one specimen of coarse-grained quartzite with several flakes removed appears to have been used as a hammerstone. Considering the knapping activity at this site, the yield of one recognized hammerstone is low indeed. This suggests the possibility of baton knapping on previously trimmed blanks.

PECKED STONE TOOLS

Inventory of pecked stone tools totals 68 manos and 36 metates.

The metates are of two general types, slab (11%) and basin (89%) (Figure 3). Most of the metates are broken or cracked, although many are whole or restorable. Many of the basin metates have been intentionally thinned and shaped by pecking the surfaces. Seventy-one percent of the metates were found in the inverted or basin down position. Those which were not were usually either disturbed or broken. Evidently, they were intentionally left in this position either to protect the grinding surface or to make the metates less conspicuous, or both. Quartzite was the most frequently used material for metates. Andesite, siltstone, limestone, diorite, gneiss, basalt, and schist occur in approximately that order of abundance.

The basin metates are generally formed from large blocks of stone, ranging up to 20,225 gm total weight. Average weight for basin metates is 11,215 gm; for slab metates, 7,103 gm. One specimen is a large basin metate

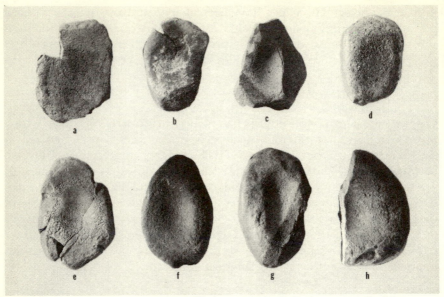

FIGURE 3   Metates from the Lone Hill site: *a-c* and *e-h*, basin metates; *d*, slab metates. (Photograph courtesy of the Arizona State Museum.)

which was worn completely through. It is possible that this milling stone was ceremonially "killed," although no evidence of burial was found. This metate did occur in an anomalous cluster of metates, on the north portion of the site, to the southeast of the trend of lithic debris.

Manos are of the one-hand variety and fall into three categories or types. Type A: modified cobble, is usally a rounded, stream-worn cobble with one or more abrasion planes. Type B: elongate-shaped, is usually somewhat rectangular, resulting from edge modification and two grinding surfaces. Type C: circular-shaped, is usually modified over the entire surface by pecking; most specimens approach sphericity.

The types of stone used for manos, in rank order, are: quartzite (34%), sandstone (28%), granite (9%), diorite, schist, and gneiss (8% each), siltstone (3%), and andesite (2%). Of the 68 manos, 53% are bifacial, 47% unifacial.

INTERPRETATION

Upon completion of sampling and analysis, the site was mapped with equal density contours using an arbitrary interval of 50 pieces of flaked stone debris per contour. The trend of flaked stone debris concentration showed nonrandom distribution (Figure 4). Separate plots of the frequency

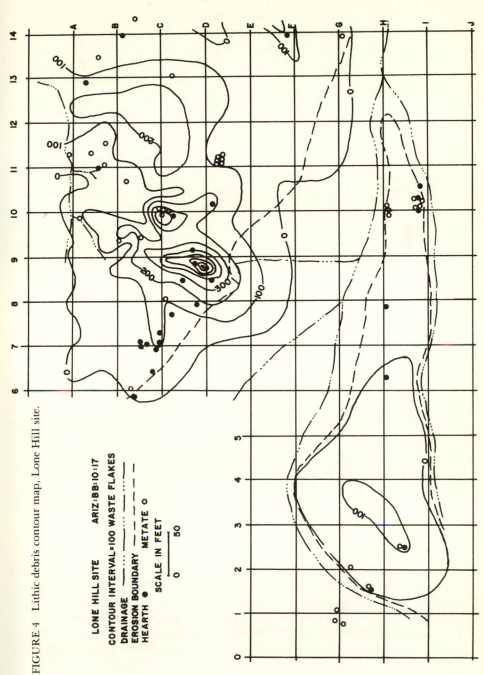

FIGURE 4 Lithic debris contour map, Lone Hill site.

LONE HILL SITE   ARIZ:BB:10:17

CONTOUR INTERVAL=100 WASTE FLAKES

DRAINAGE ....

EROSION BOUNDARY ― ― ―

HEARTH ●   METATE ○

SCALE IN FEET

0   50

and distribution of individual types of flakes were also contoured. The results of these analyses carried the same trend as the plot of total flaked stone debris and were not significant otherwise. Flaked stone debris concentrations are also correlated with the distribution of flaked stone tools and projectile points. These are probably all male-produced items. Concentrations of male-produced items at the Lone Hill site appear to be spatially segregated from female-produced or female-related items such as milling stones and hearth concentrations.

The assumption that milling stones and hearths indicate female-produced items or female-related activities is based on ethnographic data from hunting-gathering groups (Wheat, 1967: 36) and from Pueblo groups (Eggan, 1950: 131). In most groups of this type, gathering and processing of vegetable products is the work of women, whereas hunting and hunting equipment are male-associated activities and items.

CHRONOLOGY

In an attempt to obtain absolute dating for the Lone Hill Cochise site, all 27 hearths were sampled for charcoal content. Only one hearth yielded charcoal in sufficient quantity for radiocarbon analysis. The results of this sample (A-781) yield a date of 300 + 90 B.P., or about A.D. 1650. This date is inconsistent with the relative age of the material culture, and it is suggested that this hearth represents a minor, late occupation of the site (Haynes and others, 1967).

Attempts were made to secure a date by relatively new thermoluminescence technique using the limestone hearth stones from selected hearths. Dr. Noye Johnson of Dartmouth College sampled and dated the hearths on the northern portion of the site. This analysis yielded a preliminary date of 5700 B.P. (Johnson, 1965). Several assumptions had to be made in the calculation of this date, and with no radiocarbon material for cross checking, the age should be considered relative until there is further refinement of the technique in this area.

The hearths were also sampled for palaeomagnetic determination by Dr. R. L. DuBois of the University of Oklahoma. The initial results do not allow an accurate age assignment at this time.

Stylistically, the material culture can be assigned to the Chiricahua stage of the Cochise culture (Sayles and Antevs, 1941). The types and subtypes of projectile points described here correspond almost exactly with the Chiricahua–Amargosa level of Ventana Cave (Haury, 1950). Age for the Chiricahua stage ranges (depending on the source) from about 7,000 to 3,000 years ago.

Stylistic similarities with the El Riego culture phase of the Tehuacan Valley of southern Mexico (MacNeish and others, 1967) also give tentative age assignment of approximately 6,000–3,000 B.P. for the material culture of the site.

Relative dating using the similarity of the material culture, in particular the projectile points, lends support to the age of the site as suggested by the thermoluminescence analysis.

SUMMARY AND CONCLUSIONS

Statistical techniques applied to an undisturbed surface site, composed primarily of lithic waste flakes and milling stones, can produce archaeological information which has been largely ignored in previous investigations of the Cochise culture in the Southwest. A 10% random sample, applied separately to the two portions of the Lone Hill site, has produced several interpretations and results.

Statistically valid sampling and analysis of lithic waste debris has produced evidence of functionally specific areas within a site occupied by hunter–gatherers at a band level of social organization. The simplest interpretation of the nonrandom distribution of artifacts is that they reflect a division of labor between males and females at the Lone Hill site.

The low density of primary and secondary core preparation debris indicates that the Cochise occupants of the site may have pretrimmed the cores and transported them to the site for further manufacture. The high density of thinning and retouch material on the site suggests that much of the knapping activity involved artifact shaping and finishing.

The abundance of lithic debris plus finished and fragmentary artifacts with a large assemblage of milling tools argues for either an extended occupation or a seasonal camp occupied repeatedly (cf. Whalen, 1975). The placement of metates in an inverted position indicates an anticipated return, as if to a seasonal site. The concentration of lithic material in a nonrandom distribution in a seasonal site (Figure 4) can be explained as a function of (1) specific areas of a site having been selected or delegated to specific families, (2) return to the same female-owned items on each reoccupation.

The lithic industry as evidenced by both waste debris and the abundance of finished tools, leaves little doubt as to the importance of hunting as well as the utilization of vegetable resources in the lifeway of these people.

Analysis of this and other sites in this portion of the San Pedro Valley (Agenbroad, 1967) indicates that the geologic–hydrologic factors controlling site location are fourfold: (1) water source, (2) agricultural or gathering areas, (2) quarry or source material sites, and (4) vantage points. The Lone Hill site meets at least the last two criteria. The summit of Lone Hill makes an excellent vantage point from the west flanks of the valley. That the quartz seams on the hill were utilized for artifacts is substantiated in the composition of both lithic debris and finished artifacts.

ACKNOWLEDGMENTS

I would like to acknowledge the efforts of a number of individuals who assisted me in various phases of the compilation of this report. In particular, I express my gratitude to faculty members at The University of Arizona: Dr. R. H. Thompson and Dr. W. A. Longacre of the Department of Anthropology and Dr. C. V. Haynes of the Department of Geochronology. These gentlemen served as members of my thesis committee (Agenbroad, 1970). I also thank Dr. N. Johnson, Dartmouth College, for assistance in the thermoluminescent dating of the hearth stones from the site.

Students and friends assisted in much of the actual field work, mapping, and collection of surface materials. I thank the following: L. Sommers, J. Ayres, K. Adkinson, M. Womack, D. Libby, L. Bergs, M. Winters, J. Baer, E. Richardson, and P. Grebinger.

In addition, Mrs. S. Whitthorne did much of the sketching of the artifacts. Miss Helga Teiwes of the Arizona State Museum photographed the manos and metates.

Finally, I wish to acknowledge L. Carter, S. Kaylor, M. Koons, P. Ruzicka and my wife, Wanda, who typed the manuscript; and my son, Brett, who accompanied me for many hours in the field.

REFERENCES

Agenbroad, L. D. (1967) Cenozoic stratigraphy and palaeo-hydrology of the Redington-San Manuel area, San Pedro Valley, Arizona. Ph.D. dissertation, The University of Arizona, Tucson.

Agenbroad, L. D. (1970) Cultural implications from the statistical analysis of a prehistoric lithic site in Arizona. M.A. thesis, The University of Arizona, Tucson.

Bryan, K. and F. T. McCann (1943) Sand dunes and alluvium near Grants, New Mexico. *American Antiquity* 8, 281–90.

Bryan, K. and J. H. Toulouse, Jr. (1943) The San Jose non-ceramic culture and its relations to Puebloan culture in New Mexico. *American Antiquity* 8, 269–80.

Campbell, E. W. C. and W. H. Campbell (1935) The Pinto Basin site: an ancient aboriginal camping ground in the California desert. *Southwest Museum Papers* 11.

Campbell, J. M. and F. H. Ellis (1952) The Atrisco sites: Cochise manifestations in the middle Rio Grande Valley. *American Antiquity* 17, 211–21.

Dick, H. W. (1952) Evidences of early man in Bat Cave and on the Plains of San Augustin, New Mexico. In Indian tribes of aboriginal America, pp. 158–63. *Selected Papers of the XXIXth International Congress of Americanists* 31. University of Chicago Press, Chicago.

Eggan, F. (1950) *Social Organization of the Western Pueblos.* University of Chicago Press, Chicago.

Fay, G. E. (1955) Prepottery, lithic complex from Sonora, Mexico. *Science* 121, 777–8.

Fay, G. E. (1956) Peralta complex — a Sonoran variant of the Cochise culture. *Science* **124**, 1029.

Harrington, M. R. (1933) Gypsum Cave, Nevada. *Southwest Museum Papers* 8.

Haury, E. W. (1950) *The Stratigraphy and Archaeology of Ventana Cave, Arizona.* The University of Arizona Press and The University of New Mexico Press, Tucson and Albuquerque.

Haury, E. W. (1959) Association of fossil fauna and artifacts of the Sulphur Spring stage, Cochise culture. *American Antiquity* **25**, 609–10.

Haynes, C. V., P. Damon, D. Gray and R. Bennett (1967) Arizona radiocarbon dates. *Radiocarbon* **9**, 9.

Huckell, B. B. (1973a) The Gold Gulch site: a specialized Cochise site near Bowie, Arizona. *The Kiva* **39**, 105–29.

Huckell, B. B. (1973b) The Hardt Creek site. *The Kiva* **39**, 171–97.

Johnson, N. (1965) An empirical isothermal decay law for the thermoluminescence of calcite. *Journal of Geophysical Research* **70**, 4653–62.

MacNeish, R. S., A. Nelken-Terner, and I. W. Johnson (1967) *Prehistory of the Tehuacan Valley: nonceramic artifacts* 2. University of Texas Press, Austin.

Martin, P. S., J. B. Rinaldo, E. Bluhm, H. C. Cutler and R. Grange, Jr. (1952) Mogollon cultural continuity and change: the stratigraphic analysis of Tularosa and Cordova Caves. *Fieldiana: Anthropology* 40.

Rodgers, M. J. (1939) Early lithic industries of the lower basin of the Colorado River and adjacent desert areas. *San Diego Museum Papers* 3.

Sayles, E. B. (1945) The San Simon branch, excavations at Cave Creek and in the San Simon Valley, I: material culture. *Medallion Papers* 34.

Sayles, E. B. and E. Antevs (1941) The Cochise culture. *Medallion Papers* 29.

Wendorf, F. and T. H. Thomas (1951) Early man sites near Concho, Arizona. *American Antiquity* **17**, 107–13.

Whalen, N. M. (1971) Cochise culture sites in the central San Pedro drainage, Arizona. Ph.D. dissertation, The University of Arizona, Tucson.

Whalen, N. M. (1975) Cochise site distribution in the San Pedro Valley. *The Kiva* **40**, 203–11.

Wheat, M. M. (1967) *Survival Arts of the Primitive Paiutes.* University of Nevada Press, Reno.

Willey, G. R. and P. Phillips (1958) *Method and Theory in American archaeology.* University of Chicago Press, Chicago.

Windmiller, R. (1973) The late Cochise culture in the Sulphur Springs Valley, southeastern Arizona: archaeology of the Fairchild site. *The Kiva* **39**, 131–69.

Windmiller, R. and B. B. Huckell (1973) Desert culture sites near Mormon Lake, northern Arizona. *The Kiva* **39**, 199–211.

Prehistoric Social Organization in Chaco Canyon, New Mexico: An Evolutionary Perspective*

PAUL GREBINGER

Eisenhower College

It has been proposed that the social organization of the occupants of two different types of sites in Chaco Canyon, New Mexico was different. Residents of "villages" were organized according to a principle of localized corporate lineages, while residents of "towns" were organized according to a principle of dual division. I propose, as an alternative, that a rank society developed under nearly pristine conditions between A.D. 850 to 1130. The basis for the rank society was differential agricultural productivity. Some local groups that were favored by a fortuitous combination of summer thundershowers and natural catchment systems became the nucleus of the "towns." Their rights through prior use to the abundant harvests of the favored zones were the basis for the emergence of status differentiation, redistribution and ultimately craft and task specialization. Water control systems developed only after the principles of the rank society had become established and probably in response to a combination of increasing population and increasingly heavy summer thundershowers. Suggestions are presented for future research that would help test the model.

Postscript — No model is without its muddles. Two are examined. Also, the power of the model to account for further variability in the data is explored.

INTRODUCTION

This paper has developed in response to an article by R. Gwinn Vivian in which he formulates a proposition about the social organization of prehistoric inhabitants of Chaco Canyon, New Mexico. According to Vivian (1970b: 78–83) two types of sites, "villages" and "towns," were occupied by people who were organized according to two different principles of social organization. The residence units of villages were localized corporate lineages, the residence units of towns nonexogamous moieties.

The argument seems to be based on three primary observations for the time period between approximately A.D. 850 to 1130: That there is a marked physical difference between two contemporaneous types of sites; that an ap-

---

*This article was first published without postscript in *The Kiva* **39**, 3–23, and appears in this volume with permission of the Arizona Archaeological and Historical Society.

parent duality in settlement pattern and numbers of great kivas exists in some sites of the town type; and that irrigation systems are associated with only one of the two types of sites, the towns. The stimulus for the proposed contemporaneous types of organization, as Vivian notes elsewhere (1968: 29-30), comes from an hypothesis suggested by Dozier (1960) that

differences in social organization between Eastern and Western Pueblos may be explained by differences in agricultural practices, and that the bilateral character of the Tanoan kinship system is old and has no hint of a former lineage system.

While in some respects existing data do strongly support a reconstruction such as Vivian has presented, they certainly would allow others. In fact, a method of strong inference (Platt, 1964) demands that we attempt to supply alternatives, devise "crucial experiments" (in this paper suggestions for future research) and then carry out these experiments the outcome of which will allow us to refine the earlier reconstructions. It is in this spirit that I have attempted to reevaluate the existing archaeological evidence from Chaco Canyon.

Vivian's proposal treats the archaeological manifestation after A.D. 850. He shows that after A.D. 850 villages and towns began to emerge. That differences exist is evident in architecture, in some artifact types, in the burial pattern, and in the settlement pattern (Judd, 1954, 1959, 1964; Pepper, 1920; Brand and others, 1937; Kluckhohn and Reiter, 1939: Dutton, 1938; Vivian, 1965). Initially towns did not strongly differ from villages in size or in the material attributes that later distinguish them from villages. Some town sites such as Pueblo Bonito, Una Vida, Peñasco Blanco and Kin Bineola became considerably larger than the villages during the tenth century, but nothing like their maximum size.

Between A.D. 990 and 1030 a major building period was inaugurated and continued until A.D. 1124 (Vivian and Mathews, 1965: 108). The classic Chaco town sites as we know them today, including Peñasco Blanco, Pueblo del Arroyo, Pueblo Bonito, Chetro Ketl, Kin Klizhin, Kin Ya'a, Hungo Pavi, Una Vida, Wijiji, Pueblo Pintado, Old Alto, and Kin Bineola were the result of the major construction. The small village sites were also increasing during this period, but not in size as much as in number. There is impressive evidence from this period of a rapid increase in population.

A single social system organized according to the principle of ranking fits the known data from Chaco Canyon as well as the alternative Vivian has suggested. There is no need, however, to define this system in such a way that it conforms to the ideal ranked society termed a "chiefdom" by Service (1962: 143-74). Nor should we expect total conformity with the other definitions of rank society such as those suggested by Kirchhoff

(1959), Fried (1960, 1967) and Sahlins (1958, 1964). The Chaco Canyon development, by contrast, may have been closer to "pristine" (Fried, 1967: 111) than any recent example. The change to a rank society would have brought about a social system for which there was no precedent in the Anasazi Southwest and of which there might be only slight trace among historic pueblos.

AN ARCHAEOLOGICAL MODEL OF A PRISTINE RANK SOCIETY

A model of a pristine rank society in Chaco Canyon cannot be constructed by using a direct historical approach between ethnographically known rank societies among the Pueblos of North America and prehistoric communities that preceded them. Principles of ranking did not exist at the time of Spanish contact, nor have they developed in the following four centuries (Spicer, 1962; Eggan, 1950; Dozier, 1970) (See also Grebinger, 1971, for references to native social customs and institutions in selected Spanish documents). The closest approximation to such principles may have existed among Keresan pueblos. Dozier (1970: 154), referring to an earlier study by Leslie A. White, points out that,

> the Keresan pueblos had the germ of a ruling class in the medicine men, war priests, and a warrior's association. The Keresans did not, however have hereditary offices, nor was land owned by a special group but by the people in general; the resources of the land were generally available to all. Yet, ... despotic rule by the religious–political hierarchy did take place in virtually all the pueblos and across the years some Indians lost houses, property and land, and were evicted from their pueblos. Thus, considerable power was held by a central authority—the medicine men and war priests.

For the most part Keresan pueblos did not select their village chief from a specific clan as is common among Western Pueblos—Hopi, Hano, Zuni, and Acoma (Dozier, 1970: 188). Therefore, a hereditary chieftainship would not have developed among the Keresans and did not exist at the time of Spanish contact.

Furthermore, southwesternists have made no irrefutable linkages between historically known Pueblos (particularly those in New Mexico) and specific prehistoric population centers (especially those in the San Juan River drainage) (Reed, 1949; Wendorf, 1954; Wendorf and Reed, 1955; Eggan, 1950; Fox, 1967). It should be noted here, however, that Robin Fox (1967: 189–91), in his synthesis and critique of cultural continuities in the Southwest, derives Keresan pueblo population from Chaco Canyon and Mesa Verde. Consequently, even if principles of ranking had existed among the Pueblos at the time of Spanish contact, at the present time no direct historical link can be made between them and the population in Chaco Canyon. I am not without recourse, however. The syntheses of general ethnographic knowledge provided by Sahlins (1958, 1963), Kirchhoff (1959), Service (1962), and Fried (1960, 1967) can be combined with a knowledge of the logic of ranking systems in order to construct a model that accounts for a number of observations on the nature and distribution of archaeological material culture in Chaco Canyon.

The model for the development of a pristine rank society that I propose contains five major elements. First locally fortuitous combinations of climatic and topographic factors provide the basis for differential access to adequately watered agricultural land. Second, population expansion is both a response to the potential for superabundant harvests in some locales, and a force that gives rise to status differences among local groups. The first two elements of the model are dynamic or creative. The remaining three are dependent upon them. Third, as the system developed in Chaco Canyon two status groups emerged consisting of those residence units that originated in environmentally favored locales, the high status groups, and all others. The latter may also have resided within favored locales but had no claim to rights in land there. Fourth, the redistributive system developed as a mechanism of exchange to equalize the imbalance in some local groups' access to agricultural lands in favored locales. Redistribution increased in importance and the redistributive network increased in extent as the number of groups integrated by it increased, a result of expanding population. The physical expansion of the population out from the locales in which the founder groups first emerged was accompanied by a corresponding displacement of the redistributive centers. Fifth, specialization in craft production and in communal construction projects, including water control, developed as the high status group increasingly diverted productive energies toward its own ends. Each of these elements will be discussed in conjunction with a reexamination of published archaeological evidence from Chaco Canyon. A diagram of the model as it is discussed in the following pages is presented in Figure 1.

Rank societies develop where individuals or groups have differential access to natural resources, a state of disequilibrium of great evolutionary potential. Service (1962: 145–46) recognizes this fact when he points out that the development of economic specialization and redistributive networks result where local differences in the kinds of crops that can be grown or in the natural products of the land are equalized by regional exchange between economically specialized local residential units. However, it is not generally recognized that rank societies also may develop where the productive potential of agricultural lands sown to the same crops varies

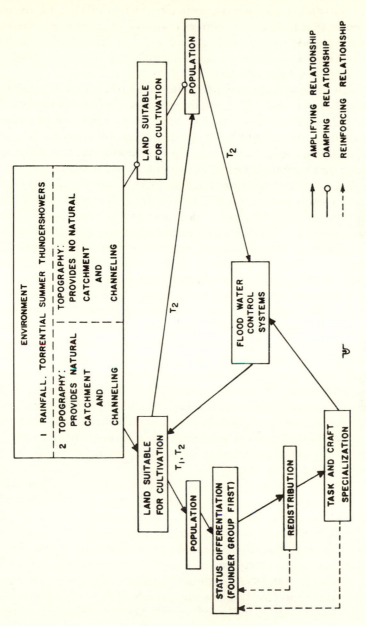

FIGURE 1 Dynamic relationships of environment, population, and social organization in the prehistoric development of a rank society in Chaco Canyon.

with a fortuitous combination of topography and climate that provide better soil, better drainage, or a more reliable water supply. In this instance, the emergence of a rank society hinges upon the claims on the abundant harvests by a founder group within a favored area. Right to the produce stems from prior use of the favored agricultural lands by the founder group (Flannery and Coe, 1968: 281–82).

Changes in the distribution of adequately watered land may result from developing climatic events. This argument is based on the assumption that Schoenwetter's studies (Schoenwetter and Eddy, 1964) in the Navajo Reservoir district 50 miles northeast may be extrapolated to Chaco Canyon (Harris and others, 1967). The chronology of climatic events in the Navajo Reservoir district includes a period of winter dominant rainfall before A.D. 800. Between A.D. 700 to 800 there is a shift to a summer dominant rainfall pattern that continues until A.D. 1100. During this period of summer dominant rainfall there is a trend of decreasing total annual precipitation that ends around A.D. 1025. The amount of annual precipitation appears to increase again between A.D. 1025 and 1100 (Schoenwetter and Eddy, 1964: 117–18). Schoenwetter (Schoenwetter and Eddy, 1964: 128) has developed a processual model of population dynamics which shows the relationships between these climatic changes and human occupation (agriculturalists) of the succession of environments that accompany them in "a specialized narrow canyon floodplain situation." According to Schoenwetter, a period of "winter dominant storms" is accompanied by an aggrading floodplain and dense tree cover. At this time the environment is occupied by "small colonizing populations." A succeeding period of summer dominant storms brings about the entrenchment of a portion of the floodplain and a decline in the tree cover. During the early stages of floodplain entrenchment population reaches its maximum size. As the summer dominant storm pattern continues the floodplain becomes completely dissected, the tree cover less dense, and the human population is forced to abandon the floodplain (Schoenwetter and Eddy, 1964: 128).

The model coincides well with what is presently known of population dynamics in Chaco Canyon. Prior to A.D. 850 there was a small Basket-maker occupation of the Canyon (Roberts, 1929; Adams, 1951; Judd, 1924). After A.D. 850 there is evidence of construction of the early and still small town sites, such as Pueblo Bonito and Una Vida (Bannister, 1965: 181–83, 196) on the north side of the Canyon, and of even smaller villages, such as the Three-C site (Vivian, 1965), on the south side of the Canyon. During the late tenth century and early eleventh century there was a tremendous increase in population as indicated by the increase of building activity throughout the Canyon (Bannister, 1965: 200–01). This would coincide with the end of the early stages of floodplain entrenchment in Schoenwetter's model. Extensive building, and presumably population increase, continued throughout the eleventh century. Early in the twelfth century building activity in the classic town sites had ceased and the population had begun to abandon the Canyon. This is the time at which Schoenwetter's Navajo Reservoir chronology truncates after 75 years of summer dominant storms and a trend to increasing annual precipitation, the effects of which were total dissection of the floodplain and lowered water tables which would have made floodplain agriculture on a large scale almost impossible.

I suggest that some local groups within Chaco Canyon found themselves in advantageous locations with respect to the crucial ingredient of successful agriculture, water. They were situated at points to which or through which runoff from small, sporadic, torrential mid-summer thundershowers was channeled by the local totography. These favored areas were located where the flatlands surrounding the canyon provided a large, continuous area for water catchment. The water then followed the natural channels of local topography into points of collection. The surfaces immediately north of the canyon between Mockingbird Canyon on the east and the point at which Escavada Wash meets Chaco Wash on the west is an area of natural catchment. The canyon wall on the north is much less severely dissected by side canyons than the Chacra Mesa on the south, but is more steep than the canyon wall formed by the northern edge of Chacra Mesa (Bryan, 1954: 10). Some of the rain that falls north of the Canyon flows directly into it over the canyon walls or through Mockingbird and Gallo Canyons. Hungo Pavi lies at the mouth of the former and Una Vida within one-half mile of the mouth of the latter. A larger proportion drains north into Escavada Wash which eventually joins Chaco Wash in the western end of the Canyon near the "town" site Peñasco Blanco. Rainfall runoff from the south periodically enters the Canyon through South Gap just across Chaco Wash from Pueblo Bonito, through Werito's Rincon opposite Hungo Pavi and through Vincente Wash in the vicinity of Mesa Fajada just opposite Una Vida. Finally, a fairly extensive basin drained by Bineola Wash is located southwest of the Canyon. The "town" site, Kin Bineola, is located in this drainage basin. In short, all five of the sites just mentioned were ideally located in proximity to large areas of arable land. The sites and the land lie within areas of natural rainfall collection.

The town sites mentioned above, Kin Bineola, Peñasco Blanco, Pueblo Bonito, Hungo Pavi, and Una Vida have early clusters of dates based on tree-ring samples from beams used in their construction. These dates range between A.D. 898 and 950 (Bannister, 1965: 200). The evidence for early construction activity at these sites is expected, as population expansion would occur first where agricultural production was most successful. The number of coresident groups within each town would increase. In time newly forming groups would find themselves farther and farther removed from direct social linkage with the founder group. During the late ninth and early tenth centuries, as population increased, there was a transformation in social organization.

A rank society cannot develop unless a single individual or a local group can capitalize on the productive advantages afforded by the environment. Service (1962: 149) describes how one man might distinguish himself by his contributions to community activities, and gain prestige among his peers. He becomes the redistributor through personal achievement. But, as Sahlins (1963) has shown, there are fundamental weaknesses in a system of redistribution that depends solely on the organizational abilities and charisma of a single individual, a "big man." The society in which there are only ephemeral big men is not far removed from what Fried (1967: 51–107) has characterized as the simple egalitarian society. The position of big man is achieved; most of his redistributive effort is expended on what is essentially self-aggrandizement. Judging from Sahlins' description, the big man does not gain much for the material improvement of those closest to him as, for example, through public works construction. His own kinsmen may not even derive a permanently improved status as a result of their association with him.

The weaknesses in the redistributive system of the type described above may be overcome where individual achievement is linked with agricultural land of outstanding productivity. An individual who distinguishes himself in community service may do so through access to resources not universally available to all, but only to him as a member of a local group that has special claim to them. An exclusive property holding principle may be based on the time of arrival and length of survival of the group that supports the redistributor. Consequently, the local group that gave rise to the redistributor can support the elevated status achieved by him through later generations of leaders. These descendants carry on the tradition of leadership even though they may not possess the organizational abilities of the individual who first launched their group into preeminence.

The founder groups could reaffirm their claims to the highly productive land by demanding the first fruits of the labor of others on the land and then, offer the produce back in a show of generosity. This might be done in the context of a religious ceremony organized and sponsored by the founder group in which the harvest is divided among the producers. Or, the founder group might acquire control of the produce of its land by regulating the acreage that each other group would be allowed to cultivate. The user would reciprocate with quantities of produce. These resources could then be redistributed in the context of ceremonies designed both to instill the value of the system of exchange and to reinforce the primacy of the founder group. The great kivas within the early towns of Chaco Canyon may have served as community redistributive centers. The association of economic function and ceremonial activity is consistent with the principle of a rank society. As Fried (1967: 141) has pointed out:

The charter of the ranking society tends to be its view of the supernatural world as represented in tales and sometimes in genealogies. Frequently the demand for certain kinds of ceremonies, logistically organized by lineage heads, big men, or chiefs, coordinates or provides the stimulus for the coordination of different sectors of the economy.

In a developing rank society as the redistributive function grows, so do the differences in status that separate the redistributor from those to whom he makes the distribution. The differentiation in status is reinforced by the use that the redistributor makes of the superabundant produce of the land. He may turn it into the increase of his immediate physical surroundings, both through the construction of specially designed quarters and the amassing of items of personal adornment (insignia of rank) that set him and his kin apart from the rest of society. Craft specialization for the purpose of providing the redistributor with these things is one usual concomitant of the rank society (Service, 1962: 148–50).

Simple clear-cut differences in status and relatively few status positions might be expected during the initial stages in the development of ranking (Sahlins, 1958: 6). Only later would such important aspects of a rank system come into play as, for example, careful accounting of "the distance of relationships between any member and the highest-ranking person of his generation" (Fried, 1967: 126). Such accounting is needed because each individual, even within a single nuclear family, may be of different rank. It becomes necessary, by keeping elaborate genealogies, to clearly separate these differences in rank.

Evidence for status differentiation and craft specialization is not abundant in Chaco Canyon, but it is tantalizing. It is well known that most of the burials that should be present at large sites like Pueblo Bonito have not been found. Pepper's and Judd's excavations have turned up fewer than 100. Normally, one of the primary indicators of differential status comes from funerary items (Fried, 1967: 112). In a rank society the status of the parents is ascribed to their children at birth. Consequently, one would expect to find the children of high ranked individuals accorded special recognition in death. Judd (1954: 328, 322–34, 336) describes burials of infants and children that were accompanied by various kinds, although never very many, artifacts. Most interesting of these is the possible burial of a macaw and child in Room 309, a "Late Bonitan" trash dump (Judd, 1954:

336). The adults among the burials in Pueblo Bonito are accompanied by pottery vessels and items of adornment, but most do not contain the quantity or the kinds of funerary items one would expect to accompany individuals of high status. A major exception to this statement is Room 33, and particularly Burials 13 and 14, uncovered by Pepper.

Both Burials 13 and 14 were discovered under a floor of boards that was found slightly more than 5 feet below the ceiling of Room 33. Above the board floor there were 12 human skulls and other bones plus large quantities of pottery vessels, shell, stone and turquoise beads and pendants, "ceremonial" sticks or staves, elaborately decorated flutes and other objects (Pepper, 1909: 197–221, 231–47). Burial 13 was accompanied by 5,890 turquoise beads, 10 turquoise pendants (which had been worn as arm and ankle ornaments), and two pottery bowls (Pepper, 1909: 222; Judd, 1954: 338). Burial 14 was accompanied by more than 15,000 turquoise, shell and stone beads and inlay sets, 689 pendants, shell bracelets, haliotis shell containers, a *Strombus* shell trumpet, a turquoise inlay basket, a small cylindrical object decorated with alternating rows of beads and pieces of shell, and "a long inlay of red stone" (Pepper, 1909: 223–31; Judd, 1954: 338). Most of the beads and pendants were apparently worn as items of adornment. Such things as a turquoise inlay basket and shell trumpet may be insignia of rank. Room 33 and its contents are described in less detail in Pepper (1920: 163–78).

Exotic items are common in the town site, Pueblo Bonito. As Vivian (1970b: 68) points out,

some ceramic forms, such as the tall cylindrical vases from Pueblo Bonito, are present only in towns, and some effigy forms have been recovered from town sites. Luxury items in towns included large quantities of turquoise in mosaic, inlay, pendant and bead form; carved and painted wood (primarily bird forms) from Chetro Ketl; painted cloisonné on sandstone; copper bells and parrots and macaws.

These items probably were made for individuals of high status and some may have had additional use in specialized ritual activities. The presence of such items in the towns but not in the villages also may be a result of status difference between people resident in these two types of sites.

A review of later masonry types in Judd (1964) and evidence suggesting that dwelling construction may have been carried out in massive preplanned operations indicate the following: there was specialization in architecture, that is, skilled masons and perhaps an individual or individuals to design the structure and to coordinate the construction; and there were sufficient food surpluses to maintain a work force that could quarry or cut, transport and shape the materials and then use them in the construction. For example, Wijiji is one of the smallest classic Chaco sites and it appears to have been constructed as a unit. Hewett (1936: 26) shows a ground floor plan containing 94 rooms. A restoration drawing of Wijiji (Hewett, 1936: 178) shows a structure of three stories. An estimate of 165 rooms for the entire pueblo was arrived at by halving the number of rooms for each above ground story. Vivian and Mathews (1966: 111) have pointed out that 15 trees were required to construct one room in Chetro Ketl. If this figure may be used for Wijiji it can be estimated that 2,500 trees would have been required in order to construct the pueblo. Although these trees probably were available within the Canyon (Bryan, 1954: 51), they still represent considerable labor in transportation alone. The large quantity of this one building material (beams) is indicative of the magnitude of building activities.

I would suggest on the basis of the evidence above that the towns were residences of individuals of high rank (although many people of lesser rank undoubtedly lived there as well). High status derived from differential access to important agricultural products. High status individuals could have funneled the available resources into the improvement and expansion of the town which would help to account for the marked differences between the two types of sites, towns and villages.

As the status differences that result from differential productivity attain the level of social rules, the social rules serve to further increase the divergence in the economic system between the high and low status groups. The function of the redistributor grows in importance. This form of organization provides for the integration of increasing numbers of individuals over a wider area. Population expansion into unfavored zones may have been possible in a rank system since the security of the redistributor's storehouse of foodstuffs would provide a buffer against years of poor crop yield. More likely, however, population increase into unfavored zones would have begun only after water control systems had been developed. Water control networks designed to direct and distribute rainfall runoff as in Chaco Canyon (Vivian and Mathews, 1965: 13–14; Vivian, 1970b: 73) would have the effect of first benefiting the occupants of the environmental zones favored with abundant runoff. To the extent that occupants of less favored zones could be included as part of the labor force employed in irrigation facility maintenance, or could find fields to cultivate in the expanding irrigation network, they too would undergo an expansion of population. They too would participate in the redistributive system, receiving goods in exchange for their effort in maintaining the water control facilities and passing the produce of their fields up to the redistributor. The development of water control may be viewed as a direct result of the redistributor's power to organize special task groups (specialization) in his own or the society's interest, or both.

The development of water control systems acted as a spur or kick that furthered population expansion. The time and place of origin are not exactly known. However, when they do appear they are found in association with town sites (Vivian, 1970b: 69). In terms of the model I am constructing they must have developed some time between the first evidence of extensive building activity in the early towns from A.D. 898 to 950 and the next period of large-scale construction which begins after A.D. 990 but does not get into full swing until early in the eleventh century. As Bannister (1965: 200–01) notes,

date clusters throughout the eleventh century, some of them synchronous and others over-lapping in time, suggest a period of continuous building activity.

During the eleventh century the size of existing town sites increased and the number of villages also increased. Fried (1967: 113) makes the cogent observation that rank society communities usually count their member-ship in the hundreds, while egalitarian bands rarely surpass 50 individuals. While no one is certain what constituted a community in Chaco Canyon, there can be little doubt that some of the town sites (which may have been only parts of a community that included other towns and villages as well) were occupied by many hundreds of individuals, perhaps thousands. One estimate of around 4,000 people by Lloyd Pierson, based on a survey of the central portion of Chaco Canyon National Monument, is cited by Vivian and Mathews (1965: 108).

Also, during the eleventh century new sites of the town type were constructed, possibly as single units in a matter of a few years. Fried (1967: 113) offers the hypothesis with respect to rank societies that:

Fairly constant population increase coupled with limitations of subsistence technology and immediately exploitable land resources tend to produce, in turn, a pattern of physical expansion, frequently in the development of satellite communities.

Possible test cases of Fried's hypothesis may be Wijiji located east of Mesa Fajada, Kin Ya'a located 30 miles south of the Canyon and Pueblo Pintado situated on the south side of Chaco Wash 17 miles east of Pueblo Bonito. Two of these sites, Kin Ya'a and Pueblo Pintado, are accompanied by the smaller village sites that have been characterized above as the residences of people who did not have high status. Of particular interest is the strong evidence that Kin Ya'a and Pueblo Pintado were connected with the Canyon proper by roads termed the Kin Ya'a Road and Chaco East Road respectively (Vivian, 1972: 12).

In spite of the small size of the three satellite town sites, the kind of expansion they represent probably would not have taken place without knowledge of water control techniques. Water control made possible an increase in population that resulted in the construction of new communities. Also, these new communities may have been dependent on water control for their subsistence or, at least, for domestic water supply. Both Kin Ya'a and Pueblo Pintado may have had no water control systems designed for agricultural purposes. They are located within or near wide valleys with sufficient drainage for floodwater farming. Also, features once interpreted as canals (Vivian, 1970b: 72–73) in the vicinity of Kin Ya'a and Pueblo Pintado have now been positively identified as roads (Vivian, 1972: 12; Vivian, personal communication). Nonetheless, there are shallow depressions in the vicinity of Kin Ya'a (Holsinger, 1901) and Pueblo Pintado (Vivian, personal communication) that may have served as reservoirs for domestic purposes. Also, there is a water control system associated with the town site Wijiji (Vivian 1972: 3; Figure 2).

One consequence of population increase and its displacement in satellites is a shift in the center of the social life of the community. This assumes that parent and satellite maintain social contact as least through the lifespan of the pioneer generation. It is not a universal rule of rank societies that offshoot communities will continue ties with the parent (Fried, 1967: 113). The construction of the isolated great kiva Casa Rinconada across Chaco Wash from Pueblo Bonito and among a cluster of village sites on the south side of the Canyon may be viewed as a mechanism that served the purpose of social integration. Kin Nahasbas, another isolated great kiva near the site of Una Vida, may be a further example of the same phonomenon (Vivian and Reiter, 1960: 106–07). On the basis of masonry types, Vivian and Mathews (1965: 109) place both of these sites in their Bonito phase which dates from A.D. 1030 to 1130+, the time period during which major population growth and expansion was taking place in Chaco Canyon. The road systems that tie Kin Ya'a and Pueblo Pintado with the Canyon proper and the Tsin Kletzin Road which has been tentatively linked with Casa Rinconada (Vivian, 1972: 12) may represent still another kind of mechanism that was designed to counteract the centrifugal effects of a shift in the social center of gravity.

There is nothing in the logic of rank systems that leads to the development of isolated great kivas. However, where ceremonial structures such as kivas exist as part of a widespread cultural tradition, as for instance in both the Mogollon and Anasazi Southwest (Vivian and Reiter, 1960), they may provide the necessary physical facility (redistributive center) for a previously established pattern of redistribution. On the basis of existing evidence from the two excavated isolated great kivas, there can be no demonstration of their use for such purposes. I think, however, that given the number of satellites established during the eleventh century in many different directions from the central part of the Canyon that other isolated great kivas will be found.

By the end of the eleventh century, one of the notable characteristics of settlement pattern was the density of sites within small areas of the Canyon. The vicinity of Pueblo Bonito and Chetro Ketl in the central portion of the Canyon is the most striking example. Large portions of the surrounding countryside which were extensively occupied during the Basketmaker period became unattractive in the Pueblo periods. Fried (1967: 112) has pointed out that in rank societies as contrasted with egalitarian societies

the actual social density of population tends to be several times the figure obtained by dividing the total units of area by the total population.

In other words, rank society populations tend to become concentrated in and exploit only small portions of the total territory available to them in any particular time period. This relationship is general where rank society economies are based on agricultural subsistence (Fried, 1967: 112). In Chaco Canyon the tendency to population concentration may be ascribed to the adaptation of rainfall runoff control systems to those areas that have been described previously as natural rainfall catchment networks.

FUTURE RESEARCH

The model that I have proposed is summarized in Figure 1. It is dynamic in that it attempts to account for the development of a rank society over a period of time, not just describe the organization as it may have existed during a particular slice of time. In this respect the model goes somewhat beyond Vivian's proposition about social organization in Chaco Canyon. The existence of a rank society as postulated can be confirmed if specific kinds of data are collected in future research there (Hill, 1970).

In order to determine whether the sequence of climatic events established by Schoenwetter in the Navajo Reservoir district also applies in Chaco Canyon, two indicators of climatic change must be examined.

1) There should be evidence of a shift from a winter dominant rainfall pattern between A.D. 700 to 800 to a summer dominant rainfall pattern in the form of an increasing proportion of nonarboreal (chenopod and amaranth) pollen relative to arboreal (pine) pollen in samples from archaeological contexts. The pattern of summer dominant rainfall should persist from A.D. 800 to 1100. It is assumed that archaeological pollen in which the proportion of weeds is high results from environmental and not cultural

factors (Lytle, 1971). It would be well to check the assumption by securing pollen samples from stratigraphic columns in areas that would not have been disturbed by man. This may be done wherever suitable exposures can be found in the canyon floor alluvium.

2) The transition from a winter dominant to a summer dominant rainfall pattern should be marked by a shift from an aggrading floodplain to a dissected floodplain. As precipitation becomes concentrated in torrential summer thundershowers, it brings about erosion and eventually the entrenchment of stream channels and lowered water tables in the floodplain. Entrenchment is often discontinuous along the course of a particular stream and may not extend to all tributary streams (Martin, 1963: 34). Consequently the effects of floodplain dissection do not necessarily mean widespread disaster for agriculturalists who depend upon a water table close to ground surface. It would be very important to determine the extent of floodplain dissection in Chaco Canyon after A.D. 800 and to correlate it with the development of water control systems. I would predict from the model of the development of rank societies presented above, that floodplain dissection was not a serious problem for the inhabitants of Chaco Canyon until perhaps the beginning of the eleventh century at which time water control devices already had been developed. The development of water control follows the rise of a rank society and is made possible by the principles of control inherent in a rank system. Furthermore, the concentration and eventual expansion of population under the rank society as it developed in Chaco Canyon was probably as instrumental in the development of water control as was environmental degradation.

The rise of the ranking principle of organization hinges on differential productivity of land in Chaco Canyon and vicinity. The differences are brought about by a change to a summer dominant rainfall pattern in combination with the natural catchment and channeling of rainfall runoff by the topography.

3) Observations of present rainfall runoff patterns should indicate areas that would have been most suitable for floodwater agriculture in the past. Chaco Canyon as well as most of the Southwest has been experiencing a cycle of floodplain dissection since the latter part of the nineteenth century not unlike the one that probably brought about the abandonment of the Canyon early in the twelfth century.

4) A further indicator of areas of natural catchment and channeling of runoff water would be the water control systems established to control floods during the eleventh century when an increase in total annual

precipitation was added to a long established pattern of summer dominant precipitation (Schoenwetter and Eddy, 1964: 117–18). It should be possible to predict the presence of one from the other.

There is no satisfactory method for estimating the amount of land in Chaco Canyon that was suitable for cultivation of crops such as corn, beans, and squash. We have no way of knowing exactly how much land was cultivated of the suitable land available.

5) If the areas of potential use for floodwater farming today can be determined on the basis of present runoff patterns, there may be some hope of estimating the quantity of land sown in crops by the prehistoric inhabitants of Chaco Canyon. Such an estimate could be made by assuming that recent Hopi agricultural practices (Hack, 1942) are similar to those employed in Chaco Canyon. The ratio of land in cultivation per capita to the total land available for cultivation among Hopi could then be applied to give a very rough estimate of the amount of land that could have been used at any one time by the inhabitants of Chaco Canyon before large-scale floodwater control techniques were developed. Some knowledge of how much land was used for cultivation after the development of irrigation can be gained from the extent of the water control systems. Vivian (1972) has already defined the nature and extent of some water control systems.

Since there is no completely satisfactory method for estimating the quantity of land suitable for cultivation (or of knowing how much land was cultivated of the suitable land available) during any one period of time, population size estimates would have to be used to show the effects of differential distribution of rainfall runoff.

6) There should be evidence of population concentration and growth in areas where local topography provides natural catchment and channeling of summer thundershower runoff. These would include the north side of the Canyon between Escavada Wash and Mockingbird Canyon, the point of junction of Chaco and Escavada Washes, the mouth of Mockingbird Canyon, the mouth of Gallo Canyon, the vicinity of South Gap, the opening of Werito's Rincon into Chaco Canyon, the area where Vincente Wash enters the Canyon and, finally, the basin drained by Bineola Wash. There should be other such areas within or in the vicinity of the Canyon. Absence of population or a decline of existing population elsewhere would be expected until population expansion and the development of water control systems made exploitation of these previously marginal lands both necessary and possible.

None of the above suggestions for critical research would establish the fact of a rank society in Chaco Canyon. They merely establish the combination of environmental factors from which a rank society may have developed. Therefore, what evidence of status differentiation, redistribution, and task and craft specialization should we search for in Chaco Canyon?

7) When the burial population of any of the classic Chaco towns is found, some of the burials should contain evidence, in quantity and kinds of associated items (insignia of rank), of status differentiation. No lavishly appointed burials should be discovered in village burial areas. There should be evidence that this pattern had its beginning probably early in the tenth century.

8) Since the rank society postulated in the model is integrated by the mechanism of redistribution, a form of exchange, there may be evidence of the integration through exchange even in the death of the redistributor. This evidence would take the form of funerary items contributed by a large number of distinct social groups. In order to assess the extent of such contributions it would be necessary to first define stylistic microtraditions within sites and between sites. The funerary items associated with individuals of high status would contain ceramics, for example, which show characteristics of the various microtraditions.

9) Relatively few positions of high status are postulated for the rank society in Chaco Canyon. Consequently, there should be evidence that the insignia of rank are localized in certain households and social groups and not others, even though these social groups are coresident in the same town. These insignia of rank may include ceremonial paraphernalia if the charter of the rank society is maintained through the ceremonial system as stipulated in the model.

It was postulated in the model that the differences between town and village site plan and architecture stem from the fact that individuals of high status reside in the towns, but not in the villages. The material increase and improvement of the town, the immediate physical surroundings of the high status group(s), is expected.

10) Exotic items such as turquoise mosaic and inlay, carved and painted wood in the form of plants and animals, copper bells, parrots and macaws, as insignia of rank, should be found only in the towns where individuals of high status reside.

11) On the basis of existing evidence, no postulates can be developed about the organization of social groups integrated by the principle of ranking. When data collected for that purpose are analyzed and interpreted, there should be evidence to indicate that such groups were the same whether resident in towns or villages. The structure of the family and higher order social units, patterns of post-marital residence, the size and composition of residence units, patterns of intergroup cooperation within a site and other aspects of social organization should be the same in both town and village.

Redistribution involves the production of more goods than are needed for immediate use, their transfer to a central repository in the control of the redistributor and, their allocation at a later time in various contexts and for various reasons. These range from religious ceremonies organized by the redistributor for no other reason than a show of his preeminent status to times of environmental stress in order to relieve a food shortage.

12) There should be evidence in town sites of larger storage facilities, or more than are usual in sites from earlier time levels or in sites of the village type. These large or numerous storage facilities should be found in association with either the residences of individuals of high status or ceremonial precincts in which redistributive ceremonies would have taken place, or both. It was postulated in the model that great kivas served as re-distributive centers.

13) Food distributed at redistributive ceremonies may have been stored near or adjacent to the isolated great kivas. (These were probably built late in the development of the rank system and after population expansion brought about a dislocation of the social center of gravity.) Existing data do not strongly support this contention, however, as Kin Nahasbas was built without immediately adjoining rooms and those adjacent to Casa Rinconada that once may have served a storage function have been weathered into oblivion (Vivian and Reiter, 1960).

14) In the isolated great kivas such as Casa Rinconada there should be evidence that the ceremonies carried out there were organized and performed by high status groups for the benefit of groups of lower status. For example, antechambers and rooms that appear to have been connected with preparation for the performance of ceremonies should contain the kinds of objects and stylistic qualities typical of high status groups. The intrusion of other kinds of objects and design styles would not be expected within these precincts.

15) The architectural style of isolated great kivas should be that of the town sites, not the villages. The person(s) of high status who organized the construction of these kivas would have them constructed by the same skilled masons who had been employed in the construction of the towns.

16) Evidence of craft specialization may be found in the form of activity areas within towns in which the production of certain exotic items was carried on, for example, ceramics in the form of effigies or bifurcated baskets and turquoise mosaic and inlay. Activity areas of this type should be found in towns only, as it was postulated in the model that individuals of high status resided in the towns.

DISCUSSION

Many forms of archaeological evidence presently available from Chaco Canyon point to the development of a rank society after A.D. 850. The exotic craft items localized in town sites and the lavish treatment of Burials 13 and 14 in Old Bonitan Room 33 are exemplary. Furthermore, Fried (1960: 720) has suggested that:

> The emergence of the superfamilial redistributive network and the rank society seem to go well with the developments he [Wittfogel, 1957] has discussed under the rubric "hydro-agriculture", in which some supervision is needed in order to control simple irrigation and drainage projects yet these projects are not large enough to call into existence a truly professional bureaucracy.

While there may be a correlation between rank society and irrigation in Chaco Canyon, I would never have proposed the rank society model if existing evidence were confined only to the irrigation systems that both Gordon and Gwinn Vivian have carefully documented (Vivian and Mathews, 1965; Vivian, 1970a,b, 1972). Furthermore, Wittfogel makes no attempt to define a specific form of social organization that would accompany hydro-agriculture. He notes only (1957: 17–18) that

> Irrigation farming .... requires radical social and political adjustments only in a special geohistorical setting. Strictly local tasks of digging, damming, and water distribution can be performed by a single husbandman, a single family, or a small group of neighbors, and in this case no far-reaching organizational steps are necessary.

Also, Millon (1962) has demonstrated that no form of centralized authority structure is necessary where even complex multicommunity irrigation is practiced. Irrigation agriculture does not necessarily presuppose a rank society. Ranking is only one possible solution to the operation of intersite irrigation systems. In the case of Chaco Canyon, however, it seems to fit other available evidence quite well.

The preceding reconstruction, in essence, postulates an increase in the complexity of social organization in Chaco Canyon. With the development of a rank society there is an increase in the importance of integrative mechanisms. I have attempted to show how a rank society might arise under the unusual environmental circumstances of a narrow floodplain. Also, I have attempted to reconstruct certain aspects of the organization of the rank society as an alternative to Vivian's proposition about social organization in Chaco Canyon. It is now possible to regard our reconstructions as alternative testable working hypotheses to which further alternatives may be added.

The chief problem that both Vivian and I have had to face in formulating our propositions has been the paucity of unequivocal data. Previously reported data are useful for stimulating thought but they have not been collected and recorded in a form that could be used in the confirmation of the propositions discussed above. Only carefully controlled data collection with the express purpose of testing hypotheses will clarify the nature of cultural development in Chaco Canyon. The problem is compounded by the difficulty of archaeologically distinguishing between the forms of social organization that have been postulated. As Fried notes (1967: 153),

the differences between egalitarian and rank society, although profound in implication, are fairly subtle in the manner in which they played out in the behavior of real people.

In fact, the primary difference between an egalitarian and a rank society is that the latter is

based upon varying increments of prestige and upon the hierarchical ordering of status positions (Fried, 1967: 183).

The existence of a principle of ranking in the prehistoric past can be demonstrated only by careful attention to the interrelationships of selectively chosen sets of data.

POSTSCRIPT

The discussion that follows is organized into four separate units. The first two deal with muddles in the model; the last two with retrodictions from the model (its power to predict past events), and how it might be used to generate test implications for further research into the Chaco phenomenon.

I

From the outset I have been uncomfortable with a key element in the model, climate change as a causal agent. There are two aspects of the climate change question that require reexamination.

The palynological studies from which Schoenwetter's chronology and model of population dynamics in a narrow floodplain were derived rest on some methodological assumptions that have not withstood recent tests (Lytle-Webb, this volume). It is no longer possible to assume that pollen derived from archaeological contexts can be used to reconstruct the nature of the environment and from that, the climate, at the time an archaeological site was occupied. In the first place, it is no longer possible to assume that the pollen rain on an archaeological site accurately reflects the make-up of the environment beyond the site itself. As Jamie Lytle-Webb has shown in her study of a contemporary Papago settlement, human activity disturbs the soil and creates optimum conditions for the growth of certain types of weeds. It happens that these are the same kinds of weeds that thrive under the disturbed soil conditions that accompany erosion and alluviation during periods of severe summer thundershowers. Secondly, pollen rain on house floors is uneven probably reflecting proximity of entry ways, smoke holes and other openings and, more important, variability in human activity. Widely divergent pollen spectra may occur in two different locations within the same structure. Therefore, a pollen sample collected from a single locus within a single archaeological feature, such as a room or house, is not likely to reflect variability in occurrence of pollen types within the feature, much less the site as a whole. In short, to the extent that Schoenwetter's interpretations are based on single samples from archaeological context rather than multiple samples from suitable exposures outside the effective range of human disturbance, I would find difficulty in accepting them as useful indicators of past environmental conditions.

If it happens on further study that no change in the pattern of rainfall distribution can be demonstrated, we shall have to search for more subtle causal factors within both environmental and cultural subsystems. It is possible that favorable location alone, *perhaps* in combination with even relatively minor changes in technological efficiency led to population increase and later developments in the Canyon.

By adopting Schoenwetter's model for the population dynamics of agriculturalists in a narrow canyon floodplain situation, I have also tacitly underwritten climate change as the sole cause of abandonment of the canyon. I think that it has been generally accepted that floodplain dissection was largely responsible for the mass exodus of the Chaco population in the twelfth century. The inference that environmental conditions had deteriorated is supported by geological evidence of arroyo cutting that seems to date late in the occupation of the classic town sites (Bryan, 1954). Given the evidence of arroyo cutting it seemed quite logical to ascribe it to the effects of a climate change such as Schoenwetter had inferred from his Navajo Reservoir district and Chuska Valley (Harris, Schoenwetter and Warren, 1967) studies. While changes in climate alone may satisfactorily account for cultural developments elsewhere, I do not think events in Chaco Canyon can be accounted for through this kind of simple causality.

Acknowledging that what follows is highly speculative, let me make a case for more complex causality. Suppose that the Chacoans through their profligate use of timber in dwelling construction had succeeded in a subtle but profound alteration of microclimatic conditions in their vicinity. Vivian and Mathews have documented the magnitude of tree use in Chaco Canyon. They estimate that the

number of trees cut for construction throughout the eleventh century would be perhaps 75,000 to 100,000 (Vivian and Mathews, 1965: 111).

They go on to point out that the timber supply was selected from young growth the removal of which

might have accelerated recession of the forest border and increased the runoff from seasonal rains (Vivian and Mathews, 1965: 111).

Erosion and floodplain dissection would be one consequence of deforestation.

But, let's go a step further. A forest maintains a cooler temperature than open grassland in part due to the fact that water retention is higher in a forest. Generally, clouds bearing rain tend to rise and pass over a hot land surface, but will drop their moisture when passing over a cooler land surface (Turk and others, 1974: 219). It may be that in removing the forest cover in the canyon and to the north and east, the Chacoans not only increased rate of runoff but decreased the amount of precipitation that might fall in any one year. Both would lead to lower effective moisture available for agricultural production. The effect of floodplain dissection as a result of too rapid runoff would be to restrict availability of arable land as Vivian and Mathews (1965: 112) have pointed out.

Chacoans adjusted in two ways. First, rainfall runoff control systems were expanded quite possibly as a means of water conservation to counteract the effect of decreased effective moisture and also to preserve land from the effects of too rapid runoff. This interpretation of the later development of water control in Chaco Canyon was developed by Gwinn Vivian (1974: 103, 109) to account for the effects of change to a summer dominant rainfall pattern as postulated by Schoenwetter. If we reject Schoenwetter's reconstruction, however, and ascribe changes in the availability of effective moisture and arable land to the dual effects of deforestation, the response of the Chacoans would be the same.

Second, we can assume that trees had become a scarce commodity by the middle of the eleventh century as an expanding population required ever more dwellings, fuel and other items of wood. The problem might have been solved in traditional Pueblo Indian fashion, by abandonment (in this case to a new timber source). However, if the model for the development of a rank society is correct, the Chacoans had already diverged from tradition. Furthermore, and this is highly significant, if Chaco towns were in the early stages of satellite community formation as postulated in the model I have developed, there would have been strong centripetal tendencies among the communities. Abandonment at this time would have required removal of all, a factor that would run counter to the fissive character of abandonment. A more likely response of Chaco leaders at this stage in the development of a rank society would have been to exploit more distant resources from the nuclear zone. After all, the fixed agricultural facilities of the Canyon had become quite well developed and were adequately productive. Further, according to the model a pattern of "employing" local labor in the context of a redistributive system had already developed. To overcome the difficulties of travel burdened with heavy objects, under the soil conditions and over the topographic obstacles of the Canyon and its vicinity, required a single innovation—the so-called "Anasazi Roadway System" (Remote Sensing Project Report, 1974). This argument is based on Romer's Rule to the effect that

the initial survival value of a favorable innovation is conservative, in that it renders possible the maintenance of a traditional way of life in the face of changed circumstances (Hockett and Ascher, 1964: 137).

A recent survey of the "great north road" that connects Chaco Canyon with the San Juan River was designed to test the proposition that roads "minimize effort in movement" (Morenon, 1975: 14). Morenon has calculated the number of calories required for an individual to walk a 13.62 km section that connects two settlements along the road. When compared with the caloric expenditure in traversing five possible alternatives to the test section, Morenon concludes that with respect to the movement of people none is significantly more efficient than the other. However, he (Morenon, 1975: 11) does allow the possibility that

certain material remains may flow along the road relatively quickly and directly over considerable distances, but this is not true of all material remains. In this case, the road may maximize the speed of flow for some materials, but not for other materials.

In short, the test is inconclusive with respect to the critical function I have postulated for the road. Tests should be designed to evaluate the energy expenditure of encumbered individuals along a prepared road surface as opposed to unimproved soil and terrain. The road should represent significant savings in energy expended in specific task performance, i.e., transportation of construction materials and the circulation of produce within the redistributive system.

II

The McElmo problem. It should be possible to incorporate the McElmo phase materials within the model. At the present time, however, existing data do not provide a basis for systematic thinking about the problem. There is a well established hypothesis to the effect that the McElmo sites represent a culturally distinct group of people who established residence in the Canyon sometime after A.D. 1050 (Vivian and Mathews, 1965: 110–1). A careful examination of the literature reveals, however, that this group of people is really a distinctive style of architecture. If we apply a rule of parsimony here, as I have tried to do in all aspects of my thinking about the Chaco phenomenon, an alternative presents itself: The McElmo phase may represent another dimension of social variability within the complex structure of a social system based on a principle of ranking. In other words, the McElmo pueblos are merely satellite communities not unlike Kin Ya'a or Pueblo Pintado. Like these Chaco towns they were constructed after A.D. 1050, and always it seems in the vicinity of arable land with the potential for development through techniques of rainfall runoff control. Also Tsin Kletzin, like the remote classic towns, is tied into the nuclear zone by a roadway (Vivian, 1972: 12) that leads directly to Casa Rinconada a possible redistributive center. And yet, I am not especially fond of this alternative either.

It is still impossible to account for the chronological and physical juxtaposition of the tri-wall structure (with associated rooms) and Pueblo del Arroyo. Furthermore, we lack any basis for comparison between the two varieties of satellite community I have postulated. The report on Kin Kletso (Vivian and Mathews, 1965) doesn't tell us much about the social structure and organization of that pueblo, there are no comparable reports from sites such as Kin Ya'a or Pueblo Pintado, and we have little or no information about how Kin Kletso compares chronologically, culturally or socially with the other McElmo phase pueblos.

III

It is possible to ascribe abandonment of sites within Chaco Canyon proper to the effects of arroyo cutting. This does not satisfactorily account for abandonment simultaneously of outlying pueblos, especially Kin Ya'a, Kin Bineola, Tsin Kletzin, Pueblo Pintado and Aztec (Chaco population). Even under present conditions of arroyo cutting dissection is often discontinuous. Some stream beds remain unentrenched. I suspect that further geological study at outlying sites will reveal no evidence of environmental deterioration. The reasons for abandonment of outlying pueblos must be sought in their social and economic integration with pueblos at the hub of the Chaco social system.

As I have postulated in the model, satellites were linked to founder groups in a redistributive network. Redistribution requires economic cooperation of diverse social units for the general welfare of all. The ties that satellites would have maintained with founder units in the early towns would have been strong, at least within the pioneer generation (Fried, 1967: 113). At the time of abandonment a significant component of the population in most satellite communities (especially the leadership) would have been of the pioneer generation. As I have pointed out above, certain technological developments in water control and roadway construction may be interpreted as attempts to maintain an existing adaptation involving several interacting pueblos, under changing environmental conditions. Following the same line of reasoning socially and economically integrated pueblos would attempt to maintain the existing adaptation by going it together even in abandonment. However, social organization based on a principle of ranking could not be maintained once the Canyon and its immediate vicinity had been abandoned. We might expect to find evidence elsewhere of short-lived attempts to reconstitute the Chaco social pattern.

IV

It is not possible on the basis of present evidence to postulate direct contact between Chacoans and Mesoamericans, especially through the mechanism of pochteca traders (e.g., DiPeso, 1968). A case for Mesoamerican trade families in Chaco Canyon must be made by careful attention to their socio-economic impact on an already well-developed rank society. If such trade were being carried on, then I would expect it to have been concentrated in the towns where highest ranking members of Chaco society resided, e.g., Chetro Ketl, Pueblo Bonito, Hungo Pavi, Una Vida, Kin Bineola and Peñasco Blanco. Traders and highest ranking local leaders would find such a relationship mutually advantageous: the traders could assure themselves a continuing supply of goods such as they required and the local leaders could provide through their lien on the labor of householder and kinsmen; the local leaders would gain a measure of prestige through their association with the persons who brought exotic goods from distant places. Further- more, local leaders could claim exclusive right to macaws for feathers and to copper bells, insignia of their rank. Of course, there should be physical evidence of the presence of traders, such as separate housing. Evidence of separate housing should not be found in satellite pueblos, only in the early classic towns where founder groups emerged.

ACKNOWLEDGMENTS

Several individuals have been instrumental in the process of transforming a few untutored ideas into their present form. Ellen Grebinger helped me see that the model should be dynamic, not static. Patricia Chase Kaufman and anonymous reviewers should be thanked for their helpful criticisms of many general and specific aspects of earlier drafts. Gwinn Vivian has provided insight, guidance and caution at crucial points in the development of the model. I haven't always followed good advice. Finally, my thanks to Sharon Urban who, in my absence, presented the Postscript to the symposium on the Chaco Phenomenon at the 49th Pecos Conference, and to Pierre Morenon for permission to quote from his paper on "Chacoan Roads and Adaptation."

REFERENCES

Adams, R. N. (1951) Half-House: a pithouse in Chaco Canyon, New Mexico. *Papers of the Michigan Academy of Science, Arts and Letters* 35, 273-95.

Bannister, B. (1965) Tree-ring dating of the archeological sites in the Chaco Canyon region, New Mexico. *Southwestern Monuments Association, Technical Series* 6 (2).

Brand, D. D., F. M. Hawley, F. C. Hibben, D. Senter, W. Bliss, R. Lister, and J. Spuhler (1937) Tseh So, a small house ruin, Chaco Canyon, New Mexico. *The University of New Mexico Bulletin, Anthropological Series* 2 (2).

Bryan, K. (1954) The geology of Chaco Canyon, New Mexico in relation to the life and remains of the prehistoric peoples of Pueblo Bonito. *Smithsonian Miscellaneous Collections* 122 (7).

DiPeso, C. C. (1968) Casas Grandes and the Gran Chichimeca. *El Palacio* 75, 45-61.

Dozier, E. P. (1960) The Pueblos of the southwestern United States. *The Journal of the Royal Anthropological Institute of Great Britain and Ireland* 90, 146-60.

Dozier, E. P. (1970) *The Pueblo Indians of North America*. Holt, Rinehart and Winston, New York.

Dutton, B. P. (1938) Leyit Kin, a small house ruin, Chaco Canyon, New Mexico. *Monographs of The University of New Mexico and The School of American Research* 7.

Eggan, F. (1950) *Social Organization of the Western Pueblos*. University of Chicago Press, Chicago.

Flannery, K. V. and M. D. Coe (1968) Social and economic systems in formative Mesoamerica. In *New Perspectives in Archeology*, edited by S. R. and L. R. Binford, pp. 267–83. Aldine, Chicago.

Fox, R. (1967) The Keresan bridge: A problem in pueblo ethnology, *London School of Economics Monographs on Social Anthropology* 35.

Fried, M. H. (1960) On the evolution of social stratification and the state. In *Culture in History: Essays in Honor of Paul Radin*, edited by S. Diamond, pp. 713–31. Columbia University Press, New York.

Fried, M. H. (1967) *The Evolution of Political Society: An Essay in Political Anthropology*. Random House, New York.

Grebinger, E. M. (1971) Topical index of some Spanish documents concerning the American Southwest, 1538–1700. M.A. thesis, The University of Arizona, Tucson.

Hack, J. T. (1942) The changing physical environment of the Hopi Indians of Arizona. *Papers of the Peabody Museum of Archaeology and Ethnology, Harvard University* 35 (1).

Harris, A. H., J. Schoenwetter and A. H. Warren (1967) An archaeological survey of the Chuska Valley and the Chaco Plateau, New Mexico. Part I: Natural science studies. *Museum of New Mexico Research Records* 4.

Hewett, E. L. (1963) *The Chaco Canyon and its monuments*. University of New Mexico Press, Albuquerque.

Hill, J. N. (1970) Prehistoric social organization in the American Southwest: Theory and method. In *Reconstructing Prehistoric Pueblo Societies*, edited by W. A. Longacre, pp. 12–58. University of New Mexico Press, Albuquerque.

Hockett, C. F. and R. Ascher (1964) The human revolution. *Current Anthropology* 5, 135–46.

Holsinger, S. J. (1901) Report on prehistoric ruins of Chaco Canyon, New Mexico. Manuscript, General Land Office, National Archives, Washington, D.C.

Judd, N. M. (1924) Two Chaco Canyon pit houses. *Annual Report of the Smithsonian Institution for 1922*, 399–413.

Judd, N. M. (1954) The material culture of Pueblo Bonito. *Smithsonian Miscellaneous Collections* 124.

Judd, N. M. (1959) Pueblo del Arroyo, Chaco Canyon, New Mexico. *Smithsonian Miscellaneous Collections* 138 (1).

Judd, N. M. (1964) The architecture of Pueblo Bonito. *Smithsonian Miscellaneous Collections* 147 (1).

Kirchhoff, P. (1959) The principles of clanship in human society. In *Readings in Anthropology* 2, edited by M. H. Fried, pp. 260–70. Thomas Y. Crowell, New York.

Kluckhohn, C. and P. Reiter (editors) (1939) Preliminary report on the 1937 excavations, Bc 50–51, Chaco Canyon, New Mexico. *The University of New Mexico Bulletin 345, Anthropological Series* 3(2).

Lytle, J. L. (1971) A microenvironmental study of an archaeological site, Arizona BB:10:3, Whiptail ruin. M.A. thesis, The University of Arizona, Tucson.

Martin, P. S. (1963) *The Last 10,000 Years*. The University of Arizona Press, Tucson.

Millon, R. (1962) Variations in social responses to the practice of irrigation agriculture. In Civilization in desert lands, edited by R. B. Woodbury, pp. 56–88. *Anthropological Papers of the University of Utah* 62.

Morenon, E. P. (1975) Chacoan roads and adaptation: how a prehistoric population can define and control its social and natural environment. Paper presented at the 40th Annual Meeting of the Society for American Archaeology, Dallas.

Pepper, G. H. (1909) The exploration of a burial-room in Pueblo Bonito, New Mexico. In *Putnam Anniversary Volume: Anthropological Essays*, edited by F. Boas and others, pp. 196–252. G. E. Steckert and Co., New York.

Pepper, G. H. (1920) Pueblo Bonito. *Anthropological Papers of the American Museum of Natural History* 27.

Platt, J. R. (1964) Strong inference. *Science* 146, 347–53.

Reed, E. (1949) Sources of upper Rio Grande culture and population. *El Palacio* 56 (6): 163–84.

Remote Sensing Project (1974) Report: an ERTS-1 image of the Chaco Canyon region, New Mexico. Manuscript, Chaco Center, National Park Service, Albuquerque. Mimeograph.

Roberts, F. H. H. Jr. (1929) Shabik'eshchee village: A late Basketmaker site in the Chaco Canyon, New Mexico. *Bureau of American Ethnology Bulletin* 92.

Sahlins, M. D. (1958) *Social Stratification in Polynesia*. The American Ethnological Society. The University of Washington Press, Seattle.

Sahlins, M. D. (1963) Poor man, rich man, big-man, chief: Political types in Melanesia and Polynesia. *Comparative Studies in Society and History* 5, 285–303.

Schoenwetter, J. and F. W. Eddy (1964) Alluvial and palynological reconstruction of environments, Navajo Reservoir district. *Museum of New Mexico Papers in Anthropology* 13.

Service, E. R. (1962) *Primitive Social Organization: An Evolutionary Perspective*. Random House, New York.

Spicer, E. H. (1962) *Cycles of Conquest: The Impact of Spain, Mexico, and the United States on the Indians of the Southwest, 1533–1960*. The University of Arizona Press, Tucson.

Turk, A., J. Turk, J. T. Wittes and R. Wittes (1974) *Environmental Science*. W. B. Saunders, Philadelphia.

Vivian, G. (1965) The Three-C site, an early Pueblo II ruin in Chaco Canyon, New Mexico. *University of New Mexico Publications in Anthropology* 13.

Vivian, G. and T. W. Mathews (1965) Kin Kletso: A Pueblo III community in Chaco Canyon, New Mexico. *Southwestern Monuments Association, Technical Series* 6 (1).

Vivian, G. and P. Reiter (1960) The great kivas of Chaco Canyon and their relationships. *Monographs of the School of American Research and the Museum of New Mexico* 22.

Vivian, R. G. (1968) A proposed reconstruction of prehistoric social organization in Chaco Canyon, New Mexico. Manuscript, Arizona State Museum, Tucson, Xerox.

Vivian, R. G. (1970a) Aspects of prehistoric society in Chaco Canyon, New Mexico. Ph.D. dissertation, The University of Arizona, Tucson.

Vivian, R. G. (1970b) An inquiry into prehistoric social organization in Chaco Canyon, New Mexico. In *Reconstructing Prehistoric Pueblo Societies*, edited by William A. Longacre, pp. 59–83. University of New Mexico Press, Albuquerque.

Vivian, R. G. (1972) Final technical letter report for prehistoric water conservation in Chaco Canyon, NSF Grant No. GS-3100, July 1, 1970 to June 30, 1971. Manuscript, Arizona State Museum, Tucson. Mimeograph.

Vivian, R. G. (1974) Conservation and diversion: water control systems in the Anasazi Southwest. In Irrigation's impact on society, edited by, T. E. Downing and McG. Gibson, pp 95–112. *Anthropological Papers of The University of Arizona* 25.

Wendorf, F. (1954) A reconstruction of northern Rio Grande prehistory. *American Anthropologist* 56, 200–27.

Wendorf, F. and E. Reed (1955) An alternative reconstruction of northern Rio Grande prehistory. *El Palacio* 62, 131–73.

Wittfogel, K. A. (1957) *Oriental Despotism: A Comparative Study of Total Power*. Yale University Press, New Haven.

A Symmetry Classification of Pueblo Ceramic Designs

DOROTHY K. WASHBURN

Peabody Museum, Harvard University

This paper is concerned with exploring an alternative to ceramic typology by which designs are classified in terms of their symmetrical structures. It is contended that while typologies can contribute only to culture histories, the study of design by a cultural universal enables investigation of problems of process and change. The attribute symmetry is (1) a basic universal component of all patterned design; (2) capable of being classified in a standardized, systematic manner; and (3) a sensitive indicator of specific cultural activities. The hypothesis that a symmetry class classification of ceramic design will reveal population group composition and interaction spheres is presented and the method is tested on three collections of Pueblo III period ceramics.

INTRODUCTION

The delimitation and measurement of occurrences of group contact, interaction, and movement has long been a methodological problem in archaeology. In the American Southwest site excavations and areal culture history reconstructions have proceeded apace for some years. However, the lack of analytical approaches relevant to situations of intercultural activity has severely curtailed our understanding of the ever changing patterns of interaction of the separate cultures. One of the critical factors has been the lack of a standardized system of artifact classification necessary for comparative studies. An analytical method which can entertain this problem will be presented in this paper.

The culture histories of the several Southwestern cultures have largely been founded upon ceramic typologies. Reference handbooks, for example Hawley's *Field Manual of Southwestern Pottery Types* (1936) and Colton and Hargraves' *Handbook of Northern Arizona Pottery Wares* (1937) were compiled to codify the designated types. However, although ceramic types provide useful guidelines to order sites in space and time, they were not designed to be and are not one-to-one equivalents with culture groups. Furthermore, since typologies are composites of co-occurring attributes, their validity depends on the degree to which different investigators can agree on a typological assignment. In an effort to solve this latter problem, some archaeologists became "lumpers" and ignored the presence of minor discrepancies from the type sherds by grouping sherds which possessed most but not all of the characteristics as one type. The "splitters," on the other hand, preferred to give new type designations to aberrant sherds. Other researchers developed new taxonomic classifications to encompass the deviants. Type-variety, ceramic group, and ceramic system were all born of such efforts.

During the past decade interest has shifted from excavations to obtain culture histories to excavations designed to elicit information concerning culture process. Such a change of focus in research objective obligates a careful assessment of the ability of the extant analytical methods to meet the new ends. In order to obtain the necessary supporting data to investigate these new problems, the study of ceramics, or of any artifact form, must undergo corresponding shifts toward the analysis of attributes selected for their role as indicators of specific aspects of cultural activity. One potential avenue of analysis involves the study of design.

Despite the tenacious adherence of most Southwestern archaeologists to the typological method there have been a number of excellent studies of ethnographic and archaeological ceramic design. One of the earliest of the ethnographic studies was Bunzel's comparison of design layouts on historic Zuñi, Acoma, Hopi, and San Ildefonso vessels (1929). She sought to delimit the range of the four styles in order to discover the degree of artistic freedom enjoyed by each potter during the composition and execution of a design. Mera examined the stylistic changes wrought by the Spanish presence on pottery produced between the sixteenth and nineteenth centuries along the Rio Grande and the Upper Little Colorado (1939). He concluded that the encomienda system of forced Indian labor may have incidentally led to the spread of design styles. The observed changes in design style and vessel shape reflected the population displacements which occurred when potters from different villages were centrally assembled to produce pots for the Spaniards' use. Chapman's studies of the changes and continuities in form and arrangement of elements on historic pottery design from Santo Domingo (1953) and San Ildefonso (1970) pueblos were early recognitions of the important interpretive role of individual decorative attributes.

Similar detailed analyses of prehistoric designs were also being carried out during the same period. Kidder and Amsden chronicled the changes in band patterns on the pottery from Pecos (1931, 1936). In another study Amsden sought to relate Hohokam and Puebloan designs through correlation of specific similarities in layout and element form (1936). Morris included a detailed description of the changes in design layout, particularly of band designs from the Basketmaker III through the Pueblo

III periods in his classic study of the La Plata valley (1939). Beals, Brainerd, and Smith subjected 50,000 Kayenta area Pueblo I-III sherds to a design element-layout analysis which they hoped would lead to

inferences . . . concerning the historical development and intercultural exchanges among the people who made the pottery (1945: 89).

More recent studies have sought not only to detail the elements and layouts utilized, but also to integrate the observed changes in design with changes in other aspects of the culture. Wasley utilized the "style of design" concept in order to coalesce pottery types into categories having broad regional and temporal significance (1959). For the Quemado, New Mexico area he subsumed 45 types within nine design styles. Similarly, Carlson defined the White Mountain Redware Tradition for an analysis of redware types from the east central Arizona, west central New Mexico area (1970) in order to demonstrate how six major design styles waxed and waned in historical succession. Smith proposed use of the term "school" (1962) to represent the variation yet homogeneity inherent in the ceramic output from a group of potters. As an example he characterized the ceramics from the Western Mound at Awatovi within the Jeddito School (1971).

Some investigators have been concerned with isolating and correlating the basic unit of design, the element, with other aspects of a cultural system in order to make inferences on the structure and functioning of that system (*cf.* Cronin, 1962; Longacre, 1964, 1970). However, ethnographic studies by Friedrich on Tarascan (1970) and Stanislawski on Hopi-Tewa practices (1969) suggest that, among certain cultural groups, the individual design element may not be significant and/or diagnostic. Particularly in the American Southwest individual design elements are widespread phenomena well known and used by many potters who work within a broad temporal range and spatial area.

Two concerns are inherent in the above research: the search for ceramic based measures of social intercourse, and the subsequent classification and analysis of these attributes. However, despite their pioneering efforts, the investigators were unable to integrate their discovery of culturally sensitive attributes to a standardized system of classification which could utilize this attribute data in comparative studies. The idea of the utility of aspects of design had been born and successfully tested but it had not yet been integrated with an analytical base that would facilitate the use of that information.

This problem can be resolved by defining attribute units which are sensitive indicators of cultural activities *as well as* standardized units of classification. Such a classification system is inherent in the well established principles of symmetry basic to the sciences of geometry and crystallography. The use of symmetry principles specifically for the study of ceramic design was first suggested by Brainerd (1942) and later explained and illustrated by Shepard in a major monograph, *The Symmetry of Abstract Design with Special Reference to Ceramic Decoration* (1948). At the time of its debut little attention was given to this new method of analysis. The typological approach continued to be utilized as the principal classification system for Southwestern ceramics. It is the purpose of this paper (also Washburn, 1977) to coordinate the use of a system of design classification based on standardized symmetry classes with a theoretical orientation that employs these units as indicators of the activities of population groups through time and space.

The principles of plane pattern generation, available in many geometry and crystallography texts (see for example, de Jong, 1959; Coxeter, 1961; Toth, 1964; and Gans, 1969) have been utilized only rarely in the study of design. The possibility of applying geometrical principles to the study of two-dimensional patterns, such as wallpaper, linoleum, tile, and textiles was pointed out in a short article by Buerger and Lukesh (1937). More significant was the work of Woods who "decoded" these principles and demonstrated their utility for the study of plane pattern designs (1935). His delineation of the classes of finite, one, and two-dimensional symmetries for pure (monochrome) and counterchanged (bicolor) patterns form the basis for the design classification system presented in this paper.

HYPOTHESIS

It is hypothesized that inter-communicating potters will produce designs which have common structural and compositional bases. These potters work within a "contact group" situation. The concept and the results of such interaction are similar to those observed by Michels in his study of Archaic and Woodland "contact networks" (1968). The homogeneous design configurations produced by the contact groups will here be referred to as "styles."

Furthermore, the lines of communication for the exchange of design ideas should be patterned after similar avenues of contact in the social, political, and economic spheres of culture. Thus, delineation of the temporal and spatial parameters of design styles should be indicative of the distributions, movements, and interactions of population groups.

It has been proposed that designs can be more efficiently and meaningfully studied through a classification based on their geometric properties. The selection of the part of the design to be subjected to symmetry analysis is crucial, since, in order to derive information on the composition and interactions of population groups, it is necessary to study an attribute of design that demonstrates definite temporal and spatial periods of presence and absence. While other ceramic attributes such as lip form, vessel shape, temper, surface finish, and paint color may be sensitive reflectors of cultural activities, it is hypothesized that the structure and composition of design are also diagnostic of certain group behavior patterns.

Design structure refers to the layout—the elementary subdivisions of the field of design. Design composition refers to the process of arrangement of elements and compositions of elements (motifs) within the structural framework. It is hypothesized that knowledge and use of certain design structures and compositional configurations are pervasive, although perhaps unconscious parts of the working knowledge of "correct" design construction techniques within a group of interacting potters. Choosing from among an almost infinite selection of design structures and element combinations available, potters within a "contact group" will follow certain traditional ways of structuring the areas to be decorated and of combining certain elements into motifs. The end result will be the consistent use of only a few of the possible layouts and element combinations. Thus, vessels which show a high degree of correlation of structural–compositional attributes are interpreted to have been produced by potters sharing the same design style. Those with lesser agreement are the result of peripheral and/or infrequent contact, trade, or recent population immigration and partial acculturation. The degree of adherence of a particular design to a specific style will be relative to the degree and type of contact experienced between the potters and the style. Delineation of this information system through the method of symmetry classification can be but one approach toward understanding the processes of social group composition and interaction.

The concept of design style has been used here in preference to "horizon" and "tradition" for several reasons. As originally defined by Willey (1945), horizon and tradition connote specific spatial and temporal parameters in a body of data that may, but do not necessarily, accompany a design style. Unlike horizon, which denotes the presence of specific artifacts or features on artifacts widespread in space but restricted in time, and tradition, which refers to a continuity of artifactual phenomena limited in spatial spread but extensive in temporal depth, all the temporal–spatial factors may be manifest in a design style in any combination. Styles may be short or long lived phenomena and may occur within a restricted or broad spatial area. Styles expand and contract through time and space as the people who produce them migrate to new areas, settle down, expand and incorporate new members, trade, bud off in small groups to neighboring valleys, dwindle in size, disperse, and are assimilated by other groups. In contrast to horizon and tradition, which are more narrowly defined concepts, styles, by their flexibility in scope, are able to more accurately mirror the range of changes which constantly are occurring within and between population groups.

The concept of design style complements the procedure of symmetry classification. Although the isolation of styles (patterned occurrences of specific structural and symmetrical constructions) is accomplished via an objective classification system, the resultant classes reflect actual patterns of potter interaction. Schapiro's definition of style best describes this scope and intent (1962: 278).

By style is meant the constant form—and sometimes the constant elements, qualities, and expression—in the art of an individual or a group . . . style is, above all, a system of forms . . . through which the personality of the artist and the broad outlook of a group are visible. It is also a vehicle of expression within the group, communicating and fixing certain values . . . It is . . . a common ground against which innovations and the individuality of particular works may be measured.

There are several important referents in the above conceptualization. First, a structural–compositional style is a *system* comprising the symmetries of elements, motifs, and layouts which are combined to form the characteristic designs of a particular group. Furthermore, a style is an *open system* constantly receiving, absorbing, rejecting, and revising new aspects from both within and without the system. Secondly, it is a form of *communication;* an unspoken yet pervasive series of normative rules of design construction promulgated by and participated in by a group of interacting potters. Within any given style individual creativity is bounded by group consensus.

Since styles may refer to specific design structural forms or compositional configurations as well as vessel color, form, or other technological properties, any one group can carry and employ more than one style. Styles are not equivalent 1 : 1 with a "culture" of the ethnographer, nor a "type" of the archaeologist. A style transcends the rigid bounds of the concept of a culture group. It refers to the products of their actions, which in inspiration, may extend beyond the limits of any one culture. Structural and compositional styles are visual manifestations of the sum of conceptualized patterns of design construction. They can be considered to be a "generative grammar" of the very basic rules of design possessed and practiced by interacting peoples.

Although the concept of style has often been utilized to describe design, extensive use of these individual studies has been limited by the absence of any precise delineations of the parameters of the styles. The definition of styles still flounders on the same problem that plagues typology. The attributes and the allowable deviations to be included within a specific style can be as debatable as those belonging to a type. The use of such a concept of style merely operates as an "umbrella" to group types or observed characteristics within a more general descriptive vehicle. However, without a standard procedure for stylistic definition, these broader descriptive categories are little better than types.

The concept of style as defined in this paper can operate as the transitional conceptual device between the investigator's classification and the real world which he seeks to describe and explain through his categorizations of it. Classifications must be objective, standardizable, and reproducible, but the cultural features which they represent are constantly changing entities. Rigid symmetry classes are suitable for the former purpose, while the concept of style best describes the latter. The use of the principles of symmetry to classify design provides a strictly uniform measure of attributes. Furthermore, because symmetry classes are not taxonomic, they avoid the implication of linked parentage among historically successive types. Thus, when designs whose structural parts have similar symmetries are grouped as a style, the concept of style becomes increasingly more meaningful and useful. Instead of merely being a broader descriptive label, "style" now can be utilized in a very specific way to characterize different cultures and their interactions.

METHODOLOGY

The proposed classification of design structure and composition is based on the property of symmetry. Symmetry describes the spatial relationship of geometrical figures around a point and or across a line axis. In this discussion comma symbols will be used to represent fundamental parts which are the basic constituents of all symmetric figures (Figure 1A). If a figure is composed of only one fundamental part it is asymmetric since it lacks point or line axes of symmetry. Symmetrical figures are composed of more than one fundamental part arranged around rotation or across reflection axes.

A symmetry operation describes the spatial movements, or transformations, necessary to superimpose a fundamental part upon its neighbor (Figure 1B). During such transformations, the size and shape of the figure remains unchanged. Pure symmetry operations involve monochrome figures (Figure 1C); whereas counterchanged patterns are

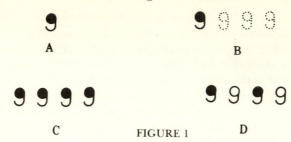

A   B

C   FIGURE 1   D

formed by the alternation of figures of identical shape but different color (Figure 1D).

All symmetry transformations involve four basic motions: translation, rotation, mirror reflection, and slide reflection. Translation involves the simple movement of a figure along a straight line axis (Figure 2A). Rotation involves the movement of a figure about a point axis (Figure 2B). Mirror reflection involves the reflection of a figure across a line axis (Figure 2C). Slide reflection involves both translation and reflection movements. The figure is first reflected across the line axis and then it is translated along the line axis (Figure 2D).

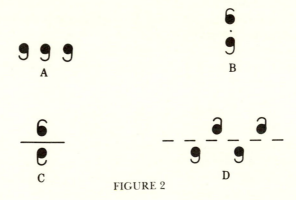

A   B

C   FIGURE 2   D

There are three design *categories* which describe plane pattern designs. Each of these is based on a different method of propagation: about a point; along one line axis; and, along two or more line axes. Finite designs are unit figures composed around a point. Figure 3A shows a finite design which has both rotation and reflection axes. The motions of translation and slide reflection cannot be utilized to generate a finite design since all symmetry operations must pass through one point central to the figure. One-dimensional designs, more commonly called bands, have only one central horizontal axis along which translation, bifold rotation, reflection, or slide reflection can occur. Figure 3B shows a band design generated by both reflections and rotations. Two-dimensional designs are based on a series of horizontal (X) and vertical (Y) axes which intersect at regular intervals forming a net. Fundamental parts are placed along and/or about these two axes and at their points of intersection. All four basic motions are compatible with two-dimensional patterns. Figure 3C shows a two-dimensional design generated by bifold rotation and longitudinal and transverse reflection. One and two-dimensional designs are called infinite since, theoretically, they can be extended indefinitely in one or two directions respectively.

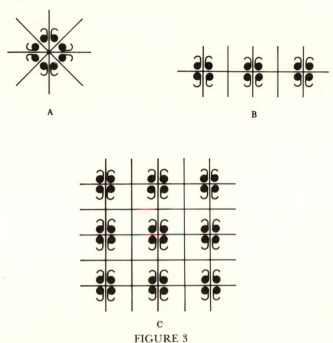

FIGURE 3

Within each of the three plane pattern categories are a series of *classes* which describe the combinations of symmetry operations that generate the particular category of design. For finite designs an unlimited number of pure and counterchanged classes are possible since there can be an infinite number of rotations around or reflections through the central point. However, only seven classes of pure patterns and 21 classes of counterchanged patterns can be generated for one-dimensional designs. The five net forms basic to two-dimensional patterns permit only 23 pure classes and 94 counterchanged classes of design. A detailed explication of the generation of all these classes forms the basis for a forthcoming monograph (Washburn, 1977). This short paper permits only a brief discussion of the principles and an illustration of the application of the method of symmetry classification.

The nomenclature utilized to describe each symmetry class is a modification of the three digit system proposed by Woods (1935). In order to separate the three categories of design, a 1- and 2- are placed in front of the symbol for one and two-dimensional designs respectively. No symbol is used for finite designs. The digit in the hundreds position corresponds to N, where N indicates the number of rotations around the principal axis. All information concerning symmetry operations along the vertical axis (Y) is stored in the units position. Similarly, all information concerning symmetry operations along the horizontal axis (X) is contained in the tens position. The digit in the tens and units position will be either a 0 or a 1. The presence of a reflection plane in any of these positions is indicated by a 1; the absence by an 0. The superscript 2 above the two reflection and rotation digits indicates that counterchange accompanies the indicated symmetry operation *within* the figure. The subscript 2 after the reflection digits indicates counterchange *between* figures along that axis. Counterchange between the rotation units will be indicated by a subscript 1 for counterchange along the vertical axis, a subscript 2 for counterchange along the horizontal axis, and a subscript 3 for counterchange along both vertical and horizontal axes. The presence of an X and/or Y after the three digit number indicates the presence of slide reflection along either the X and/or Y axis. A superscript 1 above the proper X or Y designator indicates slide reflection along that axis; a subscript 1 indicates slide reflection between axes. Counterchange along the slide reflection axes is indicated by a superscript 2 above the X or Y for counterchanged slide reflection along one axis, and a subscript 2 for counterchanged slide reflection between slide reflection axes.

In order to demonstrate the above classification procedure, a hypothetical one-dimensional design has been constructed (Figure 4A). The construction of a design involves a sequential process of choices among the repertoire of structures and elements. Analysis of the design involves the study of the symmetrical configurations of each stage of assembly of the design parts. First, the field of design, or the area to be decorated on the vessel is delineated. Then the basic structural lines are drawn in order to subdivide this area into the regular spaces which will be elaborated by motifs and elements. The end result of this process is the design structure, or layout. In Figure 4A the field of design is a band which has been subdivided into panels. Since the rectangular panels have bifold rotation as well as longitudinal and vertical axes of reflection, they have Class 1-211 symmetry. If figures composed of single elements or simple combinations of elements comprise the design, they are placed directly within the framework. Sometimes, however, the structure undergoes further subdivision before the figures are added. Complex motifs composed of a number of elements may simply be placed within the framework or may be part of the structural subdivisions. For example, within each panel in Figure 4B is a bifold rotational black figure with two stepped triangular ends that will coincide with each other after a rotation of 180°. This motif has Class 1-200 symmetry (Figure 4C). Interlocking in bifold rotation position with each of the solid stepped ends are hatched units of similar form. However, because they are not exactly the same shape as the solid units, they are not in perfect counterchanged bifold rotation with them. This use of color reversals for effect rather than perfect superposition will be called "false counterchange."

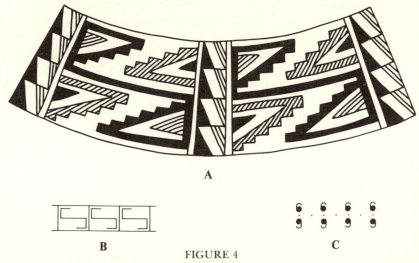

A

B

FIGURE 4

C

The two forms of counterchange are compared in Figure 5A and 5B. Solid figures are indicated by solid lines; hatched figures by dotted lines. Figure 5A illustrates true counterchange. Since all Y figures are the same shape, the dotted Y rotates 180° and is perfectly superimposed upon the solid Y. However, in Figure 5B the figures not only alternate in color but also in shape. Therefore, only the *effect* of color alternation is present. To generate this particular design, the solid unit rotates 180° into a solid unit and the dotted to the dotted by skipping the intervening figure of a different shape and color. True counterchange again is exemplified in the panel dividers in design Figure 4A. Two rows of right triangles are opposed; one is solid black, the other hatched. A bifold rotational motion moves the row of hatched triangles into the solid row and vice versa. This motif has Class 1-2^{2}00 symmetry.

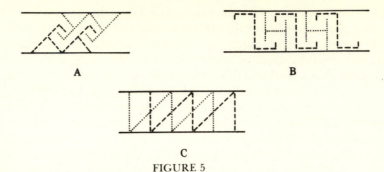

C

FIGURE 5

Design 4A also illustrates a procedure of design construction, the "continuous line" technique characteristic of late Puebloan design. During the composition of the two opposing rows of triangles in the panel dividers the potter did not draw each row separately, but drew two large, overlapping zigzags between the two banding lines. Thus the same design was achieved with a highly sophisticated economy of line (Figure 5C).

The symmetry of the whole design can be the same as or different than the symmetries of the constituent parts. The latter characterizes the symmetry of Figure 4A. Although there is bifold counterchange of figures and elements within each panel, the symmetry motion used to move the design from one panel to the next is pure bifold rotation, Class 1-200. The black bifold unit rotates 180° into the succeeding black bifold units; the hatched unit rotates 180° into the succeeding hatched unit.

ANALYSIS AND RESULTS

From the above example it should be clear that a design can be and usually is composed of structures and motifs that possess different symmetries. In fact, the possible number of element–structure symmetry combinations is virtually endless. What is thought to be significant is that certain groups consistently utilized specific combinations of structures and elements. Through a symmetry classification of design it is possible to recognize these selected patterns of design composition as stylistic representatives of specific population groups.

In order to demonstrate the proposition that regional design styles can be isolated by symmetry classifications and, furthermore, that these styles can be useful indicators of cultural process and change, it is necessary to examine, compare, and correlate data from all periods and areas of the Southwest. For the purposes of illustration in this paper three Pueblo III period collections have been subjected to symmetry analysis. One comes

from the Upper Gila area near Quemado, New Mexico, one from the El
Morro Valley near Ramah, New Mexico, and the third from Salmon ruin,
Bloomfield, New Mexico. The Upper Gila collection includes 158
polychrome and black-on-white designs from four sites. St. Johns
Polychrome and Tularosa Black-on-white are the most common types
represented. Thirty-four designs on both polychrome and black-on-white
vessels were studied from three El Morro Valley sites. One hundred and
eight-four designs, predominantly Mesa Verde Black-on-white, have been
examined from the Salmon site.

According to the hypothesis, ceramics from adjacent areas should possess
a high number of similarities in design structure and composition.
Conversely, ceramics from more distant areas should display fewer
similarities. Since the Upper Gila and El Morro Valleys are only about 50
air miles distant, a comparison of these collections should reveal the high
degree of similarity between designs from neighboring areas. Likewise, the
marked disparities between distant groups producing different styles will
be revealed in the comparison between designs from the west central New
Mexico and Four Corners area.

There will be shared characteristics among the three collections since
they all were produced by members of the Anasazi tradition. This common
base is manifest in the bias toward one prevalent design category, one-
dimensional, and one design structure class, bifold rotation. One-
dimensional designs appear as 75% of the Upper Gila sample, 88% of the El
Morro sample, and 64% of the Salmon ruin sample (Table 1). Furthermore,
within this category, 43% of the Upper Gila designs, 40% of the El Morro
designs, and 67% of the Salmon ruin designs have Class 1-200 symmetry
(Tables 2-4). The line graph in Figure 6 clearly shows this preference for
Class 1-200 structured designs. In addition, many of the Class 1-100 designs
from the Upper Gila and El Morro samples are actually imperfect Class 1-
200 structures since the motion intended was often technically reduced
because of slight differences in the shape of the figures.

TABLE 1

Frequency distribution of the three design categories in the Upper Gila, El Morro, and the
Salmon ruin collections

Site	Design category	Finite		One-dimensional		Two-dimensional		Total number observed
		Number observed	%	Number observed	%	Number observed	%	
Upper Gila		8	5	119	75	31	20	158
El Morro		2	6	30	88	2	6	34
Salmon		11	6	117	64	56	30	184

Discovering Past Behavior

TABLE 2
Frequency distribution of designs in design classes within the Finite category of design

Site \ Design class	200 Number observed	%	211 Number observed	%	400 Number observed	%
Upper Gila	4	50			3	38
El Morro			2	100		
Salmon	2	18			7	64

Site \ Design class	411 Number observed	%	600 Number observed	%	Total number observed
Upper Gila	1	12			8
El Morro					2
Salmon	2	18			11

TABLE 3
Frequency distribution of designs in design classes within the One-Dimensional category of design

Site \ Design class	1–100 Number observed	%	1–200 Number observed	%	1–110 Number observed	%	1–101 Number observed	%
Upper Gila	23	19	52	43			8	7
El Morro	5	17	12	40	1	3	1	3
Salmon	4	3	79	67	2	2		

Sites \ Design class	1–211 Number observed	%	$1\text{–}100x^1$ Number observed	%	1–201 Number observed	%	Total number observed
Upper Gila	26	22	2	2	8	7	119
El Morro	11	37					30
Salmon	15	13	2	2	15	13	117

TABLE 4

Frequency distribution of designs in design classes within the Two-Dimensional category of design

Site	Design class — 2–100 Number observed	%	2–200 Number observed	%	2–201x_1^1 Number observed	%	2–200x_1y_1 Number observed	%
Upper Gila	2	6	15	49	5	16	4	13
El Morro							2	100
Salmon			16	29	7	13	31	55

Site	Design class — 2–211 Number observed	%	2–211x_1y_1 Number observed	%	2–411 Number observed	%	Total number observed
Upper Gila	1	3	1	3	3	10	31
El Morro							2
Salmon			2	3			56

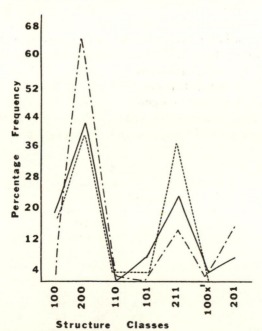

FIGURE 6 Frequency distribution of seven classes of One-Dimensional design in the classification of design structure. Solid line, Upper Gila designs; dashed line, El Morro designs; dot-dashed line, Salmon designs.

It could be argued that the close correlation between the three samples revealed in Figure 6 negates the value of symmetry classes as indicators of differences between contact groups. A chi-square test of independence was performed to test the null hypothesis that the distribution of symmetry classes in the three design categories was independent from the three localities. With a chi-square value of 12.59 and four degrees of freedom, the p-value of $< |02$ allows rejection of the null hypothesis and reinforces the conclusion that there are significant differences in the use of the different structure classes by the potters from the three areas.

The Upper Gila and El Morro collections were studied to test the ability of symmetry analysis to demonstrate similarities as well as differences between designs produced by two populations who lived and worked within the sphere of one broad-based contact group. Although the El Morro sample is much smaller, the similarity of the designs from both areas is obvious. Seventy-five percent of the Upper Gila and 88% of the El Morro designs are one-dimensional, and of these, 43% and 40% respectively have Class 1-200 symmetry of their structures. Due to the similar distribution of the one-dimensional structure classes used by these two populations, a chi-square test of independence should support a null hypothesis of no association between design structures and the two locations. For the purposes of this analysis the data were grouped into four classes—the three most prevalent structure classes (Class 1-100, 1-200, and 1-211) and a fourth class consisting of all other infrequently used classes. The chi-square value of 3.615 with three degrees of freedom corresponds to a p-value of $\sim.30$ which confirms the null hypothesis.

A common characteristic between the Upper Gila and the El Morro areas was the use of a counterchanged color scheme. Table 5 shows the distribution of the uses of the three types of color arrangements as well as an "other" category for those designs which do not fall into one of the three

TABLE 5

Frequency distribution of the three kinds of color arrangement within the seven classes of One-Dimensional design

Site \ Color	Pure		True counterchange		False counterchange		Other		Total number observed
	Number observed	%	Number observed	%	Number observed	%	Number observed	%	
Upper Gila	7	6	21	18	22	18	69	58	119
El Morro	1	3	4	13	16	54	9	30	30
Salmon	110	94	2	2	5	4			117

color forms. It is clear that potters in the Upper Gila and El Morro areas use some form of counterchange to structure their designs more frequently than do potters at Salmon ruin. The use of false counterchange was particularly popular at the El Morro sites—54% of the designs were so constructed.

Although Figure 4A is a hypothetical design, it was composed of structures and motifs that illustrate the hallmarks of the El Morro design style. The sense of color alternation between hatched and solid figures was maintained throughout the design, inclusive of the individual filler elements. Thus, if the main motifs were counterchanged, all other adjacent elements would always be of alternate colors.

Symmetry analysis can also reveal particularistic differences between two collections belonging to the same style. For example, Tables 2–4 and Figure 6 show a greater use of Class 1-211 by the El Morro area potters. This may reflect a skewed representation of all the classes due to the small sample size. Alternatively, it could be indicative of one aspect of the uniqueness of the El Morro relative to the Upper Gila design style. Both areas produced designs in counterchanged style. However, the El Morro potters apparently preferred to structure them by Class 1-211 as well as by Class 1-200.

Secondly, no El Morro designs were based on Class $1\text{-}100x^1$ or Class 1-201 structures. Since slide reflection is inherent in both of these classes, the absence of the use of this motion is notable. Thirdly, the execution of many of the El Morro designs was not nearly as precise as that on the Upper Gila designs. Hatching, line overlaps, crudely outlined and filled figures, asymmetric elements of varying shapes in sequence, poor space planning between figures, absence of fillers, and the composition of figures without the use of the "continuous-line" construction technique made the El Morro potters' products artistically inferior and easily separable from those of the Upper Gila area. Such local differences within a style are usually masked if the ceramics are typed. In the above case, the counterchanged polychrome designs from both sites would be classified as St. Johns Polychrome and the black-on-white designs would be classified as Tularosa Black-on-white.

More important, this method of classification has served to highlight an important conceptual difference in the way two populations chose to determine the visual effect of their designs. Since similar design elements were used by both groups, a design element study would not necessarily discern the difference in compositional style. Furthermore, since even many of the same basic design structures were used for the designs from both areas, they could not be distinguished by studying their pure symmetries alone. In this case it was necessary to analyze the frequency distribution of counterchanged symmetries to confirm the markedly different character of their styles.

In the foregoing example, two collections were studied which represented the products of potters working within the same design style. Symmetry analysis can also be utilized to contrast designs from distant areas whose potters may experience only sporadic interaction. A standard typological study would assign such vessels to different types thereby implying totally different origins. However, no population is ever long in total isolation and all populations interact with groups both near and far to some extent. Consequently, even designs from distant groups should share some similar aspects as well as possess characteristics totally unique. It is contended that a symmetry classification can more accurately characterize this situation. For example, although counterchanged designs typify the west central New Mexico area, this compositional technique did reach the Four Corners area. Six percent of the Salmon ruin designs are counter-changed. A more detailed analysis of a larger sample will be necessary before it can be concluded whether these vessels were produced in the Cibola area and traded into the San Juan or whether they were produced at Salmon ruin. In either case, their presence at Salmon ruin is a record of some form of interaction between the two areas. The line graph in Figure 7 shows the different distributions of the use of the three forms of color arrangement—pure, true counterchange, and false counter-change—among the three areas. The preferences for monocolor designs at Salmon ruin stands in clear contrast to the use of counterchanged constructions at the Upper Gila and El Morro sites.

The existence of markedly different compositional styles in the Salmon ruin and the west central New Mexico area (Upper Gila) was confirmed by a chi-square test. In this case the data were grouped into four structure classes (Classes 1-200, 1-100, 1-211, 1-201) and a fifth "other" class consisting of the three infrequently used structure classes. The chi-square value of 26.57 with four degrees of freedom corresponds to a p-value of < 001.

Other differences between the Salmon ruin and the Upper Gila areas include a slightly higher percentage frequency of two-dimensional designs at Salmon ruin (Table 1). These were well planned patterns based on large numbers of repeats of the figures along the multiple horizontal and vertical axes. In contrast, the two-dimensional designs produced by the Upper Gila potters were really only extensions of band designs which were classified as two-dimensional due to the technical presence of two horizontal axes. Furthermore, 71% of the two-dimensional patterns from Salmon ruin were based on a slide reflection structure, a motion which was conspicuously infrequent among the Upper Gila and El Morro area designs.

During the same period, populations belonging to different cultural

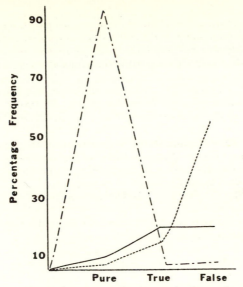

FIGURE 7   Frequency distribution of designs among the three color arrangements for the seven classes of One-Dimensional design. Solid line, Upper Gila designs; dashed line, El Morro designs; dot-dashed line, Salmon designs.

traditions composed very different designs. To the south and west the Hohokam preferred two-dimensional designs which covered almost the entire design field of the vessel. In contrast, the relatively few two-dimensional designs found on Upper Gila and Salmon ruin area vessels are always placed within a band layout. To the south, the Mimbres finite designs based on mirror reflections consist of figures of animals, insects, and humans in the bottom center of large bowls. Finite designs are infrequently found among the Anasazi, and when present, are usually based on the motion of rotation.

In short, potters do execute design styles unique to different areas and periods. Within a contact group situation, constant cross-fertilization of design ideas occurs. Conversely, cultural traditions discrete in space as well as in cultural heritage have distinctly different stylistic histories. It has been the purpose of this paper to demonstrate how the methodology of symmetry analysis can illuminate such problems in a systematic, standardized, and more meaningful way.

ACKNOWLEDGMENTS

I wish to thank the Peabody Museum, Harvard University for access to the Upper Gila collection; C. R. Redman of the Cibola Archaeological Research Project for access to the El Morro collection; and C. Irwin-Williams of the Salmon Ruins Project for access to the Salmon collection.

REFERENCES

Amsden, C. A. (1936) An analysis of Hohokam pottery design. *Medallion Papers* 23.

Beals, R. L., G. W. Brainerd and W. Smith (1945) Archaeological studies in northeast Arizona. *University of California Publications in American Archaeology and Ethnology* 44(1).

Brainerd, G. W. (1942) Symmetry in primitive conventional design. *American Antiquity* 8, 164–6.

Buerger, M. J. and J. S. Lukesh (1937) Wallpaper and atoms: how a study of nature's crystal patterns aids scientist and artist. *Technology Review* 39, 338–42.

Bunzel, R. L. (1929) The Pueblo potter. *Columbia University Contributions to Anthropology* 3.

Carlson, R. L. (1970) White Mountain Redware: a pottery tradition of east central Arizona and western New Mexico. *Anthropological Papers of The University of Arizona* 19.

Chapman, K. M. (1953) The pottery of Santo Domingo pueblo: a detailed study of its decoration. *Memoirs of the Laboratory of Anthropology* 1.

Chapman, K. M. (1970) The pottery of San Ildefonso pueblo. *School of American Research Monograph Series* 28.

Colton, H. S. and L. L. Hargrave (1937) Handbook of northern Arizona pottery wares. *Museum of Northern Arizona, Bulletin* 11.

Coxeter, H. S. M. (1961) *Introduction to Geometry*. John Wiley, New York.

Cronin, C. (1962) An analysis of pottery design elements, indicating possible relationships between three decorated types. In Chapters in the prehistory of eastern Arizona, edited by P. S. Martin, pp. 105–14. *Fieldiana: Anthropology* 53.

Friedrich, M. H. (1970) Design structure and social interaction: archaeological implications of an ethnographic analysis. *American Antiquity* 35, 332–43.

Gans, D. (1969) *Transformations and Geometries*. Appleton-Century Crofts, New York.

Hawley, F. (1936) Field manual of prehistoric southwestern pottery types. *University of New Mexico, Bulletin* 291.

de Jong, W. F. (1959) *General Crystallography: A Brief Compendium*. W. H. Freeman, San Francisco.

Kidder, A. V. and C. A. Amsden (1931) The pottery of Pecos, Vol. 1. *Papers of the Phillips Academy Southwestern Expedition* 5.

Kidder, A. V. and A. O. Shepard (1936) The pottery of Pecos, Vol. 2. *Papers of the Phillips Academy Southwestern Expedition* 7.

Longacre, W. A. (1964) The ceramic analysis, and sociological implications of the ceramic analysis. In Chapters in the prehistory of eastern Arizona, II, edited by P. S. Martin, pp. 110–25 and 155–70. *Fieldiana: Anthropology* 55.

Longacre, W. A. (1970) Archaeology as anthropology: a case study. *Anthropological Papers of The University of Arizona* 17.

Mera, H. P. (1939) Style trends of Pueblo pottery in the Rio Grande and Little Colorado cultural areas from the sixteenth to the nineteenth century. *Memoirs of the Laboratory of Anthropology* 3.

Michels, J. W. (1968) Settlement patterns and demography at Sheep Rock Shelter: their role in culture contact. *Southwestern Journal of Anthropology* 24, 66–82.

Morris, E. H. (1939) Archaeological studies in the La Plata district, southwestern Colorado and northwestern New Mexico. *Carnegie Institution of Washington, Publication* 519.

Schapiro, M. (1962) Style. In *Anthropology Today*, edited by S. Tax, pp. 278–303. University of Chicago Press, Chicago.

Shepard, A. O. (1948) The symmetry of abstract design with special reference to ceramic decoration. Contributions to American Anthropology and History 47, *Carnegie Institution of Washington, Publication* 574.

Smith, W. (1962) Schools, pots, and potters. *American Anthropologist* **64**, 1165–78.

Smith, W. (1971) Painted ceramics of the western mound at Awatovi. *Papers of the Peabody Museum of Archaeology and Ethnology* 38.

Stanislawski, M. B. (1969) Hopi-Tewa pottery making: styles of learning. Paper presented at the 34th Annual Meeting of the Society for American Archaeology, Milwaukee.

Toth, L. F. (1964) Regular figures. *International Series of Monographs on Pure and Applied Mathematics* 48.

Washburn, D. K. (1977) A symmetry analysis of upper Gila area ceramic design. *Papers of the Peabody Museum of Archaeology and Ethnology* 68.

Wasley, W. W. (1959) Cultural implications of style trends in southwestern pottery: Basketmaker II to Pueblo II in west central New Mexico. Ph.D. dissertation, The University of Arizona, Tucson.

Willey, G. R. (1945) Horizon styles and pottery traditions in Peruvian archaeology. *American Antiquity* **11**, 49–56.

Woods, H. J. (1935) The geometrical basis of pattern design, Parts I, II, III. *The Journal of the Textile Institute, Transactions* 26.

A Synthetic Model of Archaeological Inference*

MICHAEL B. SCHIFFER

The University of Arizona

Despite the many programmatic statements in the literature concerning how best to derive archaeological inferences, very little is actually known about the logico-empirical structure of inferences and their justification. Based on the three basic problems that must be resolved in the justification of any inference, a synthetic model is presented that details the general structure of inference justification. The basis of the model is three sets of archaeological laws, correlates, c-transforms, and n-transforms. The model is illustrated by examination of the uxorilocality residence inferences of Hill and Longacre. In more general applications of the model, the problem of the subjective element is laid comfortably to rest and processes of learning archaeological laws are discussed.

The basic question that underlies this paper is: How do archaeologists acquire knowledge of the past? This question can be interpreted in two ways. The first is the procedural or methodological aspect of knowledge acquisition, and the second is the logico-empirical structure of the justification of knowledge (Harvey, 1969). In other words, one may be interested in the processes of gaining knowledge or in the products of knowledge, or both.

The processes of knowledge acquisition have been the subject of many recent papers in archaeology. Beginning with the early work of Thompson (1958), archaeologists have provided several models of the processes used to generate understanding of the past (Binford, 1968a, 1968b; Clarke, 1968; Fritz, 1968, 1972; Fritz and Plog, 1970; Grebinger, 1971; Hill, 1970a, 1972; Mayer-Oakes, 1969; Swartz, 1967; Tuggle, 1970; Tuggle, Townsend and Riley, 1972; and others). The most recent work by Fritz (1972) is an important synthesis which will serve for a considerable period of time to acquaint archaeologists with the major issues in general methodology.

In stark contrast to the adequate understanding of archaeological procedure stands the rather poor understanding of the product and justification of archaeological inference. In the context of the "methodological debate" (Hill, 1972) the nature of the laws which underlie and make credible the substantive applications of all methodologies has

---

*Portions of this paper appear as Chapter 2 in *Behavioral Archeology*, Academic Press, New York and are reproduced here by permission of the publisher.

not been discussed, nor have the ways in which these laws are logically related to one another, to the data, and to knowledge of the past. In this paper I propose a general answer to the question of how archaeologists gain knowledge of the past. The nature and function of general types of archaeological laws are examined. A synthetic model of inference is presented in which these law types and their interrelations are specified. Several other topics relevant to archaeological epistemology are also investigated, including the subjective element in archaeological inference and the processes of law acquisition.

DEFINITIONS

Some preliminary definitions are in order. *Archaeological knowledge* is defined as consisting of the laws that are employed implicitly or explicitly to retrieve knowledge of the past from archaeological data. In confining the meaning of archaeological knowledge to sets of laws, I do not imply that other kinds of knowledge are unimportant. I simply desire to discuss the portion of the conceptual repertoire of archaeology that consists of *lawlike* statements. Archaeological knowledge is largely covert at this stage in the development of archaeology, and therefore it is necessary to digress at this point and explain more fully my use of the term "law" in connection with these archaeological principles.

Philosophers of science employ "law" as a technical term to denote certain relational statements having empirical content which function as major premises in the explanations of a discipline. Nagel (1961) refers to them as "experimental laws," while Hempel (1966) uses the designation "cover law." In applications of these terms, no connotations of immutability or compulsion need inhere. Laws are simply one kind of relational statement which function (in conjunction with other information) to explain or predict empirical phenomena. Probabilistic laws are, of course, encompassed by this formulation. For purposes of this paper, the philosophical perspective on laws is maintained. A law is a statement relating two *or more* operationally defined variables (adapted from Hempel, 1966). Because many relational statements of archaeological knowledge possess these properties and also function to explain and predict empirical phenomena, the appropriate designation in the absence of any other specific term is *law*. This usage naturally leaves one ample room to subject all such relational statements to discussion, retesting, or in most cases extraction from the literature and initial testing. *Relational statement, principle,* and sometimes *lawlike statement* are used here as synonyms for law as just defined. Archaeological knowledge, then, consists of these kinds of principles.

An *inference* is a descriptive statement of high probability about past cultural behavior or organization. By this definition, a positively tested hypothesis becomes an inference. *Inference justification* is the archaeological knowledge and data—and their structure—that give an inference its credibility.

THE SYNTHETIC MODEL

The basic problem in constructing this synthetic model is to determine the general nature of archaeological knowledge. The model presented here is based on what I suggest is the archaeological knowledge required to solve the problems which confront every archaeologist as a result of the three basic properties of archaeological data:

1) they consist of materials in static spatial relationships;
2) they have been output in one way or another from a cultural system, and
3) they have been subjected to the operation of noncultural processes.

Because a solution to each of these problems must be reached in the justification of any inference, three sets of laws, or at least assumptions within each problem domain, are employed. I now present the basic problems in greater detail and discuss the corresponding law sets.

CORRELATES

Let us begin by visualizing an ongoing cultural system. Such a system consists of material objects, human actors, foods, fuels, and is manifest in the repetitive occurrence of activities. What one pictures is a system of action—of energy transformations and material flows occurring in space. If the human participants and all other energy sources completely halt their actions, the activities cease, as does the operation of the behavioral system. What remains (assuming no modification by other processes) is the closest conceivable approximation to a "fossil" of a cultural system—its material elements in a system-relevant spatial matrix. While most archaeologists would gratefully accept a site produced under those conditions, when confronted by one, there would still be a major problem left to solve by the application of laws before inferences could be made.

Because the data themselves are totally silent and do not apprise the archaeologist of the ways artifacts once participated in a behavioral system or how they reflect the organization of that system, a set of relational statements must be acquired and applied to the materials. These statements relate behavioral variables to variables of material objects or spatial relations (Binford, 1962: 219; Struever, 1968: 134; Adams, 1968: 210; Ascher, 1962: 360). They may also involve organizational variables. Such statements have the important property of being operationally definable and, therefore, testable in an ongoing cultural system. Principles of this sort, without which no archaeologist could possibly know anything about the operation of a cultural system—past or present—by observing its material objects and their spatial relations are here termed "correlates." I have elsewhere referred to these laws as "arguments of relevance" (Schiffer, 1972a, 1972b), but that usage is misleading. In a strict sense, all principles that serve to link an inference to specific archaeological observations are arguments of relevance (Binford, 1968a: 23, 1968b: 273).

One important kind of correlate relates variables of behavior to variables of material objects. Such correlates are often (but not exclusively) used to infer the manufacturing operations that produced an element, or the use to which it was put. Statements that relate the fracturing properties of a lithic material and the particular applied forces to attributes of the resultant products and byproducts are examples. Crabtree's (1968) experiments on the removal of blades from polyhedral cores have produced many correlates of this type:

Assuming that obsidian has been properly preformed into a core with ridges, the platform is ground until it has the appearance of frosted glass. . . . The pressure crutch has been made, and the specimen is now ready for removal of the first blade (Crabtree, 1968: 463). Blade types are governed by the manner in which the pressure tool is placed on the edge of the core. The triangular blade is made by directly following one ridge, and the trapezoidal type is made by positioning the tip of the pressure tool in line with but between, two ridges (Crabtree, 1968: 465).

Armed with this correlate (and several others not made explicit), an investigator examining materials in the hypothetical stalled cultural system could recognize the attributes of certain artifacts and waste products as indicative of a particular kind of manufacturing behavior. Or looked at another way, if he were seeking to identify this kind of behavior, the application of the correlate would readily produce test implications.

Correlates are often exceedingly complex and may involve multiple variables of behavior, system organization, spatial relations and material objects (see Rathje, 1973, for an example of a correlate relating social mobility to status symbols). The terms "behavioral–material" or "behavioral–spatial–material" or any other meaningful combination may be applied to these laws. Despite the potential complexity of both laws and terminology, all correlates function in inference justification by allowing the derivation or identification of some aspects of an operating cultural system from knowledge of those aspects, spatial and material, which would be or are present in the archaeological record.

C-TRANSFORMS

The formulation and use of correlates is the procedure that archaeologists employ to solve the problem posed by the nonbehavioral nature of archaeological data. The second problem, solutions to which also lie embedded in the justification of any inference, requires the construction and use of laws that relate variables of an ongoing cultural system to variables describing the cultural deposition or nondeposition of its elements.

It is possible to define the nature and function of these laws more precisely by returning to the hypothetical cultural system. If the operation of the energy sources resumes, one notes that continuous activity results in periodic outputs of exhausted tools, waste products of food and fuel consumption, obsolete items, and others. Items discarded during the normal operation of a cultural system constitute the major source of the archaeological record. Another source of materials that begins a path to the archaeological record is de facto refuse, produced when the inhabitants abandon a site and leave usable materials behind (Schiffer, 1972b).

The general problem of cultural formation processes typified by normal outputs, de facto refuse, and other sources is taken into account by laws of the cultural formation processes of the archaeological record (Schiffer, 1972b). These principles permit an investigator to specify the ways in which a cultural system outputs the materials that may eventually be observed in archaeological context. Application of these laws is necessary to relate the past qualitative, quantitative, spatial, and associational attributes of materials in systemic context to materials deposited by the cultural system. Such laws are termed c-transforms.

Unfortunately, c-transforms are the most seriously embedded principles of archaeological knowledge; the necessity of their use is generally unacknowledged and a very few of them have been made explicit (Schiffer, 1972b). One hypothesis that functions within the c-transform domain is that

... with increasing site population (or perhaps site size) and increasing intensity of occupation, there will be a decreasing correspondence between the use and discard locations for all elements used in activities and discarded at a site (Schiffer, 1972b: 162; emphasis in original).

Employing this principle (untested though it is) one can justify the use of data from limited activity sites (Wilmsen, 1970) to postulate locations of past activity performance, since most elements of such a site are discarded at their locations of use (assuming no modification of spatial relationships by subsequent processes). Many inferences which rest on similar c-transforms are found in Binford, and others (1970) and Brose (1970); in both of these monographs the assumption of a correspondence between use and discard locations for many classes of debris is made.

Other c-transforms relate quantititative variables of a cultural system to quantitative variables of cultural deposition. For example, Howells (1960) developed several c-transforms which allow the reconstruction of site population size through the use of data from the retrieved burial population.

Superficially, c-transforms resemble correlates. At one level they both apply to the dynamics of ongoing cultural systems. But only c-transforms contain information about system outputs, such as discard rates, discard locations, loss probabilities, burial practices, and others. *Only c-transforms can be used to predict the materials that will leave systemic context.*

N-TRANSFORMS

The last major problem presented by the nature of archaeological data concerns the post-occupational changes in site and artifact morphology caused by noncultural processes, such as wind, water, rodent activity, chemical action. Noncultural formation processes are taken into account in inference justification by the use of principles which I designate n-transforms. *N*-transforms are the most highly developed area of archaeological knowledge, and there are many explicit laws. As two simple examples of n-transforms, I note that pollen is preserved in acidic soil, while bone is destroyed in acidic soil (all other variables constant). Other examples of n-transforms may be found in works by Clark (1960), Hole and Heizer (1973), and others. All n-transforms allow the archaeologist to predict the interaction between variables of culturally deposited materials and variables of the noncultural environment in which the former materials are found.

The relationships between c-transforms and n-transforms are portrayed in Figure 1.

STIPULATIONS

It has been argued thus far that archaeological knowledge consists of correlates, c-transforms, and n-transforms. These three sets of laws permit a complete "transformation" to be made between materials in archae-

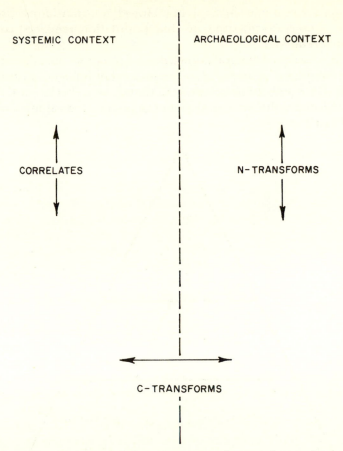

SYSTEMIC CONTEXT   ARCHAEOLOGICAL CONTEXT

CORRELATES   N-TRANSFORMS

C-TRANSFORMS

FIGURE 1   The domains of correlates, *c*-transforms, and *n*-transforms.

ological context and materials in their past systemic context. To complete the synthetic model of inference, several elements must be added. In the first place, one must often make assumptions within the domains of the three law sets. These additional but necessary bits of information are here termed "stipulations." I have deliberately refrained from calling these bits of information "assumptions." The point to be emphasized is that they are assumed or stipulated only in a specific inference justification; in principle, stipulations are subject to independent testing. Assumptions, on the other hand, seem never to be tested.

Stipulations convey information about other conditions that were present in the past. These may pertain to the cultural system under study, its natural and cultural environment, or even to subsequent cultural systems. As an example, in applying Howell's *c*-transforms discussed earlier, it is necessary to stipulate that population remained constant during site occupation.

In addition to archaeological knowledge, stipulations, and the inference itself, the completed synthetic model requires that inference justification include statements about observations made on the archaeological record. Figure 2 illustrates this structural model of archaeological inference and inference justification.

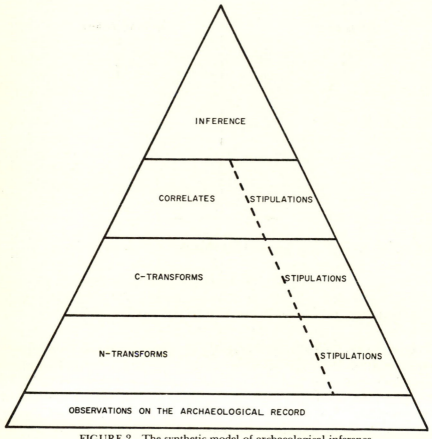

FIGURE 2   The synthetic model of archaeological inference.

ARCHAEOLOGICAL EXPLANATION

The synthetic model specifies that the explanation of archaeological observations is achieved when they are shown to be the expectable consequence of the relevant laws and initial conditions (see also Fritz and Plog, 1970; Watson, LeBlanc, and Redman, 1971). The inference itself and stipulations are seen as the relevant initial and boundary conditions, while correlates, *c*-transforms, and *n*-transforms constitute the laws. Together, these statements function to explain aspects of the archaeological record. In other words, a given behavioral or organizational property, other features of a past cultural system and its environment, post-depositional variables, and the relevant laws provide the conditions to account for (or allow the prediction of) aspects of material items and their interrelationships in the present. When coupled to stipulations and laws, an inference is justified to the extent that it makes certain archaeological observations expectable. Of course, alternative inferences and explanations are never precluded.

THE UXORILOCALITY INFERENCE

Abstract discussions of types of laws and logical relations are seldom adequate to explain a model and its uses. Therefore, I shall attempt to illustrate the synthetic model by analyzing a specific inference with respect to its underlying justification. The inference to be examined is the identification of uxorilocal residence (units) at Carter Ranch site (Martin, *et al.*, 1964; Longacre, 1968, 1970a) and Broken K pueblo (Martin, Longacre and Hill, 1967; Hill, 1970b). These inferences stand particularly vulnerable to close examination because many of the underlying principles and stipulations have been published previously by Longacre and Hill. In this discussion I treat only that part of the justification that concerns the spatial distribution of ceramic design elements. In addition, problems of the contemporary occupation of residence areas and the statistical interpretation of nonrandom patterning are not discussed. And finally, no alternative inferences and justifications are presented that could account for the same archaeological phenomena.

Longacre (1970a: 28) states the major hypothesis (a correlate) as follows:

Social demography and social organization are reflected in the material system. In a society practicing postmarital rules stressing matrilocality, social demography may be mirrored in the ceramic art of female potters; the smaller and more closely tied the social aggregate, the more details of design would be shared.

The next statement that "differential relative frequencies of designs may suggest the delimitation of various social aggregates" (Longacre, 1970a: 28) does not follow as directly as Longacre implies. In this example he attempts to spell out the nature of some of the correlates that underlie his analysis. What he does not present, nor does Hill, are the important remaining correlates and transforms that are embedded in the justification of this inference.

The incomplete presentation of the uxorilocality inference justification by Longacre and Hill has had an impact on research undertaken after and stimulated by their early published statements (Longacre, 1964; Hill, 1966). Stanislawski (1969a: 30), for example, has set out among the modern Hopi to examine "...the method of Hopi pottery training, and the association of family unit and pottery style or type." This research, while important in its own right, is completely irrelevant with respect to testing the laws justifying the uxorilocality inference (see also Longacre, 1970b). Had Stanislawski attempted the analysis undertaken here with benefit of the synthetic model, he would have discovered an essential implicit stipulation (which can also be represented as a correlate). This stipulation is that the social unit of pottery manufacture is the same as or a subset of the social unit of pottery use. This is certainly not the case among the modern Hopi. Most of their pottery has been made for export since the ceramic art was revived there before the turn of the last century; only a very few pots are actually used by Hopi households. And although Stanislawski (1969b: 12) is aware of these conditions, the implications seem to escape his notice. I suspect that if one were to excavate a modern Hopi village, such as Sichomovi, after it had been abandoned, one would have difficulty in demonstrating that pottery had been made there in the twentieth century. Only under the above conditions of use–manufacture social unit relationship would one expect designs to be transmitted intergenerationally within a localized social unit.

In addition to the stipulated relationship between the social units of pottery manufacture and use, an implicit c-transform (or stipulation) underlies this inference. The tables presented by Hill (1970a: 39, 1970b: 63) and Deetz (1965: 93) purport to represent relationships between post-marital residence patterns and the intrasite spatial distribution of female- and male-associated style elements. Such relationships totally omit factors of cultural deposition. Hill (1970b) has termed these relationships "correlates," and they do meet the definition for correlates presented above. Such statements relate a behavioral aspect of a cultural system (marital residence pattern) to material variables (ceramic design elements) and spatial variables (design element distributions). As such, they contain no terms that deal with aspects of the archaeological record.

Using such principles, one might be able to infer residence pattern by examining design element distributions in a modern community (making the appropriate stipulations), but only by inclusion of c-transforms and n-transforms (or stipulations within those domains) can one make a complete linkage to archaeological observations. Unless one assumes that at least some pottery was discarded or abandoned at the location of pottery use, there are no reasons whatsoever to expect the occurrence of a non-random distribution of design elements in the rooms where the pottery was used. This aspect of the inference justification has to date been overlooked but is as essential to the rigorous explanation of the data and the justification of the inference as any other aspect. Limitations of space prevent a detailed presentation of the complete justification for the uxorilocality inference. But the entire justification as I have reconstructed it is presented in Table 1.

Examination of Table 1 illustrates that the entries in any of the law domains can be presented as either a stipulation or a relational statement. A stipulation can be readily changed into the respective relational statement;

TABLE 1

The uxorilocality inference and its justification

INFERENCE: Localized uxorilocal residence units

CORRELATES	STIPULATIONS
1) If there is uxorilocality, and the social unit of pottery manufacture is the same as or a subset of the social unit of pottery use, and there is matrilineal transmission of style, then uxorilocal units will be equivalent to design units and there will be more sharing of designs within units than between units.	1) The social unit of pottery manufacture is the same as or a subset of the social unit of use.
2) If the social unit of pottery manufacture is the same as or a subset of the unit of use, and women make the pottery, then there will be matrilineal transmission of style.	2) Women make the pottery.
3) If uxorilocal residence units are localized, then by (1) and (2) above, there will be differential relative frequencies of design elements in the community corresponding to the various uxorilocal residence units.	

C-TRANSFORMS	STIPULATIONS
	1) Some pottery is discarded or abandoned at its location of use and the design elements on this pottery are a representative sample of the design elements made by the manufacture unit.

TABLE 1—cont

N-TRANSFORMS	STIPULATIONS
1) Pottery paste and fired-on design elements are preserved under most soil conditions. Items will remain at their locations of discard unless there is post-occupational disturbance of the site.	1) There is no post-occupational disturbance of the site.

ARCHAEOLOGICAL OBSERVATIONS
1) At the site in question, there will be differential distributions of pottery design elements across residential areas.

that is, it becomes a law which specifies the former stipulated information in one term and one or more additional variables of the past system under examination in its other term. This leads through another logical path to the archaeological data. For example, the stipulation that the use and manufacture social units are related could be transformed into a general statement: in villages where pottery is made without wheels or molds and there is no intervillage exchange of the pottery under question, the social unit of pottery manufacture is the same or a subset of the social unit of pottery use. One can then either stipulate that the conditions for the applicability of this law are met (such as handmade pottery with no external exchange) or produce other correlates and transforms that specify which sets of data at that site would tend to confirm the presence of these prior conditions. Of course, all inference justifications must contain at least one correlate.

This discussion is not intended to be the last word on the uxorilocality inference—other reconstructions are both possible and desirable (see Binford, 1968c: 270; Watson, 1971: 34-7; Allen and Richardson, 1971). Relevant tests of the actual principles that justify it must still be produced, as Longacre (personal communication) is now attempting. However, the examination of the inference with benefit of the synthetic model has indicated what some of these additional principles might be.

SUBJECTIVE ELEMENT

Turning from specific applications of the inference model, I shall now examine more general issues of archaeological epistemology on which the model may be expected to shed some light. It is now possible to lay to rest the stubborn issue of the role of the subjective element in archaeological inference. In the first sustained study of the subject, Thompson (1956, 1958) argued that inference contains a subjective element. He (1958: 4) states:

The ability to recognize the indicative quality of the data is therefore a first requisite for the archaeologist who hopes to reconstruct the context of the specimens which he discovers. This ability is, of course, subjective; it is often described as the "feel" which an investigator has for the material.

Not only does the subjective element play a part in allowing the archaeologist to recognize the "indicative qualities" of the data, but it is also said to influence the selection of the "probative data" against which the probability of the inference is measured (Thompson, 1958: 8). The large role that Thompson assigns the subjective element leads directly to his (1958: 8) conclusion that

The final judgment of an archaeologist's reconstruction must therefore be based on an appraisal of his professional competence, and particularly the quality of the subjective contribution to that competence.

Employing the synthetic model, we are in a position to determine precisely what this subjective element is. If archaeological knowledge is composed of several sets of law statements, one can explain variations in the ability of different investigators to offer inferences for a particular body of data ("recognize the indicative quality") by suggesting that they possess or apply these sets of laws differentially. This is analogous to explaining some of the variations in speech among members of a community by hypothesizing that they possess different sets of generative rules. An archaeologist who has internalized a wide variety of correlates, c-transforms, and n-transforms has a greater ability, in Thompson's terms, to recognize the indicative qualities of the data. Or, in the jargon of the new archaeology, such an archaeologist is capable of generating numerous test implications for a hypothesis.

Archaeologists who consistently display these abilities are known in the profession as "competent." Their inferences and tested hypotheses are usually accepted without a rigorous exegesis of the underlying principles. But, by employing the synthetic model, one is led to ask appropriate questions about the nature of the laws underlying an inference and their linkage to other elements of the inference justification. Use of the model in this way will lead to the possibility of evaluating reconstructions and explanations independently of the investigator who offered them. Sound scientific method demands not that we constantly retest and repeat the work of our colleagues, but that we be able to do so if the need arises. In short, archaeologists do exhibit different abilities both to generate inferences from data and derive implications from hypotheses; these differences can be explained in terms of the differential possession and use of archaeological knowledge.

A problem that is directly implied by the above discussion concerns the means by which correlates, c-transforms, and n-transforms are acquired, especially if such principles are implicit. In advanced scientific disciplines, most laws are explicit and can be learned by the diligent study of textbooks (Kuhn, 1962). This is not yet the case in archaeology. Even if one internalized every law contained in archaeological textbooks, he would be incapable of generating from the data all the knowledge of the past which we claim is accessible. Conspicuously absent in all introductory textbooks (e.g., Hole and Heizer, 1973; Fagan, 1972; Rouse, 1972) or in any texts, for that matter, is a section or sections describing the archaeological knowledge required to infer some aspects of a past cultural system.

Clearly, the laws composing archaeological knowledge must be acquired by prospective archaeologists, but the question is: How? I believe that the process of law acquisition is not unlike the way a child learns the grammar of a language. After ploughing through a large sample of site reports and syntheses, a student unconsciously proposes and internalizes trial relational statements to account for the linkage between data an investigator presents and his inferences about the past. These relational statements correspond to what I have termed correlates, c-transforms, and n-transforms.

Because archaeological knowledge rarely reaches the printed page and resides primarily in the conceptual framework of individual investigators, there is no shortcut method of learning these principles beyond the laborious and wasteful task of reinventing them while reading and comprehending the archaeological literature. The nonpresentation of laws is perhaps the most efficient way to write site reports, syntheses, and interpretive papers, but in the absence of good textbooks we are left without an efficient means of enculturating aspiring archaeologists. More importantly, we cannot take stock of the conceptual progress of archaeology or easily determine the undeveloped areas of archaeological knowledge. I suggest that future writers of textbooks will have to devote much more space to listing and illustrating the use of relational statements of archaeological knowledge. I envision, for example, several introductory texts covering separately many complex subjects in reconstruction, such as social organization, lithic technology, and subsistence. Such texts would be nothing less than catalogs of law statements with examples of their applications to specific archaeological situations and some discussion about the extent to which they had been tested.

CONCLUSION

In this paper, I have attempted to lay bare the general structure of inference justification and the nature of archaeological knowledge. Despite the many ways that archaeologists have devised to gain knowledge of the past, the basic structure of inference justification seems to be the same.

Some of the important features of the synthetic model are:

1) All descriptive statements about the past—inferences and tested hypotheses—are part of a complex explanatory framework which accounts for aspects of the archaeological record.

2) Some of the laws in these explanations—correlates and *c*-transforms—are laws of cultural dynamics.

3) All knowledge of the past is inference in the sense that there is no epistemically tenable or otherwise useful distinction between direct or indirect knowledge of the past. All knowledge of the past acquired through archaeological means is made accessible by the use of laws.

Once the many principles constituting the three areas of archaeological knowledge are made explicit and subjected to testing, archaeology will advance conceptually and cumulatively at a rapid rate. Too few of the implicit laws now in use are really adequate for the interpretive tasks assigned to them. As more of these principles are made explicit and others are originated by archaeologists, we will find ourselves turning increasingly to ethnoarchaeology, simulations, and experimental studies of all sorts to test posited laws—correlates, *c*-transforms, or *n*-transforms.

ACKNOWLEDGMENTS

A shortened version of this paper was read at the 37th Annual Meeting of the Society for American Archaeology, May 4, 1972, Bal Harbour, Florida. I thank Annetta Cheek, Paul F. Grebinger, Michael E. Levin, H. A. Luebbermann, Jr., Charles G. Morgan, William L. Rathje, J. Jefferson Reid, James T. Rock, Raymond H. Thompson, and David R. Wilcox for commenting on earlier drafts of this paper. This study was carried out while the author held an N.S.F. Graduate Traineeship in the department of anthropology at The University of Arizona. Louis Gregoire drew Figure 1, and Sharon Urban drew Figure 2.

REFERENCES

Adams, W. Y. (1968) Invasion, diffusion, evolution? *Antiquity* **42**, 194–215.

Allen, W. L., and J. B. Richardson III (1971) The reconstruction of kinship from archaeological data: the concepts, the methods, and the feasibility. *American Antiquity* **36**, 41–53.

Ascher, R. (1962) Ethnography for archaeology: a case from the Seri Indians. *Ethnology* **1**, 360–9.

Binford, L. R. (1962) Archaeology as anthropology. *American Antiquity* **28**, 217–25.

Binford, L. R. (1968a) Archeological perspectives. In *New Perspectives in Archeology*, edited by S. R. and L. R. Binford, pp. 5–32. Aldine, Chicago.

Binford, L. R. (1968b) Some comments on historical versus processual archaeology. *Southwestern Journal of Anthropology* **24**, 267–75.

Binford, L. R. (1968c Methodological considerations of the archeological use of ethnographic data. In *Man the Hunter*, edited by R. B. Lee and I. DeVore, pp. 268–73. Aldine, Chicago.

Binford, L. R., S. R. Binford, R. Whallon, M. A. Hardin (1970) Archaeology at Hatchery West. *Society for American Archaeology, Memoir* 24.

Brose, D. S. (1970) The Summer Island site: a study of prehistoric cultural ecology and social organization in the northern Lake Michigan area. *Case Western Reserve University Studies in Anthropology* 1.

Clark, J. G. D. (1960) *Archaeology and Society: Reconstructing the Prehistoric Past*. Methuen, London.

Clarke, D. L. (1968) *Analytical Archaeology*. Methuen, London.

Crabtree, D. E. (1968) Mesoamerican polyhedral cores and prismatic blades. *American Antiquity* **33**, 446–78.

Deetz, J. (1965) The dynamics of stylistic change in Arikara ceramics. *Illinois Studies in Anthropology* 4.

Fagin, B. M. (1972) *In the Beginning: An Introduction to Archaeology*. Little, Brown, Boston.

Fritz, J. M. (1968) Archaeological epistemology: two views. M.A. thesis, University of Chicago, Chicago.

Fritz, J. M. (1972) Archaeological systems for indirect observation of the past. In *Contemporary Archaeology*, edited by M. P. Leone, pp. 135–57. Southern Illinois University Press, Carbondale.

Fritz, J. M. and F. T. Plog (1970) The nature of archaeological explanation. *American Antiquity* **35**, 405–12.

Grebinger, P. F. (1971) Hohokam cultural development in the middle Santa Cruz Valley, Arizona. Ph.D. dissertation, The University of Arizona, Tucson.

Harvey, D. (1969) *Explanation in Geography*. Edward Arnold, London.

Hempel, C. G. (1966) *Philosophy of Natural Science*. Prentice-Hall, Englewood Cliffs, N. J.

Hill, J. N. (1966) A prehistoric community in eastern Arizona. *Southwestern Journal of Anthropology* **22**, 9–30.

Hill, J. N. (1970a) Prehistoric social organization in the American Southwest: theory and method. In *Reconstructing Prehistoric Pueblo Societies*, edited by W. A. Longacre, pp. 11–58. University of New Mexico Press, Albuquerque.

Hill, J. N. (1970b) Broken K pueblo: prehistoric social organization in the American Southwest. *Anthropological Papers of The University of Arizona* 18.

Hill, J. N. (1972) The methodological debate in contemporary archaeology: a model. In *Models in Archaeology*, edited by D. L. Clarke, pp. 61–108. Methuen, London.

Hole, F. and R. F. Heizer (1973) *An Introduction to Prehistoric Archeology*. Holt, Rinehart and Winston, New York.

Howells, W. W. (1960) Estimating population numbers through archaeological and skeletal remains. In The application of quantitative methods in archaeology, edited by R. F. Heizer and S. F. Cook, pp. 158–80. *Viking Fund Publications in Anthropology* 28.

Kuhn, T. N. (1962) *The Structure of Scientific Revolutions*. University of Chicago Press, Chicago.

Longacre, W. A. (1964) Archaeology as anthropology: a case study. *Science* 144, 1454–5.

Longacre, W. A. (1968) Some aspects of prehistoric society in east-central Arizona. In *New Perspectives in Archeology* edited by S. R. and L. R. Binford, pp. 89–102. Aldine, Chicago.

Longacre, W. A. (1970a) Archaeology as anthropology: a case study. *Anthropological Papers of The University of Arizona* 17.

Longacre, W. A. (1970b) Current thinking in American archeology. In Current directions in anthropology, edited by A. Fischer, pp. 126–38. *Bulletins of the American Anthropological Association* 3(3), pt. 2.

Martin, P. S., W. A. Longacre, and J. N. Hill (1967) Chapters in the prehistory of eastern Arizona, III. *Fieldiana: Anthropology* 57.

Martin, P. S., J. B. Rinaldo, W. A. Longacre, L. G. Freeman, Jr., J. A. Brown, R. H. Hevly, M. E. Cooley (1964) Chapters in the prehistory of eastern Arizona, II. *Fieldiana: Anthropology* 55.

Mayer-Oakes, W. J. (1969) Towards a theoretical framework for systematic archaeological operations. Manuscript, Arizona State Museum Library. Xerox.

Mayer-Oakes, W. J. (1970) Comments on analytical archaeology. *Norwegian Archaeological Review* 3, 12–16.

Nagel, E. (1961) *The Structure of Science*. Harcourt, Brace and World, New York.

Rathje, W. L. (1973) Models for mobile Maya: a variety of constraints. In *The Explanation of Culture Change*, edited by C. Renfrew, pp. 731–57. G. Duckworth, London.

Rouse, I. (1972) *Introduction to Prehistory: A Systematic Approach*. McGraw-Hill, New York.

Schiffer, M. B. (1972a) Cultural laws and the reconstruction of past lifeways. *The Kiva* 37, 148–57.

Schiffer, M. B. (1972b) Archaeological context and systemic context. *American Antiquity* 37, 156–65.

Stanislawski, M. B. (1969a) The ethno-archaeology of Hopi pottery making. *Plateau* 42, 27–33.

Stanislawski, M. B. (1969b) What good is a broken pot? *Southwestern Lore* 35, 11–18.

Struever, S. (1968) Problems, methods and organization: a disparity in the growth of archeology. In *Anthropological Archeology in the Americas*, edited by B. J. Meggers, pp. 131–51. The Anthropological Society of Washington, Washington, D.C.

Swartz, B. K. (1967) A logical sequence of archaeological objectives. *American Antiquity* 32, 487–97.

Thompson, R. H. (1956) The subjective element in archaeological inference. *Southwestern Journal of Anthropology* 12, 327–32.

Thompson, R. H. (1958) Modern Yucatecan Maya pottery making. *Society for American Archaeology, Memoir* 15.

Tuggle, H. D. (1970) Prehistoric community relationships in east-central Arizona. Ph.D. dissertation, The University of Arizona, Tucson.

Tuggle, H. D., A. H. Townsend, and T. J. Riley (1972) Laws, systems, and research designs: a discussion of explanation in archaeology. *American Antiquity* 37, 3–12.

Watson, P. J., S. A. LeBlanc, and C. L. Redman (1971) *Explanation in Archeology*. Columbia University Press, New York.

Wilmsen, E. N. (1970) Lithic analysis and cultural inference: a Paleo-Indian case. *Anthropological Papers of The University of Arizona* 16.

Chipped Stone and Human Behavior at the Joint Site

MICHAEL B. SCHIFFER

The University of Arizona

Chipped-stone data from the Joint site, a Pueblo III ruin in the Hay Hollow Valley of east central Arizona, are used in a demonstration of how explicit consideration of cultural formation processes can enhance activity reconstructions. It is pointed out that in the conceptual frameworks of both culture history and processual archaeology, cultural formation processes are treated in a cursory and misleading fashion. A new framework, based on the principles of behavioral archaeology, is presented and explicit models are built of Joint site cultural formation processes. Inferences about chipped-stone activity locations obtained by factor analysis of Joint site secondary refuse data, while in no sense definitive, do illustrate the utility of this approach to the study of the past.

INTRODUCTION

In this paper I describe some of my investigations into prehistoric human behavior at the Joint site, a Pueblo III ruin in the Hay Hollow Valley of east central Arizona (Figure 1). The Joint site was excavated in the summers of 1970 and 1971 by the Southwestern Expedition of the Field Museum of Natural History under the direction of the late Paul S. Martin. The site comprises 36 rooms, distributed among a 27-room main unit, a 6-room minor unit, and three outlying, semisubterranean kivas, in addition to numerous extramural deposits (Figure 2). The best current estimate for period of occupation based on dendrochronology (Wilcox, 1975; Schiffer, 1973) and radiocarbon (Schiffer, 1973) is A.D. 1200–1275.

The Joint site excavation was designed to be an experiment in the organization of an archaeological project. We reasoned that, because archaeological sites are scarce resources and should only be exploited (i.e. excavated) for problem-oriented research purposes, one potential conservation measure would be to apply more than one research design to the same site. Three very different research designs prepared by Frederick Gorman, John Hanson and myself were operationalized during the excavation of the Joint site (Hanson and Schiffer, 1975). The results of our experiment in archaeological organization are reported elsewhere (Hanson and Schiffer, 1975; Gorman, this volume).

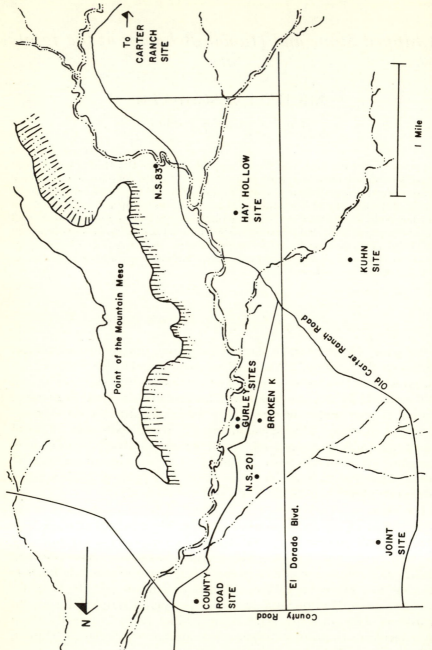

FIGURE 1 Map of the Hay Hollow Valley showing the Joint site in relation to other excavated sites and major physiographic features.

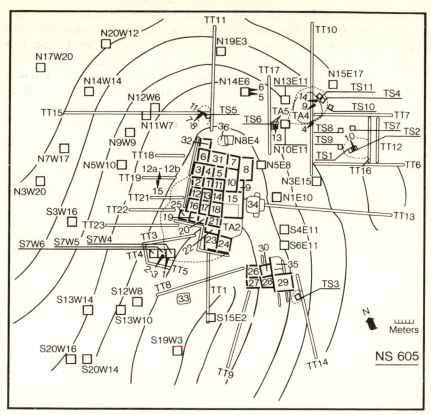

FIGURE 2 Map of the Joint site displaying major excavation units.

The research design I applied to the Joint site developed out of, but partially in reaction to, the studies in processual archaeology carried out by Hill (1970) and Longacre (1970) at the Broken K pueblo and Carter Ranch sites, both of which are also in the Hay Hollow Valley (see Figure 1). These pioneering investigations had firmly established the utility of the now oft-repeated assumption that archaeological remains are patterned in a manner reflecting past human behavior. I had no quarrel with this assumption when taken in its most general sense. Yet I felt uneasy with a more specific, largely implicit version which leads to the expectation that artifacts are broken and discarded at their locations of use (Schiffer, 1975a). It seemed to me that, in the uncritical use of this assumption, a major domain of behavioral variability pertaining to the formation of the archaeological record was being overlooked. A genuine behavioral archaeology (Reid, 1973; Schiffer, 1973) requires that a more general, flexible framework be developed to encompass the variability introduced into the archaeological record by various formation processes (Schiffer, 1972; Schiffer and Rathje, 1973; Schiffer, this volume).

My researches at the Joint site have been directed toward establishing and testing this more general framework for both reconstructing the past and explaining the facts of the archaeological record. Before turning to the specifics of my Joint site research design and results, I will address several general topics. The first, cultural formation processes and transformations, presents major features of the new framework for viewing the relationship between past behavior and the archaeological record. The second topic considers how culture historians and processualists in the American Southwest have treated these relationships. Finally, I return to show how the Joint site project provides evidence for the utility of explicitly considering how a cultural system produces archaeological remains.

THE GENERAL FRAMEWORK FOR A BEHAVIORAL ARCHAEOLOGY

Let us begin with a statement of the obvious and follow out some of its not-so-obvious implications: A past cultural system and its archaeological record are different phenomena. This distinction can be reinforced analytically by the description of cultural materials in terms of two contexts. The *systemic context* (Schiffer, 1972) refers to the participation of material items in a behavioral system. The statement that "women ground maize with manos and metates in habitation rooms" pertains to the systemic context of manos, metates, maize, women, and rooms. On the other hand, the *archaeological context* (Schiffer, 1972) refers to materials that are no longer part of an ongoing behavioral system. For example, "manos, metates, and maize are found in floor association in the larger rooms" is a statement about the archaeological context of these items.

Naturally, the systemic context of archaeological sites is no longer observable and it must be approximated by the archaeologists' models. However, in studies of modern material culture, experimental archaeology and ethnoarchaeology, the systemic context is directly observable and need only be reported.

Both contexts can be described in terms of formal, quantitative, spatial and relational variables. Descriptions of the systemic context pertain to behavioral properties, while archaeological context descriptions relate to a static, 3-dimensional arrangement of objects, residues, and noncultural materials on and in the ground.

Although noncultural formation processes, such as soil deposition, rodent burrowing, and bacterial attack of organic materials, play an important role in the formation of any archaeological context, and must be taken into account when data are gathered and reconstructions are offered (Schiffer and Rathje, 1973; Schiffer, this volume; Reid, Schiffer and Neff, 1975). I am concerned here primarily with the cultural processes responsible for forming the archaeological record. Cultural formation processes (Schiffer, 1972, 1973) are the activities that are responsible for many aspects of the archaeological context. In fact, a major type of cultural formation process can be simply defined as the activities that transform materials from systemic context to archaeological context. For example, when wornout tools are discarded, when the dead and their grave accompaniments are buried, when items are accidentally lost, and when (often usable) items are simply abandoned as an activity area is vacated, materials have been transformed from systemic to archaeological context.

In the discussions that follow several general types of refuse, defined in terms of cultural formation processes, are used extensively. *Primary refuse* (Schiffer, 1972) is material which has been discarded at its location of use. Waste material which has no location of use is primary refuse when discarded at its location of production. *Secondary refuse*, on the other hand, consists of items which have been transported away from their locations of use and discarded elsewhere (Schiffer, 1972). Both primary and secondary refuse are produced by normal system operation at an activity area; that is why the term *discard*, with its connotation of intention, is emphasized. Materials of these refuse types were determined to be no longer of use and, therefore, discarded by the occupants of an activity area. The third type of refuse, *de facto*, is produced by a very different process. De facto refuse is produced when the occupants of an activity area abandon it leaving behind often usable artifacts (Schiffer, 1972). De facto refuse, then, consists of the materials which were in systemic context just prior to activity area abandonment. (It should be noted that these refuse types and processes do not exhaust all of the possible ways by which materials may be transformed from systemic context to archaeological context.) Quite clearly, each type of refuse or combination of refuse types may contain data appropriate for answering only some kinds of systemic context questions. For example, one would not plot the distribution of secondary refuse on a site and claim that it represents past activity areas (other than discard activities).

Consideration of various cultural formation processes leads to an appreciation of the differentiated nature of archaeological remains and also to a reevaluation of generally accepted assumptions about how the archaeological context is produced. For example, we can now cast out statements to the effect that the patterning of remains in a site *directly* reflects the structuring of past activities and social groups there. We can substitute instead the proposition that the archaeological context is a distorted reflection of the systemic context. Such distortions are caused, in part, by cultural formation processes. But these distortions can be taken into account and corrected by constructing appropriate conceptual and methodological tools to act as lenses through which aspects of the systemic context can be perceived by observing aspects of the archaeological context. Just as all information needed to produce a sharp print is encoded in even the most poorly focused negative, the information for reconstructing the past is encoded in the structure of the present. Instead of applying holographic restoration techniques, we apply c-transforms, the laws describing the regularities of cultural formation processes (Schiffer, 1973; Schiffer and Rathje, 1973), to eliminate the distortions introduced by cultural formation processes.

The ways in which c-transforms are used in "transformation procedures" to establish relationships between the two contexts of archaeological materials form the core of behavioral archaeology's program for reconstructing the past (Reid, 1973; Reid and Schiffer, n.d.; Reid, Schiffer, and Neff, 1975; Schiffer, 1973, and this volume). Quite clearly the archaeological context and systemic context are not equivalent; and this fact poses the basic problem faced by all archaeologists: How does one relate the archaeological and systemic contexts? Although one might be tempted to suggest that relationships are established by "transforming" the archaeological context into systemic context, this is true only in a metaphorical sense. The task is one of modeling with c-transforms the transformations wrought by cultural formation processes on systemic materials to produce the archaeological context. When one successfully models or specifies the nature and effects of these processes, then, and only then, can the two contexts of remains be rigorously related. Throughout the remainder of this paper, reference is made to the "transformation problem." It should be understood that in "transforming" the present into the past, one is accounting in terms of c-transforms for the transformations of the past into the present by cultural formation processes. Transformation procedures consist of the methods and principles by which transformations are effected.

Reid and I have elsewhere proposed a general model of the transformation procedure (Reid, 1973; Reid and Schiffer, n.d.; Reid, Schiffer and Neff, 1975; Schiffer, 1973, and this volume); in this paper I shall present only its bare and simplified outlines and one contrived example to set the stage for considering how the transformation problem has been handled in southwestern archaeology and how it was handled in my part of the Joint Site Project.

Transformation procedures are simply the principles and methods used to explicitly account for properties of the archaeological context in terms of cultural (and noncultural) formation processes. Transformations are of two types and both depend in part on *c*-transforms. *Systemic transformations* link systemic context information to relevant units of analysis, while *identification transformations* relate or operationalize units of analysis (e.g. refuse types) to units of observation (proveniences) in the archaeological context. In this paper I am concerned principally with systemic transformations.

AN EXAMPLE OF TRANSFORMATION PROCEDURES: POTTERY AT A SITE

In this example, an archaeologist is dealing with a sedentary agricultural village that has been transformed into an archaeological site. The archaeologist is given no information about the cultural formation processes responsible for creating the site; these must be identified independently if specific systemic context questions about the remains are to be answered. It is assumed that the entire site has been excavated and that all discarded and abandoned pottery, the artifact class of interest, has been recovered.

SPATIAL TRANSFORMATIONS OF THE POTTERY

At the village, two homogeneous classes of pottery, bowls and jars, were found in archaeological context. What kinds of transforms must be applied to these materials in order to answer the systemic context question: Where were jars normally used? The presence of a number of formerly sturdy dwellings at this site leads the archaeologist to suspect that it may have been inhabited year-round and supported a population of perhaps several hundred. Based on these inferences, which have been presumably established through the use of other relevant archaeological laws and transforms, the archaeologist deduces that substantial amounts of secondary, as well as some primary and de facto refuse would have been produced by this village. This follows directly from the c-transform that as the intensity of occupation and the population size of an activity area increase so will the ratio of secondary to primary refuse produced (adapted from Schiffer, 1972: 162).

The next step requires the archaeologist to identify the various kinds of refuse that have been recovered. Although primary and de facto refuse would be of most interest, through past experience the archaeologist knows that they might not be fully representative of the pottery in use during the systemic context of an activity location. Therefore, it is necessary to also utilize secondary refuse. By means of an identification transformation the archaeologist can specify attributes of the provenience units that are likely to contain refuse of one type or another. Primary refuse would occur on use surfaces (which need to be independently identified). For example, if sweeping and refuse removal were not performed with the utmost rigor in dwellings, one would likely find some sherds embedded in floors or resting on floors in areas, like corners, which had low foot traffic. If primary refuse is successfully identified, then use locations can be readily derived on the basis of a spatial *equivalence transformation*. In other words, because primary refuse is discarded at its location of use, present location of an artifact equals its past location of use. Activity locations, though not exclusively of use, are determined by a similar transformation applied to de facto refuse. De facto refuse would be expected to consist largely of serviceable items deposited on the last-abandoned use surfaces. Whole or restorable cooking pots found in a hearth would be examples of de facto refuse abandoned at its location of use. Other instances of that same type of cooking vessel might also be recovered stacked against a dwelling's wall. In the latter case, these de facto refuse vessels might have been abandoned at their locations of storage.

Deposits of secondary refuse in a sedentary community are usually characterized by a high density of material occurring in great variety. Such materials are usually broken, worn-out, or incomplete. When one has identified a secondary refuse area by means of this or other identification transformations, he is then ready to apply more complex spatial transformations. For example, the spatial transformation of nonequivalence, use areas contributed to the nearest secondary refuse area, provides a link between an object in secondary refuse with its location of use in the past. (It should always be kept in mind when devising transformations that one is attempting to account for the present properties of the archaeological record in terms of the behavioral systems of the past.) Archaeologists have not given sufficient attention to developing these transformations—some even imply that ascertaining activity locations from secondary refuse is impossible (Redman, 1973). As I shall show in the Joint site discussion below, one can determine activity locations from secondary refuse material by developing more sophisticated c-transforms.

QUANTITATIVE TRANSFORMATION OF THE POTTERY

One can ask questions about quantitative variables of the systemic context of the pottery from the hypothetical village and illustrate the role of quantitative c-transforms. For example, how much pottery was used during the occupation of this village? Since one deals most often with sherds—not pots—in archaeological context, present sherd counts must be transformed into jar or bowl counts of the systemic context. This is effected by means of a quantitative and formal transformation. By assembling representative whole pots and comparing the weight of whole vessels and sherds one is able to derive ratios of sherd production, such as 50 ounces of sherds per jar. These ratios are then multiplied by the total weight of sherds to yield total vessel counts (Baumhoff and Heizer, 1959).

Let us suppose that it is possible to determine the total number of bowls or jars that were discarded. In itself, such information does not reveal much about the systemic context. One might wish to ask another systemic context question, such as: How many bowls were in use by a household, on the average, during the occupation of the site? To answer this question, another quantitative c-transform is applied (from Schiffer, 1973: 105):

$$T_D = \frac{kct}{L}$$

where,

T_D = total quantity of discarded bowls

k = average quantity of bowls in use by a household

c = number of households

t = occupation span of site

L = uselife of bowls.

By substituting in the equation the known quantity—total amount of discarded pots—and using c-transforms and other relevant laws on additional archaeological data to determine values of the remaining variables, one can solve for the approximate number of vessels in use by a household.

IMPLICATIONS OF THE POTTERY EXAMPLE

First, a ratio of 20 bowls per jar in archaeological context does not signify that 20 bowls were in use for every jar in a past household. Such an inference derives from the application of an equivalence transformation to quantitative variables; that is, quantities in the archaeological context equal quantities in the systemic context. This kind of equivalence transformation is often made implicitly—and therein lies the danger. It is often not a justifiable transformation procedure.

A second implication of this example is that items that are spatially associated in archaeological context were not necessarily associated during a process of systemic context, such as manufacture or use. Conversely, elements spatially associated in a systemic process are not necessarily associated in archaeological context. Again, implicitly made equivalence transformations, in this case of spatial variables, are to be avoided if the locational aspects of systemic context materials are to be successfully described.

Both implications underscore the risks in using implicit transformations. When such transformations are employed, assumptions of equivalence between systemic context and archaeological context variables are nearly always included. Equivalence transformations are only appropriate in a very limited number of circumstances; when applied to other situations they usually result in erroneous statements about the systemic context.

TRANSFORMATION PROCEDURES IN SOUTHWESTERN ARCHAEOLOGY

In the preceding section an outline of the transformation problem was presented. The purpose of this section is to consider how the transformation problem has been handled in Southwestern archaeology. This discussion is carried out in the context of examining briefly and in very general terms the two major paradigms, "culture history" and "culture process," that have guided research in Southwestern archaeology. In discussing these paradigms, it is necessary to summarize and simplify the work of many investigators. Consequently, the generalizations put forth apply not to individual archaeologists, but to two ways of doing archaeology.

CULTURE HISTORY

Culture history studies began in earnest during the second decade of this century with the work of Kroeber, Nelson, Kidder, Spier, Hough, and others (see Taylor, 1954). The dominant, but by no means exclusive, questions asked by culture historians concern chronology and the relationship of archaeologically defined cultures. For example,

1) What pottery types, archaeological features, and other cultural phenomena are earlier or later than others?
2) How do the relationships of these cultural materials in space and time indicate development and interaction of archaeological cultures?

A set of important transformation assumptions are employed by investigators attempting to answer these questions. For example, the law of stratification, stating that later deposits overlie earlier ones, was used to establish temporal relationships between many archaeological features. Examples are the replacement of pithouses by pueblos in the Anasazi region (Kidder and Guernsey, 1919) and the sequence of Hohokam house types documented at Snaketown (Gladwin and others, 1937). Many other innovative techniques for establishing sequences of deposition have been employed (for example, Burgh, 1959).

Another assumption about cultural formation processes employed by the culture historians is that refuse disposal subsystems were simple and produced homogeneous deposits differing only in time or culture. An implicit transformation—used on an intersite basis—that underlies these studies is that of an equivalence in space, quantity, and form between materials in their archaeological and systemic contexts. In other words, objects were discarded on the sites where they were used or manufactured; different proportions of items between sites reflect differences in systemic patterns, and cultural formation processes did not modify forms beyond recognition, as might occur through recycling.

The assumptions of equivalence between archaeological and systemic contexts when applied on an intersite basis favored the use of specific techniques of data retrieval. Probability sampling of sites was not considered to be a very serious problem since refuse was assumed to be largely homogeneous, except for possible differences in time or culture. Emphases in fieldwork included the excavation of trash mounds to determine the succession of artifact types and block excavations in architectural features to find evidence of stratification. In any event, the emphasis was on vertical control to reveal stratification. Dominant forms of analysis focused on techniques of assemblage comparison, usually conducted on an unformalized basis (Gladwin, 1934). Stage classifications were also employed (Kidder, 1924). The results of these studies were integrated into a framework which explained changes through time and variability in space as resulting from diffusion, migration, and independent invention.

The results of culture history studies, based on the assumption of intersite equivalence in archaeological and systemic contexts are impressive in many respects. Research in culture history has provided descriptions of the archaeological record for many areas of the Southwest, outlined the sequence of major events, generated explanatory hypotheses, and provided a temporal framework in which other questions could be consistently asked. The advent of computers, multivariate analyses, and especially theoretical innovations has led to a reexamination of questions long held in abeyance for lack of appropriate methodological tools.

CULTURE PROCESS

These other questions began to be consistently asked in the Southwest during the 1960's by archaeologists interested in culture process. These investigators are primarily concerned with the reconstruction of activities, activity locations, social organization, and discovery of the processes of culture change. Specifically, the questions asked by investigators, such as Hill (1970), Longacre (1970), and F. Plog (1974) working in the Hay Hollow Valley, include:

1) What activities were conducted at a site?
2) Where on the sites were they performed?
3) How did processes of adaptation to regional cultural and environmental factors affect the activities and social organization of a community?

Assuming, as the processual archaeologists had to, that social organization and behavior are reflected in the material remains of cultural systems, they also implicitly accepted the assumptions of equivalence which had guided several earlier generations of investigators. For the first time, however, these equivalence assumptions were applied on an intrasite basis. It was assumed that the locations of items in a site reflect the locations of their use, that the relative quantities of items in different parts of a site reflect intensity or duration of the activities conducted there, and finally, that cultural formation processes had no significant effect on the formal properties of remains.

These assumptions led to a preference for techniques of broad horizontal excavation of both architectural and extramural site areas. Such expansive excavations were designed to expose artifact and feature distributions, thus reflecting—by the equivalence assumptions—activity locations of the past. Special emphasis was placed on the description and recovery of artifacts associated with occupation surfaces.

Many of these studies have been aided by complex computer routines employing multivariate analytic techniques. The results thus obtained have proved to be extremely stimulating, especially to researchers in other geographic areas concerned with increasing our knowledge of the past (Clarke, 1968). However, many reasonable doubts can be raised concerning the validity of some specific reconstructions, especially where cultural formation processes produced remains which depart from the equivalence assumptions. Nevertheless, these studies have conclusively demonstrated, particularly at Broken K pueblo (Hill, 1970) and the Carter Ranch site (Longacre, 1970; Brown and Freeman, 1964), that the remains within a site are neither homogeneous nor randomly distributed and that deposits within a site vary along dimensions other than time or culture.

DISCUSSION

These examples from Southwestern archaeology illustrate the close relationship between transformation assumptions, problem foci, and techniques of data gathering and analysis. However, neither the cultural historians nor the processualists have apparently appreciated the varied nature of cultural formation processes and their effects. I certainly do not suggest that all or even many of the transformations made in the past were unfounded. However, once the question is raised, it becomes difficult to evaluate past inferences about historical events, behavior, and organization without devising some way of independently measuring the cultural formation processes that operated.

Southwestern archaeology, like New World archaeology in general, has gone from the one extreme of considering the remains at a site to be largely undifferentiated rubbish to the other extreme of believing that most remains directly reflect activity locations of the past. Neither view is adequate for achieving the behavioral and organizational understanding of past cultural systems that most archaeologists now seek. It was with these questions in mind that I approached the reconstruction of behavior at the Joint site.

THE JOINT SITE STUDY

The general transformation framework presented above was applied to answer specific questions about activities and activity locations within the systemic context of the chipped stone assemblage from the Joint site. The examination of these behavioral questions was aimed not at producing specific systemic context statements about these remains but at illustrating the general transformation procedures. The questions I asked of the chipped stone assemblage were:

1) Where did the activities of various stages of chipped stone tool manufacture take place?

2) What were the most frequent activities in which chipped stone tools were used?

3) Where were various functionally distinguished chipped stone tools used?

The reconstruction of activities and activity areas is most easily accomplished using certain varieties of refuse. Primary and de facto refuse can readily provide information on activity locations. However, refuse of these types may be produced only in small quantities by a sedentary community that sequentially abandons its behavioral spaces. Further, primary and de facto refuse are often difficult to identify. In order to maximize the probability of answering my systemic context questions, I also designated secondary refuse deposits as containing relevant data. Initially, I had no idea of how to transform such data into activity and activity area inferences.

In order to retrieve data from these refuse types at the Joint site, we applied a multiphase sampling program (Binford, 1964; Redman, 1973; Hanson and Schiffer, 1975) to rooms and extramural areas. Through familiarity with other sites in the region, we knew that primary and de facto refuse were deposited on room floors, and that secondary refuse was deposited in the fill of early abandoned rooms, on surfaces below the floors of late constructed rooms, and in extramural areas. Two strata, rooms and extramural areas, each having substrata, were defined. Rooms were randomly sampled within classes based on floor area as determined from exposed wall measurements. A 2% stratified random sample of extramural areas within classes based on differential density of surface artifacts was obtained. With information gained from the 2% sample and a series of backhoe trenches, a second phase of excavations was conducted to sample previously untouched secondary refuse areas. The completed sample of extramural areas at the Joint site probably contains excavation units from every major deposit of secondary refuse.

Identification transformations for primary and de facto refuse were only crudely developed; emphasis was placed on recording all remains in contact with room floors on the assumption that they were primary or de facto refuse. These identification transformations were only partially successful. Materials can come into direct contact with a floor through a variety of cultural and noncultural formation processes. Such material could be primary or de facto floor refuse, primary, secondary, or de facto roof refuse, or even secondary refuse from the fill (Schiffer and Reid, 1975; Schiffer, 1973; S. Plog, 1973). The confidence with which artifacts can be identified *after* excavation as primary and de facto refuse is limited in this case. Thus, our lack of care in the field in asking and answering questions necessary for delineating observational units (proveniences) relevant to the refuse types of interest placed limits on the kinds of transformation I could successfully apply to the data. Even so, the actual counts of chipped stone artifacts in floor association were quite low; this suggested that insufficient primary and de facto refuse were available for reliable transformations.

My solution to the problem of working with contaminated and infrequent primary and de facto refuse types was to concentrate on building a transformation model applicable to secondary refuse. I sought to experiment with the possibility that secondary refuse could be made to yield information on general behavior patterns within the systemic context of the chipped stone. Secondary refuse areas as a whole were made the focus of transformation model development.

Before the transformation procedures and results are described, it is necessary to discuss briefly the major types of activity area which occurred at the Joint site. Fortunately, a good deal of information on the use of space has been accumulated from study of other pueblos in the Hay Hollow Valley, such as Carter Ranch (Longacre, 1970) and Broken K (Hill, 1970). On the basis of this information and archaeological evidence from the Joint site, five gross types of activity area were defined.

At Broken K pueblo, Hill (1968, 1970) found an association between large rooms, mealing bins, and firepits. Rooms with these features are said to have been the location of diverse habitation activities. Smaller rooms which lack these features are considered to have been storage rooms, primarily for foodstuffs. A similar pattern of room size and feature association, probably representing the same functional room classes, is found at the Joint site (Hanson and Schiffer, 1975). Based on a chi-square test, rooms with a floor area greater than 7.5 m² tend to occur with firepits, while those below this figure do not ($p < .05$). Although the cutoff point between the two classes differs slightly from the 6.6 m² found at Broken K (Hill, 1968), it is likely that gross patterns of space utilization were similar.

Habitation activities, such as cooking and some others involved in food preparation, would most likely occur in close proximity to a hearth. I therefore assume that the presence of a firepit in a room indicates that habitation activities took place there, unless the room is also semi-subterranean. In the latter case, it probably served a special function as a kiva. The absence of a firepit indicates that a room functioned primarily as storage, although in Rooms 17, 7, and 29 food preparation activities are indicated by the presence of mealing bins (see Figure 2). Despite the crudeness of these room-use divisions, they are adequate to define major variations in the use of interior space at the Joint site.

In addition to habitation rooms, storage rooms, and kivas, two other major kinds of activity space are found at the Joint site. Because many rooms were entered by the roof only (Wilcox, 1975), the roof of the pueblo would almost automatically have become an activity area. Other outdoor but nonarchitectural areas of the site contain past activity surfaces, as indicated by the firepits in Test Area 2 (Figure 2).

In attempting to devise transformations for the assemblage of chipped stone from the Joint site, I considered the following activity areas to be of interest: roofs, habitation rooms, storerooms, kivas, and extramural areas. I believe these to be the major classes of activity space in which activities were repetitively performed and from which secondary refuse areas received their materials.

The basic aim of any transformation procedure is to relate the archaeological and systemic contexts by modeling the formation processes to which the material under study was subjected. In the case of secondary refuse deposits at the Joint site, achievement of this goal centered on the question: How were secondary refuse deposits related to past activity areas? The dispersed patterning of secondary refuse locations indicated no direct relationships to suspected activity areas (Figure 2). Further, during excavation it became apparent that all secondary refuse areas contained the same inventory of materials; thus I was uncertain about the existence of sufficient variability between deposits for hypothesizing relationships among activity areas and secondary refuse areas. But as Binford (1972) has pointed out, units with identical artifact inventories can still contain important variability in relative frequencies useful in studies of covariation.

Assuming that this variability inhered in the data, I asked the question: by what cultural formation processes could a variety of activity areas, such as habitation rooms, storerooms, kivas, roofs, and plazas, give rise to several dozen discrete secondary refuse areas containing the same artifact types but in varying relative frequencies? My answer to this question was in the form of a hypothetical c-transform: if activity areas contribute refuse largely, but not exclusively, to the nearest secondary refuse deposit, and if the spatial configuration of activity areas is such that all are likely to be represented in any secondary refuse deposit, then a pattern of similar artifact inventory with variable relative frequencies will occur among the secondary refuse areas. A factor analysis of the secondary refuse samples should isolate covarying artifact types discarded from the same type of activity area. This model is based on the assumption that artifacts from the same type of activity area are discarded in constant proportion to one another.

I tested this transformation model on simulated data. A site with four discrete types of activity area, 36 secondary refuse areas, and 40 different tool types—ten per activity area—was constructed on paper. Based on the cultural formation process assumption that these four activity areas contributed differentially to secondary refuse areas, a set of tool frequency data was generated by means of refuse contribution coefficients and a general equation (another c-transform) that relates activity performance to refuse production (Schiffer, 1975b). Factor analysis of the simulated data with varimax rotation (Nie, Bent, and Hull, 1970) yielded the four expected factors consisting of the proper tool types.

Despite the encouraging results of this test, I was uncomfortable with the assumption that activity areas were completely differentiated. In few communities is the segregation of activities in space so rigid. To bring the transformation model closer to reality, I produced ten additional sets of simulated data in which the amount of activity sharing—and hence artifact sharing—between activity areas was varied. The ten sets of data were factor analyzed in the same manner (Schiffer, 1975b). In an analogous situation, Binford and Binford (1966: 245–6) predicted that common artifacts would load equally on the multiple factors which produced them. This prediction was confirmed by analysis of simulated data up to a point. The results indicated that when more than 20% of the assemblage is used in all activity areas, the common artifacts turn up only in the first factor while later factors contain sets of tools used exclusively in one or another activity area. On the basis of these tests (more fully described in Schiffer, 1975b), confidence was gained in the transformation model. I readily concede, however, that this model is still too simple. Nonetheless, since it has produced promising results, other investigators may be stimulated to look at their data in terms of the processes by which it was formed, and to develop more satisfactory models.

Before applying this model to the Joint site data, it was necessary to classify the 29,693 chipped stone artifacts in a manner reflecting functional (or use) variation, and to conduct studies of raw material usage that could guide the choice of variables for input to the factor analysis. The chipped stone tools were classified into 55 types. These are broken down into 16 unifacially modified, eight bifacially modified, 24 use modified, and seven unmodified types. The attributes used to define these types relate to artifact size, angle of the working edge, degree of modification, and specific modifications of manufacture or use (Schiffer, 1973). Based on their possession of various attribute states, all tool types were assigned *potential* uses. These are the generalized activities that a tool could have carried out by virtue of its form. A classification deriving from the relationships of these attributes should provide at least a coarse measure of *actual* uses (*cf.* White and Thomas, 1972).

These 55 types can occur in any of three raw materials: quartzite, chert, and chalcedony. Studies of reuse and preferential raw material selection for types led to the discovery of significant patterns and formed the basis for the choice of variables. Chalcedony, a relatively rare (6.10% of all tools), imported material was used more economically than the more accessible and abundant chert (83.47%) or quartzite (10.43%). There was a tendency for large tools, such as large utilized flakes and shatter, and hammerstones, to be made from quartzite. Quartzite was less amenable to fine flaking, as revealed by its infrequent use in retouched tools. On the other hand, chert and chalcedony were used for almost all tool types. The data and tests supporting these generalizations are presented elsewhere (Schiffer, 1973). Based on these results, the variables factor analyzed included utilized flakes and shatter, unutilized by-products of tool manufacture, and other tool types which occur in relative abundance. The counts of flakes and shatter within edge-angle-size classes were combined by raw material, then the chert and chalcedony totals were summed. Quartzite tools, having slightly different use patterns, were kept separate. Debitage was kept segregated by raw material, but several infrequently occurring types were not analyzed. Other composite variables were made to eliminate infrequently occurring types and to reduce redundancy in the classification.

A total of 42 variables including both debitage and tools, distributed among 33 samples of secondary refuse and probable secondary refuse was subjected to factor analysis. These data are presented elsewhere (Schiffer, 1973). The result was five factors, of which the first three are easily interpreted when variables with factor loadings below .60 are deleted. Table 1 presents the results of this factor analysis, while tool descriptions and potential uses are listed in Table 2.

TABLE 1
The SPSS variables that load at 0.60 or above on each of five factors

Factor 1	Factor 2	Factor 3	Factor 4	Factor 5
VAR082	VAR011	VAR008	VAR086	none
VAR091	VAR014	VAR009		
LGMED	VAR164	VAR010		
LGLO	VAR166	VAR011		
MEDLO	VAR167	VAR012		
SMMED	VAR169	VAR013		
SMLO	VAR170	VAR088		
QLGMED	LGHI	VAR091		
QLGLO	MEDHI	QSMHI		
QMEDMED	QLGHI			
QMEDLO	HAMCOB			
QSMMED	RETSCR			
QSMLO	SAW			
HAMCOR				

TABLE 2

Descriptions and potential uses of chipped stone types used as variables in SPSS factor analysis. Variables labeled only by letters are composite types. The first segment of the variable label (other than a Q) refers to artifact size, measured as the maximum area when lying flat (LG = greater than 17.4 cm², MED = 8.8–17.4 cm², SM = 3.5–8.7 cm²). The second segment denotes edge angle (HI = greater than 65°, MED = 45°–65°, LO = less than 45°). (A prefix of Q indicates that the material is quartzite)

Variable label	Raw material	Description	Potential uses
VAR008	chert	core	none (chipping waste)
VAR009	chert	decortication flake	none (chipping waste)
VAR010	chert	mini-shatter	none (chipping waste)
VAR011	chert	trim flake	none (chipping waste)
VAR012	chert	false-start core	none (chipping waste)
VAR013	chert	shatter	none (chipping waste)
VAR014	chert	waste flake	none (chipping waste)
VAR082	chert	unifacial retouched flake	shaving, scraping (wood, plant)
VAR086	quartzite	core	none (chipping waste)
VAR088	quartzite	mini-shatter	none (chipping waste)
VAR091	quartzite	shatter	none (chipping waste)
VAR164	chalcedony	core	none (chipping waste)
VAR166	chalcedony	mini-shatter	none (chipping waste)
VAR167	chalcedony	trim flake	none (chipping waste)
VAR169	chalcedony	shatter	none (chipping waste)
VAR170	chalcedony	waste flakes	none (chipping waste)
LGHI	chert, chalcedony	utilized flakes and shatter	heavy scraping, shredding (hides, wood, plant)
LGMED	chert, chalcedony	utilized flakes and shatter	heavy scraping (hides, wood, plant)
LGLO	chert, chalcedony	utilized flakes and shatter	heavy cutting (skin, meat, hide, plant)
MEDHI	chert, chalcedony	utilized flakes and shatter	medium scraping, shredding (hide, wood, plant)
MEDLO	chert, chalcedony	utilized flakes and shatter	medium cutting (skin, meat, plant)
SMMED	chert, chalcedony	utilized flakes and shatter	light scraping (hide, wood, plant)
SMLO	chert, chalcedony	utilized flakes and shatter	light cutting (skin, hide, meat, plant)
QLGHI	quartzite	utilized flakes and shatter	heavy scraping, shredding (hide, wood, plant)
QLGMED	quartzite	utilized flakes and shatter	heavy scraping (hide, wood, plant)
QLGLO	quartzite	utilized flakes and shatter	heavy cutting (skin, meat, hide, plant)
QMEDMED	quartzite	utilized flakes and shatter	medium scraping (hide, wood, plant)

TABLE 2—*contd*

Variable label	Raw material	Description	Potential uses
QMEDLO	quartzite	utilized flakes and shatter	medium cutting (skin, meat, plant)
QSMHI	quartzite	utilized flakes and shatter	light scraping, shredding (hide, wood, plant)
QSMMED	quartzite	utilized flakes and shatter	light scraping (hide, wood, plant)
QSMLO	quartzite	utilized flakes and shatter	light cutting (skin, hide, meat, plant)
HAMCOB	chert, quartzite	battered cobble	chipping, pounding (stone, bone)
HAMCOR	all types	battered core	pounding (stone, bone)
RETSCR	chert, chalcedony	unifacial retouched flake	medium scraping (hide, wood, plant)
SAW	chert, chalcedony	unifacial retouched flake	cutting (bone, wood)

Factor 1 contains a large sampling of utilized flakes and utilized shatter of all sizes and all but the steepest edge-angles. Also indluded are a single unifacially retouched tool type, battered cores, and one type of quartzite waste shatter. All of these types but one has been used, probably for light-, medium-, and heavy-duty cutting and scraping of meat, hides, and plant material. Battered cores could have been used to roughen the grinding surfaces of metates, or to break bone for marrow extraction, or tool manufacture. These activities probably comprise the major tasks which would have been performed by a sedentary Puebloan community practicing a mixed subsistence strategy. For this reason and because Factor 1 accounts for the lion's share of the variance (72.2%), I suggest that these activities were performed in most activity areas.

Factor 2 consists primarily of chert and chalcedony debitage. In addition, three tool types with steep edge angles, and a hammerstone, saw, and re-touched scraper type occur. These findings suggest a set of tools used to make other tools, such as projectile points, arrows, bows, and other hunting equipment. Steep-edged scrapers would be useful for shaping wood or other dense material. Saws would come in handy to work wood and bone. These activities may have taken place in kivas and on roofs. This inference rests on the assumption that in order to use the chalcedony as economically as possible, it would have been desirable to have a great deal of control over all products of chipping activity. Such control would have been facilitated by activity performance close to the location of raw material storage, presumably in rooms.

Factor 3 includes predominantly the unutilized waste products of chert and quartzite tool manufacture, and suggests the manufacture of tools from these materials. This set of activities may have occurred on roofs and in other exterior areas. Both materials can be quarried on the site in nodules of workable size, and at least some chipping would be expected to have occurred near these quarry locations.

The locations where the activities of Factors 2 and 3 were performed have not been definitely identified. Attempts to test the location hypotheses with suspected primary and de facto refuse have been inconclusive thus far. Clearly, the need to exclude infrequently occurring artifact types, the obvious vagaries of trying to measure function, the lack of adequate control over recycling, and insufficient and misidentified primary and de facto refuse all contribute to the difficulty of deriving certain conclusions about the activities and activity areas within the systemic context of the Joint site chipped stone assemblage. Additional studies utilizing other data classes and more sophisticated transformation procedures will be required to develop more detailed inferences in which greater confidence can be placed. Nevertheless, this preliminary study has made a small first step toward transforming the Joint site chipped stone from archaeological context using just secondary refuse. But more importantly, it has indicated that fruitful results can be obtained from analysis of data (secondary refuse) usually thought to be intractably silent on the subject of activity areas. The modest degree of success achieved is due to the explicit consideration of cultural formation processes with the general transformation model of behavioral archaeology.

CONCLUSION

In this paper I have described my approach to the reconstruction of human behavior at the Joint site. This approach is based on the assumption that the formation of the archaeological record provides the key to understanding the past. The cultural formation processes of the archaeological record, once almost entirely ignored, are now properly coming to the forefront of theoretical and experimental studies in archaeology. The Joint site is one of the first test cases of a framework for a behavioral archaeology which has as its core the modeling of the cultural formation processes responsible for one's data. Although the application of this framework to the chipped stone data from the Joint site has produced neither startling discoveries nor definitive answers, productive questions are being asked. It is hoped that future studies on Joint site data and elsewhere with a refined and expanded framework will lead to greater insights into human behavior of the past.

ACKNOWLEDGMENTS

I thank the members of the Southwestern Expedition who participated in the Joint Site Project: (1970) D. Burkenroad, M. Ester, G. Goode, J. Goode, F. Gorman, D. Gregory, J. Hanson, M. Hanson, R. Hevly, J. Johnson, C. Maley, S. Ott, P. Parker, M. Powers, J. Rick, W. Sampson, S. Saradyar, A. Schiffer, J. Schaefer, and S. Tracz; (1971) S. Anderson, D. Andrews, R. Barber, S. Cox, A. Engstrom, J. Hanson, M. Hanson, M. Henderson, E. Hirvela, S. James, J. Justeson, B. Lehner, J. Moore, A. Schiffer, P. Smith, D. Thompson, S. Tracz, C. Wiley, and H. Wong. I especially thank the late Paul S. Martin for support through the Field Museum of Natural History and the National Science Foundation (Grants GS2381 and GY4601), and for his constant encouragement. The University of Arizona provided computer time on a CDC 6400. This research was undertaken while I held an N.S.F. Traineeship in the department of anthropology at The University of Arizona. I thank Paul F. Grebinger and John A. Hanson for providing useful, and sometimes even amusing, comments on an earlier draft of this paper.

REFERENCES

Baumhoff, M. A. and R. F. Heizer (1959) Some unexploited possibilities in ceramic analysis. *Southwestern Journal of Anthropology* 15, 308–16.
Binford, L. R. (1964) A consideration of archaeological research design. *American Antiquity* 29, 425–41.
Binford, L. R. (1972) Model building—paradigms, and the current state of Paleolithic research. In *An Archaeological Perspective*, by L. R. Binford, pp. 252–95. Seminar Press, New York.
Binford, L. R. and S. R. Binford (1966) A preliminary analysis of functional variability in the Mousterian of Levallois facies. In Recent studies in paleoanthropology, edited by J. D. Clark and F. C. Howell, pp. 238–95. *American Anthropologist* 68(2), pt. 2.
Brown, J. A. and L. G. Freeman, Jr. (1964) A UNIVAC analysis of sherd frequencies from the Carter Ranch pueblo, eastern Arizona. *American Antiquity* 30, 162–7.
Burgh, R. F. (1959) Ceramic profiles in the western mound at Awatovi, northeastern Arizona. *American Antiquity* 25, 184–202.
Clarke, D. (1968) *Analytical Archaeology.* Methuen, London.
Gladwin, H. S. (1934) A method for designation of cultures and their variations. *Medallion Papers* 15.
Gladwin, H. S., E. W. Haury, E. B. Sayles, and N. Gladwin (1937) Excavations at Snaketown, material culture. *Medallion Papers* 25.
Hanson, J. A. and M. B. Schiffer (1975) The Joint site—a preliminary report. In Chapters in the prehistory of eastern Arizona, IV. *Fieldiana: Anthropology* 65, 47–91.
Hill, J. N. (1968) Broken K pueblo: patterns of form and function. In *New Perspectives in Archeology*, edited by S. R. and L. R. Binford, pp. 103–42. Aldine, Chicago.
Hill, J. N. (1970) Broken K pueblo: prehistoric social organization in the American Southwest. *Anthropological Papers of The University of Arizona* 18.
Kidder, A. V. (1924) *An Introduction to the Study of Southwestern Archaeology.* Phillips Academy, Andover.
Kidder, A. V. and S. J. Guernsey (1919) Archaeological exploration in northeastern Arizona. *Bureau of American Ethnology, Bulletin* 65.
Longacre, W. A. (1970) Archaeology as anthropology: a case study. *Anthropological Papers of The University of Arizona* 17.

Nie, N., D. H. Bent and C. H. Hull (1970) *Statistical Package for the Social Sciences*. McGraw-Hill, New York.

Plog, F. (1974) *The Study of Prehistoric Change*. Seminar Press, New York.

Plog, S. (1973) Variability in ceramic design frequencies as a measure of prehistoric social organization. Manuscript, Department of Anthropology, University of Michigan, Ann Arbor.

Redman, C. L. (1973) Multistage fieldwork and analytical techniques. *American Antiquity* 38, 61–79.

Reid, J. J. (1973) Growth and response to stress at Grasshopper pueblo, Arizona, Ph.D. dissertation, The University of Arizona, Tucson.

Reid, J. J. and M. B. Schiffer (n.d.) Toward a behavioral archaeology (in preparation).

Reid, J. J., M. B. Schiffer and J. M. Neff (1975) Archaeological considerations of intrasite sampling. In *Sampling in Archaeology*, edited by J. W. Mueller, pp. 209–24. The University of Arizona Press, Tucson.

Schiffer, M. B. (1972) Archaeological context and systemic context. *American Antiquity* 37, 156–65.

Schiffer, M. B. (1973) Cultural formation processes of the archaeological record: applications at the Joint site, east-central Arizona. Ph.D. dissertation, The University of Arizona, Tucson.

Schiffer, M. B. (1975a) Behavioral chain analysis: activities, organization, and the use of space. In Chapters in the prehistory of eastern Arizona, IV. *Fieldiana: Anthropology* 65, 103–19.

Schiffer, M. B. (1975b) Factors and "toolkits:" evaluating multivariate analyses in archaeology. *Plains Anthropologist* 20–67: 61–70.

Schiffer, M. B. and W. L. Rathje (1973) Efficient exploitation of the archeological record: penetrating problems. In *Research and Theory in Current Archeology*, edited by L. Redman, pp. 169–79. John Wiley, New York.

Schiffer, M. B. and J. J. Reid (1975) A system for designating behaviorally-significant proveniences. In The Cache River Archaeological Project: an experiment in contract archaelogy, assembled by M. B. Schiffer and J. H. House, pp. 253–5 *Arkansas Archaeological Survey Research Series* 8.

Taylor, W. W. (1954) Southwestern archaeology, its history and theory. *American Anthropologist* 56, 561–75.

White, J. P. and D. H. Thomas (1972) What mean these stones? Ethno-taxonomic models and archaeological interpretations in the New Guinea Highlands. In *Models in Archaeology*, edited by D. L. Clarke, pp. 275–308. Methuen, London.

Wilcox, D. R. (1975) A strategy for perceiving social groups in puebloan sites. In Chapters in the prehistory of eastern Arizona, IV. *Fieldiana: Anthropology* 65, 120–59.

Inventory Operations Research in Southwestern Prehistory:
An Example from East Central Arizona

FREDERICK J. E. GORMAN
Boston University

Prehistoric management of technological inventories at a PIII pueblo is investigated in terms of operations research to determine the direction of cultural process at the general systems level. A framework for observation and measurement of system trends is discussed in terms of behavioral information and control. Dynamic metaphors are presented which analogize known trends of natural systems and hypothetical trends of cultural inventory systems. Selected prehistoric technological inventories are analyzed as behavioral information systems. This specific system problem is translated into the language of general systems by defining archaeological characteristics of the information system in terms of (1) the time–space resolution of system environments, (2) automata theory of discrete relations between these and (3) classification of the external environment. The state-transition structure of inventory management is examined and stable homeostats are isolated. Stable inventory management policy suggests that certain theories about culture process need to be modified.

In this paper, general systems theory is applied to the problem of determining the direction of change in technological inventory management strategies employed by the prehistoric occupants of a well-defined archaeological site. An inventory system is simply a system which stores items that have functions at various points in time (Churchman, 1971:215). Inventory management, a branch of operations research, is assumed to be a primary dimension of culture process and an attempt is made to derive a dynamic metaphor which analogizes directional change in cultural and natural systems. The general systems approach is necessary because the theory of general systems itself is based on the assumption that the processes of behavior in physical, biological and cultural domains of the universe can be modelled in terms of principles common to all.

PREHISTORIC ACTION AND INFORMATION PROCESS: THE GENERAL SYSTEMS FRAMEWORK OF TREND ANALYSIS

The isolation of process in natural and cultural systems depends on the analyst's ability to measure change in either matter–energy or information over time. One form, action process, involves the movement of

matter-energy through a sequence of system states. Another form, information process, involves change in information from one system state to
the next. Change in communicated phenomena is usually called
"information-processing" or "communication" while change in observed
phenomena is often referred to as "statistical mechanics," "statistical
thermodynamics," or "structural mechanics" in systemic context. The investigation of either action or information process in anthropological
studies has been a matter of preference since matter–energy and
information always flows together in systems (Miller, 1971:281). However, system-specific forms of matter–energy are characterized by specific
patterns of information, but not the reverse, which leads some theorists to
believe that information is the basic measure of system behavior.

   The isolation of information process entails assumptions and measurements which are fundamentally different from those used to derive action
process. An understanding of four basic features of information systems is
necessary to follow the course of investigation in this paper.

   1) Information process is essentially stochastic in nature and is
concerned with change in the likelihood that one or more quantities will
interactively associate with another, while action process is deterministic,
because it focuses on change in the amount by which one or more
quantities determine another.

   2) The major characteristic of the set of information measures is one of
linear system response to a stochastic process input. Much of the simplicity
and elegance of information as a linear response is based on the additive
function of logarithmic transformations of factorial relations which bound
the possible interactions among elements in a set. This function permits
arithmetic summation of average interaction potential per element which
would otherwise be expressed as a cumbersome power function. It should
be apparent that information systems are part probabilistic and part
deterministic; that is, they are statistical–mechanical systems. Here it is
essential to know that the statistical–mechanics of cultural inventory
management trends are evaluated as dynamic information systems, which
in   turn   are   compared   to   the   information   conveyed   by   the
statistical–mechanics of physical and biological systems trends.

   3) The symmetry characteristic of element relations noted above permits isolation of the information behavior of the system as a *whole*, rather
than in terms of its parts (Ashby, 1972), as is necessary in causal analysis of
deterministic action systems. This is reflected in the fact that relational
symmetry in information systems implies concern with the idea of self-
generated control of behavior which is reflected in the restricted
exploitation of a set of possibilities. Information is the essential

component of any control system and information–theoretic studies of human behavior are primarily concerned with control problems (Edwards, 1964). The investigation of directional change in amounts of control which characterize the self-organization program of human information systems requires evaluation of the *redundancy, self-organization or negentropy* function. The statistical–mechanical behaviors of natural and cultural systems that are well organized (i.e. contain much redundancy or negentropy) are highly predictable and little information is gained by observing them; perfectly organized systems are incompletely predictable in theory and their behaviors provide no information at all (Miller, 1968: 123). It is the direction of change in the amount of self-organization through a sequence of system states which permits assignment of culture process to a position in the domain of linear system trends.

4) The type of information which may be applicable to the solution of the widest range of operations research problems in archaeology at present concerns the interaction of system entities that are *discrete* and *finite*.

These four criteria restrict the general system model of inventory management to what has been variously termed a "dynamic homeostatic system" (Wood and Matson, 1973)' a "machine with input" (Ashby, 1972), or "information teleology" (Gorman, 1973). The usefulness of the homeostatic model as compared to the alternative general systems approach, namely the "complex adaptive system" (Buckley, 1968) or "teleological information" model (Churchman, 1971), has been questioned by several archaeologists. The main question concerns the relationship between the meaning or purpose of system organization and the stability of system regulators where both are assumed to exist in homeostatic models and are to be demonstrated in complex adaptive systems (Watson, LeBlanc and Redman, 1971: 67–73, Wood and Matson, 1973: 676–8).

The nature of stability and purpose is considered an empirical question to be resolved by an examination of trends in the regulation or control of natural and cultural systems in the next section.

TRENDS IN PHYSICAL, BIOLOGICAL AND CULTURAL SYSTEMS

The construction of dynamic metaphors as hypotheses which have unambiguous test implications entails an evaluation of physical, biological and cultural system trends in terms of linear system process. In this framework matter–energy relations are characterized by the statistical–mechanical interaction of random variables: we are dealing always with a set of relevant theoretical possibilities that is usually wider than the actual case during any given interval of time (Ashby, 1956: 3). Since the quantity contained in one set may (in theory) *vary independently* of the other in any state-transition, this principle can be used to generate eleven linear system processes which describe the trends of all known and unknown linear systems. Only five of these are listed below as hypotheses in the form of dynamic metaphors. Each is restricted to a known trend in a natural system and its inventory management analogue.

CLOSED PHYSICAL SYSTEMS

Closed physical systems move toward statistical equilibrium, from larger aggregates of potential element interaction to a smaller number. This is defined alternately as the predominance of the occurrence of the more probable sorts of aggregates over the less probable (Rapoport, 1968: 137). Directional change is toward decrease in negentropy or amount of order in interaction. The behavior of gases as explained by the second law of thermodynamics provides an example of this kind of system trend.

   An inventory management system exhibits a similar trend when the cost of storing various types of items in equal availability situations remains constant through time, while the cost of inconvenience incurred when differentially available kinds of items are demanded from inventory increases (see Churchman, 1971: 165). The amount of organization or the task potential of this storage policy declines as the cost of procuring items from inventory rises. The determinant of process itself in both the system trend and the management analog is unchanging and interaction that is specifically resistant to change is automatically selected (Ashby, 1968a, b).

OPEN PHYSICAL SYSTEMS

This system trend is the reverse of the closed physical system process. An open physical system may be conceptualized by imagining a situation in which "grains of sand are poured into a container" (von Foerster, 1960). System movement is from smaller aggregates of potential interaction to a larger number. Directional change is toward increase in negentropy or amount of order in interaction.

   An analogous trend in inventory storage policy may exist when the cost of storing various items in equal availability increases through time, while the cost of inconvenience in procuring differentially available types of items remains constant. The task potential of this inventory storage policy increases as the cost of item procurement declines. In both cases, the determinant of process itself is changing and in interaction that is specifically susceptible to change is selected.

CLOSED BIOLOGICAL SYSTEMS

Less familiar is the "progressive similarity" trend of relatively closed biological communities. Here, increasing environmental stress on a population of organisms composed of few common species (having large numbers of individuals) associated with numerous rare species (having few individuals), results in the reduction of the number of rare species and increases the predominance of the few common species (Odum, 1971: 141). In terms of statistical mechanics, this biological trend may be phrased as the shift from a larger number of theoretically available sets of potential interaction between species to a smaller number. This is an example of evolutionary selection upon preexisting sets of variety in which biotic energy declines.

An analogous process occurs in inventory management when the rate of decrease in the cost of storing various kinds of items in equal availability situations exceeds the declining cost of inconvenience incurred when needed types of items are differentially available. The decrease in the task potential of this inventory storage policy and the nature of the determinant of this system process are similar to those defined in the discussion of closed physical systems above.

OPEN BIOLOGICAL SYSTEMS

The "progressive differentiation" (von Bertalanffy, 1969) of organismic components or "increasing speciation" in an evolutionary community of organisms form two aspects of a well-known trend in living systems. White (1949: 367) applied this principle to conceptualize culture process as a system trend toward "greater organization, greater differentiation of structure, increased specialization of function, higher levels of integration and greater degrees of energy concentration."

An analogous trend in inventory management occurs when the cost of storage of various items in equal availability situations increases at a rate that exceeds increase in the cost of inconvenience incurred when demanded types of items are differentially available. The task potential of storage policy increases as the cost of item procurement declines. The nature of the determinant of process itself is similar to the one defined in the discussion of open physical systems above.

OPEN BIOLOGICAL SYSTEMS—THERMODYNAMICS AND HOMEOSTASIS

Knowledge of thermodynamic processes and homeostasis in biological systems is largely restricted to the study of organisms in their environments. A basic distinction exists between "reversible thermodynamics" which implies an equality of negentropy or energy in organismic input and output at any state (Rapoport, 1968) and "irreversible thermodynamics" (Rosen, 1972) or "energy capture" which implies an inequality of negentropy in organismic output and input, where greater amounts of the first quantity serve to minimize the system-wide production of entropy. Steady-state minimization forms the homeostatic trend of organisms as complex adaptive systems.

The analogy between organismic process and inventory management is complex because it entails conceptualization of linked "Ashby machines" where an artifact inventory (machine) as prehistoric living system output is linked to a subsistence inventory (machine) as system input. Thus we are required to deal not only with the amount of task potential or organization in artifact storage, but also the amount of organization in subsistence storage. The latter is indirectly given by the ratio of the cost of storing various floral and faunal species in equal availability situations to the cost of inconvenience in procuring differentially available species from inventory. Cultural system production of disorganization or entropy may be subject to steady-state minimization in a situation where the amount of organization in subsistence management is consistently greater than the amount of task potential or organization in the management of technological inventories.

Lower level homeostats may operate, however, in the inventory management of both artifacts and subsistence items, or in one type of inventory but not the other, or may not operate in either. The management analogue of organismic process has four variants. (1) Sequential values of task potential in artifact storage and organization in subsistence storage are both homeostatic and identical in the case of reversible thermodynamic trends. Alternatively, in irreversible thermodynamic process these values define parallel trajectories in a phase-plane. (2) Sequential values of task potential in artifact storage and organization of subsistence storage are identical but nonhomeostatic in the case of reversible thermodynamics. In the case of irreversible thermodynamics these values are neither homeostatic nor identical. Steady-state minimization is not a likely result of the latter process. (3) Sequential amounts of task potential in artifact storage are homeostatic and are lower than nonhomeostatic values of subsistence organization as a process that is analogous to irreversible thermodynamics alone. (4) A reverse situation is possible in which nonhomeostatic values of task potential in artifact storage are lower than a sequence of homeostatic values of subsistance storage organization. This process is also analogous to irreversible thermodynamics alone.

In order to analyze a prehistoric technological inventory system as a behavioral information system a procedure (Klir, 1969: 95) for solving special system problems using the general systems theory is followed. Translation of the problem by input mapping to the language of general systems forms the initial requirement and is satisfied by defining the archaeological characteristics of the behavioral information system in a classification of systems proposed by Klir (1969: 69–257).

As the archaeological quantities which are being dealt with in this analysis are measurable, the behavioral information system is termed *physical*. Part of this physical system is *real* because one inventory variable (object size) contains values which really exist. The remainder of the physical system is conceptual because nominal variables used in the analysis of inventory (object use-state, shape, function, use-wear and material) contain discrete values whose existence can be defined by reference to the classification. (Discrete information systems are the only type which can deal with qualitative and quantitative scales in an interchangeable manner free of bias.) The system is characterized by a classification of inventory variables as input which is finite in size and structure (or is characterized by a limited number of variable relations). Both the conditions suggest that the interaction between the internal environment of the behavioral information system and its external environment of inventory variables is *relatively closed*, such that the paths of interaction between the two can be accurately defined.

ENVIRONMENTS OF THE BEHAVIORAL INFORMATION SYSTEM

Both the internal and external environments are of immediate relevance to the behavioral information system because they constitute the *time–space specification* of the system. These are the set of architectural units at the Joint site (Figure 2) which contained the excavated artifact inventories that are partitioned according to their membership in a prehistoric activity interval. The Joint site is a 36 room single story peublo situated in the Hay Hollow Valley, east central Arizona (Figure 1).

It is located near the Broken K pueblo (Hill, 1970) and at a greater distance from the Carter Ranch site (Longacre, 1970) and may have been partly contemporaneous with both. Prehistoric cultural activity at the Joint site has been estimated by means of radiocarbon (Schiffer, 1973) and dendrochronological (Wilcox, 1975) analyses to have lasted from A.D. 1120

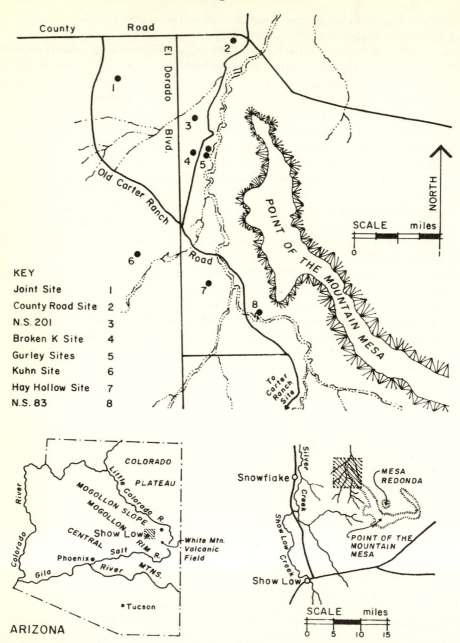

Joint Site   1
County Road Site   2
N.S. 201   3
Broken K Site   4
Gurley Sites   5
Kuhn Site   6
Hay Hollow Site   7
N.S. 83   8

FIGURE 1   Location of the Joint site, east central Arizona. Adapted from Martin *et al.* (1964) and Schiffer (1973).

to 1275. Chronological interpolation (Hanson, personal communication) of the palynological sequence (Hevly, Ward and Van De Graff, n.d.) permits an approximate interval estimation of A.D. 1160–1320. Archaeological items and features which characterize the Joint site are described in the literature (Hanson and Schiffer, 1975; Wilcox, 1975; Schiffer, 1973). The portion of the external environment which is the object of this investigation are two artifact inventories represented by 920 groundstone and 121 bone tools. Input values of the variables which define these tool inventories simulate the response behavior or output of the information system in any given state. Spatial resolution of this external environment entails quantitative bias, for only 69% (25/36) of the room universe (Figure 2) was excavated for this study.

The effect of this partial representation cannot be estimated since the sampling distribution of information itself is not known (Frick, 1968: 183). Temporal resolution of the external environment also entails qualitative bias which is reflected in the stratigraphy of inventory items recovered from the floor (0–5 cm) and the level above (6–20 cm) in each sampled room. This "floors vs. fill" problem continues to complicate archaeological interpretation and has stimulated new contextual research (Schiffer, 1972). An attempt is made in this analysis to control the input of floor versus fill inclusive artifact materials. The assumption is made that inventory items recovered from 0–5 cm and, alternatively, 0–20 cm above the floor of each room are associated with its abandonment. The effect of this differential input on the behavior of the information system in its various states is presented in Table 3, and is interpreted later.

The internal environment of the behavioral information system is given by the set of its internal states. Each internal state is defined as a discrete set of contemporaneous rooms at the Joint site. Each internal state determines an instantaneous set of external object values that describe the inventories of groundstone and bone tools which are processed by the information system. The sequence of these internal states (Table 1) comprises the information system *program* of temporary behavior.

This program also constitutes part of the memory of the system and is discussed later. Temporal resolution of the internal states entails three qualitative biases which must be specified because it is here that the traditional problem of archaeological time-space assignment confronts any system analysis of past cultural behavior. Definition of a sequence of internal states in terms of separate periods of time requires the use of a constant chronological trait or continuous index at the general systems level. The relative pollen chronology of architectural units at the Joint site is the only index available at present which meets this continuity requirement. It is based on samples randomly selected from floor quadrat strata in

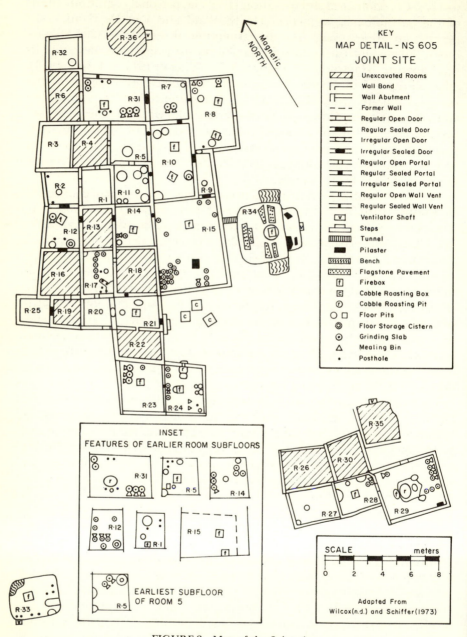

FIGURE 2   Map of the Joint site.

TABLE 1
Internal states of the system[a]

	S^{-5}	S^{-4}	S^{-3}	S^{-2}	S^{-1}	S^0
R02	1	0	0	0	0	0
R03	1	0	0	0	0	0
R05	1 (U)	0	0	0	0	0
R12	1 (U)	0	0	0	0	0
R21	1	0	0	0	0	0
R33	1	0	0	0	0	0
R13	1*	1*	0	0	0	0
R16	1*	1*	0	0	0	0
R19	1*	1*	0	0	0	0
R01	1 (L)	1 (L)	1 (U)	0	0	0
R17	1	1	1	0	0	0
R18	1*	1*	1*	0	0	0
R20	1	1	1	0	0	0
R25	1	1	1	0	0	0
R36	1*	1*	1*	0	0	0
R04	1*	1*	1*	1*	1*	0
R11	1	1	1	1	1	1
R14	1 (L)	1 (L)	1 (U)	1 (U)	1 (U)	1 (U)
R07	0	0	1	0	0	0
R06	0	0	1*	1*	1*	0
R08	0	0	1	1	1	0
R09	0	0	1	1	1	0
R10	0	0	1	1	1	0
R31	0	0	1 (L)	1 (U)	1 (U)	0
R32	0	0	1	1	1	0
R15	0	0	1	1	1	1
R34	0	0	0	1	1	1
R22	0	0	0	0	1*	1*
R23	0	0	0	0	1	1
R24	0	0	0	0	1	1
R26	0	0	0	0	1*	1*
R27	0	0	0	0	1	1
R28	0	0	0	0	1	1
R29	0	0	0	0	1	1
R30	0	0	0	0	1*	1*
R35	0	0	0	0	1*	1*
%	0.67	0.50	0.76	0.82	0.70	0.69

[a] Key:
S^{-5} = A.D. ± 1160–1205±
S^{-4} = A.D. ± 1205–1230±
S^{-3} = A.D. ± 1230–1250±
S^{-2} = A.D. ± 1250–1265±
S^{-1} = A.D. ± 1265–1285±
S^0 = A.D. ± 1285–1320±

1 = inclusion in state set
0 = exclusion from state set
(U) = uppermost floor
(L) = lower subfloor
* = not excavated
% = resolution level

the excavated rooms (Figure 2). Ratios of Pine to Juniper, small pine to large, and arboreal to nonarboreal pollen were employed in analysis (Hevly, Ward and Van De Graff, n.d.). Chronological interpolation of the pollen sequence (Table 1) conflicts with tree-ring dates from two of the six rooms (R06, 21/R09, 10, 31, 34) which yielded wood specimens that have been examined. The pollen sequence conflicts with most of the radio-carbon dates (Wilcox, 1975) obtained from the Joint site. The latter produced the least satisfactory results of the three dating techniques and is not considered further here.

The pollen chronology is based on a stratigraphically biased sample of floor levels within certain architectural units at the site, because the chronology pertains to the uppermost floors or terminal occupation surfaces alone. Pollen data from the earlier subfloors of six rooms (Figure 2, inset) are presently unavailable. Subfloors of rooms in which occupation of uppermost floors terminated in a state later than the initial one (R01, 14, 15, 31) were assigned to the preceding internal state of the system. Inspection of Table 1 shows that the portion of the state sequence S^{-3} to S^0 (A.D. $\pm$ 1230–1320$\pm$) is probably the least biased because it contains the fewest number of arbitrary inclusions of subfloors.

In order to measure the *time–space resolution* of the set of internal states of the system in terms of the degree to which an excavated room sample represented any activity interval, it was necessary to assign unexcavated rooms to various internal states. These assignments were less objective because they entailed manipulation of architectural evidence to infer oc-cupational contemporaneity. Certain unexcavated rooms (R04, 06, 18) were directly accessible to adjacent rooms, and were also part of the same or an adjacent architectural complex. These were assigned to the range of sequential states diagnostic of the dated rooms. A similar logic permitted assignment of unexcavated rooms (R13, 16, 19) characterized by sealed access to adjoining excavated rooms where the latter represent a range of sequential states. The remaining unexcavated units (R22, 26, 30, 35) were assigned to the states of adjacent dated rooms on the basis of architectural similarity (Figure 2). The percentage of excavated rooms listed in each column of Table 1 is the estimated level of time–space resolution for the set of internal system states. It also serves as the resolution level of the external object environment since recovery of groundstone and bone artifacts (in whole or fragmentary condition) was fairly thorough.

AUTOMATA THEORY OF DISCRETE RELATIONS BETWEEN CULTURE SYSTEM ENVIRONMENTS

The behavioral information system is also a member of the class of discrete general systems, because its internal states and its external inventory variables acquire a finite number of discrete values which are known to the system only at discrete instants in time. This condition is specified for the internal states of the system in the previous section. The additional requirement that relations between discrete variable values be expressed by equations in a particular logic algebra is satisfied by application of the theories of sets and combinatorics entailed in the calculus of the information measures. The four basic measures are given below.

The cost of storing various kinds of items in equal availability situations is measured in terms of *maximum information for an inventory* as the greatest theoretical value that may be ascribed to a set of categorical alternatives. It is given by

$$H_{\max} = \mathrm{Log}_2 n \tag{1}$$

where n is the number of inventory types that occur. Inventory management in this condition is chaotic because formal patterning as the degree of organization or predictability is absent.

The cost of inconvenience incurred when types of items are demanded from inventory and are differentially available is measured in terms of *actual average information per inventory type,* and is given by

$$H = -\sum_{i-1}^{n} p(i)\,\mathrm{Log}_2\,p(i) \tag{2}$$

where n is the number of types that occur, p is the relative frequency of occurrence, and i equals the ith type. Actual average information results from the operation of restraint on the variety of type associations in inventory that are otherwise possible.

The cost of procuring items from inventory is measured in terms of *relative entropy* or *disorder* which is given by the ratio

$$h = H/H_{\max} \tag{3}$$

in which (H) is the actual average information and $(H_{\max})$ the maximum information. Relative entropy is the measure of inventory management dynamics because it acquires meaning only as successive intervals of activity are compared in living or dead cultural systems.

Finally, the amount of task potential in inventory storage policy of any state is measured in terms of *organization, redundancy* or *negentropy* of information. This value is given by

$$r, o = 1 - h \tag{4}$$

in which (h) is the relative entropy. Organization of information is simply the amount of certainty with which some patterning (inventory type associations) never occurs relative to what might occur in a situation where all possibilities exist (Nauta, 1972: 112). Organization (or control) considerations are complementary to those of energy in any living or non-living system where energy and control reflect the limits of task performance (Edwards, 1964: 2). The model used to analyze the behavior of the information system is selected from automata theory, and the type which is compatible with the archaeological framework of investigation is the *finite-memory automaton* (Klir, 1969: 100).

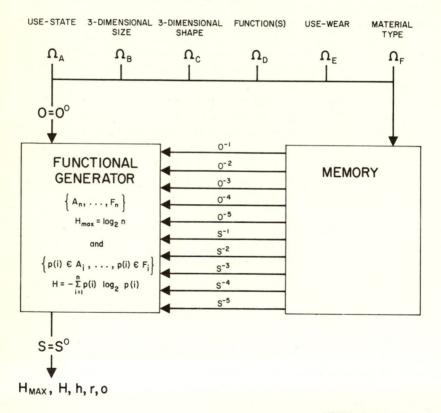

FIGURE 3   Flow model of the finite-memory automaton.

This model machine (Figure 3) is applicable to the analysis of discrete system relations which can be specified in terms of a finite set of inventory stimuli and responses with a given function. The memory preserves some past discrete values of the input inventory variables to apply them later to the functional generator as the system moves through its sequence of internal states. This delay element makes provision for the fact that the membership of individual architectural units (and the variable values of their inventory contents) in a sequence of internal states may or may not be affected by state transition (see Table 1). Thus, the informational response at a given time is uniquely determined by the inventory item stimulus at the same time and by some past item stimuli from the memory. The abstract theory of automata (Klir, 1969: 100) is directly relevant to archaeological applications because directional change in the behavior of the system is investigated in terms of the state transition structure defined as the set $(H|_{max}, H, h, r, o)$ of transitions between states where a single internal stimulus is associated with a single transition (Table 4).

CLASSIFICATION OF THE EXTERNAL SYSTEM ENVIRONMENT

The difference in assumptions which underlie the isolation of prehistoric action and information results from different nonexperimental solutions to the problem of modeling archaeological systems as black box systems in which "quantities cannot be forced to take any required sequence of values and whose classification to inputs and outputs is unknown" (Klir, 1969: 65). Assumptions of a positivist rather than empirical nature (Hill and Evans, 1972) must underlie archaeological classification of both action and information variables. Partitioning of archaeological action variables, however, is conditioned by the a priori assumption that the behavior of the culture system environment (nature, technology, society, ideology or any subset of these, depending on the investigation) is random. The classification of action variables is accepted on the basis of extracting deterministic nonrandom behavior from a system environment. The concept of information as a theory of selection from an uncertain environment entails no prior assumption about the nature of environmental patterning in terms of statistical hypothesis. In this framework, relevant external archaeological quantities are assumed to exist in the environment of the prehistoric culture system as discrete but uncertain forms. The basis for accepting a set of variables is the maximization of information which the classification conveys about the environment. Information in this context is maximized to the degree that conditional uncertainty is reduced.

The discussion of classification of the external system environment is restricted to inventories of technological items alone. My investigation of the informational characteristics of the detailed inventories of floral and faunal subsistence remnants excavated from the architectural units of the Joint site (Hevly, Ward, Van De Graff, n.d.) is incomplete and will be reported elsewhere.

The specific problem which oriented the inventory classification of groundstone and bone tools was one of determining attributes which might logically condition the *potential performance* of prehistoric tasks within the architectural units, since the universe of actual task performance remains unknown. Concern with task-conditioning factors required that inventory variables be mutually exclusive, independently sortable and descriptively exhaustive of each artifact. Only six variables satisfied the requirement where any combination of two or more might conceivably affect potential task performance. Every object was classified in terms of variable: use-state; three-dimensional size; three-dimensional geometric shape; function(s); use-wear and material composition. Each variable specified a sample space on which an information-bearing inventory of relevant discrete values was defined (Figure 3). Each object was assigned exclusively to one discrete value in each of the six separate inventory variables. Clearly, each artifact is characterized by only one of a finite number of possible use states, or possible size, shapes, functions and so on.

In constructing the classification of the inventory, discriminant redundancy was controled at each stage of the procedure. For example, bone and groundstone artifacts were classified as separate populations because of obvious redundancy in linkages between material composition and function. The classification is time-invariant in that an attempt was made to separate object discrimination from the contextual bias of room provenience. It was also necessary to control redundancy in the partitions of discrete values within each inventory variable because most of the variables specified more than one dimension of observation and measurement (such as three-dimensional size). This required three stages of analysis in which (1) the discrete values of each dimension were partitioned separately, (object length, width, thickness, for example), (2) discrete combinations of values were derived from the object distributions in matrices of two, three, or four dimensions, and (3) discrete combinations of values were evaluated in terms of the information conveyed by their conditional distribution. A conservative approach to interpretation was adopted. Discrete combinations were accepted as values of an inventory variable when knowledge of the values of one dimension reduced conditional uncertainty about the other dimensions at the .25–.50 interval of confidence. Partitions of variable values in the critical regions beyond this interval were arbitrarily rejected as indicative of classificatory randomness or redundancy respectively.

It was necessary to evaluate the degree to which the inventory variables themselves were mutually exclusive and independently sortable. Consequently measurement was made of the degree to which knowledge of the discrete values of any one inventory variable reduced the conditional uncertainty contained in each of the remaining variables. Different critical regions of classification rejection were adopted at this more inclusive level of discrimination. Reduction of conditional uncertainty among the groundstone tool inventory variables was accepted at the .02–.49 interval of confidence, and among the bone tool inventory variables the .08–.75 interval was accepted.

Inventory variables and their values were derived from computer applications of the Uncertainty Coefficient subroutine of the FASTABS program in the SPSS package (Nie, Bentley and Hull, 1970).

The operational definitions used to attain a reasonable degree of unambiguous classification differed according to the nature of each inventory variable. Variable use-state of objects is limited to four discrete values because only two kinds of observations which are dichotomous and complementary could be made with any consistency. An object might be physically complete or in a broken state. Prehistoric objects may have been used for one or several purposes independently of physical condition.

Variation in object size was thought to be the outcome of a number of multiple independent causes, specifically the other variables such as material, function, wear and use-state. Multiple independent causality implies the selection of measure intervals which generate normal distributions of object thickness, width and length. Maximum measurements (in millimeters) of these dimensions were recorded independently and the appropriate normality of object distribution and closest approximation to the smallest number (5) of intervals required of a normal distribution. Intervals of the selected limit for each of the three object size measures were then combined to form discrete values of this inventory variable.

Consistency in classification of three-dimensional object shape was perhaps most difficult to achieve. Each object was positioned with respect to its major use-plane and geometric shapes of opposite ends, sides, and planes were defined in terms of paired permutations of straight, concave or convex edges. A straight edge was used to resolve ambiguities.

Artifacts from the Joint site displayed a bewildering variety of primary and alternate functions. Investigation of groundstone and bone tool functions by means of experimental analogy and microscopic analysis of wear led to the conclusion that only one third of each object population could be assigned to standard southwestern single-purpose archaeological functions with any confidence. In certain cases groundstone pestle mortars were alternately used as hammerstones or as manos, mealing bin sides were used or unused metates, portable metates served as crude griddles, and some manos also functioned as grinding pallettes or shaft abraders. Bone tools were also characterized by multiple functions in many cases. Certain cloth weaving awls were subsequently used as either fine or coarse-coil basket awls, or as fiber mat-plaiting awls; other coarse-coil basket awls were later used as leather perforaters and a hair/blanket pin was altered for use as a coarse-coil basket awl. Primary and alternate object functions were assigned on the basis of diagnostic features gleaned from the literature (DiPeso, 1956, 1958; Martin, Rinaldo and Longacre, 1961) and microscopic wear patterns.

Observations of object use-wear were restricted solely to abrasion through use of object surfaces and were independent of evaluations of the shape or wear patterns diagnostic of object function. Objects exhibited planar or nonplanar abrasion on planar or nonplanar surfaces. Discrete combinations of various object abrasions and various object surfaces formed the values of this inventory variable.

Discrimination of the material composition of groundstone tools was aided by knowledge gained from an intensive investigation of building materials forming the architecture of the Joint site (Tracz, 1970). Architectural categories of sandstone were used in the classification of tool materials because it was intuitively apparent that certain varieties had been selected for strength, grit, micaceous inclusion and stain color which were likely to have resulted from differential prehistoric weathering. Other groundstone tool materials (such as petrified wood, quartzite, basalt) were readily distinguishable. Bone tool materials were sorted by anatomical element and taxon to the level of order only. Combinations of element and taxonomic affinity formed the discrete values of this inventory variable.

The final phase of classification of the external environment of the behavioral information system entailed an evaluation of the degree to which the discrete values of each inventory variable approached the most efficient discrimination or coding possible in theory given the same element frequencies. This must be undertaken to evaluate the degree to which the intrinsic structure of information (that part which has discriminate value) is affected by extrinsic structure as additional unwanted information that is unavoidably contained in the ensemble as "noise" (Legendre and Roberts, 1972: 570). This distortion is caused by inconsistent "lumping" and "splitting" of discrete values and it is reflected in the uneven relationship between the number of discrete elements and their relative frequencies. Unacceptable amounts of informational distortion must be reduced as much as possible by redefining variable values which compose the ensemble. The Huffman (binary) coding technique is used to determine the amount of efficient discrimination expressed as the percentage ($h*$) of the greatest average binary information per inventory variable ($H*$) represented by the actual average information per value of the inventory variable. The binary coding technique has been illustrated in an application to the inventory of design elements of ceramics from the Joint site (Justeson, 1973). It will suffice to note that the binary code ($H*$) is based on the notion of symbol length, which is the number of binary digits required to isolate any discrete value of the variable, and, the concept that probabilities of different symbol length should form a geometric series descending from the probability of shortest symbol to the longest (Herdan, 1966: 274). The discrimination efficiency value ($h*$ = $H/H*$) should approximate unity if the classification is adequate, but the converse does not necessarily hold, which means that the coding technique is only a check which can rule out a set of variable values (Justeson, 1973).

All of the major kinds of information conveyed by the inventory variables over the excavated population of groundstone and bone tools from the site are listed in Table 2 to permit insight into the static patterning of the inventory and its variable discrimination coefficients ($h*$).

TABLE 2

Static information and discrimination coefficients of variables in the technological inventories

	Groundstone artifacts						
	Use-state	Size	Shape	Function	Wear	Material	Grand mean
H_{max}	2.0000	6.0000	6.3576	5.6147	3.1699	3.8074	4.4916
H	1.6589	4.7179	5.4119	4.2758	2.8548	2.9874	3.6571
h	0.8295	0.7863	0.8513	0.7615	0.9006	0.7846	0.8190
r, o	0.1705	0.2137	0.1487	0.2385	0.1994	0.2154	0.1810
$h*$	0.9527	0.9807	0.9727	9.7770	0.9347	0.9406	

	Bone artifacts						
	Use-state	Size	Shape	Function	Wear	Material	Grand mean
H_{max}	2.0000	5.0875	6.0000	4.7004	4.0875	2.5850	4.0767
H	1.7508	4.2434	5.5674	4.0796	2.7242	1.7539	3.3457
h	0.8529	0.8341	0.9279	0.8679	0.6665	0.6785	0.8046
r, o	0.1471	0.1659	0.0721	0.1321	0.3335	0.3215	0.1954
$h*$	0.9645	0.9763	0.9751	0.9567	0.9638	0.9825	

THE STATE TRANSITION-STRUCTURE
OF INVENTORY MANAGEMENT

The program of temporary behavior (Table 3) may be examined in terms of its state-transition structure (Table 4). The interpretation is subject to several qualifications. Foremost among these is the sensitivity of informational change in the system program.

TABLE 3

System program of average temporary information behavior[a]

		Groundstone tools		Bone tools	
		Floor alone	Floor and level above	Floor alone	Floor and level above
S^{-5}	H_{max}	3.7941	4.0575	2.4369	3.7374
	H	3.3096	3.4944	2.3189	3.1314
($\pm$ 1160–	h	0.8629	0.8586	0.9397	0.8181
1205$\pm$)	r, o	0.1371	0.1414	0.0603	0.1819
S^{-4}	H_{max}	3.5274	3.8171	1.3900	3.3155
	H	3.1766	3.3431	1.3627	2.8242
($\pm$ 1205–	h	0.8976	0.8750	0.9728	0.8345
1230$\pm$)	r, o	0.1024	0.1250	0.0272	0.1655
S^{-3}	H_{max}	4.2466	4.3450	2.8511	3.8642
	H	3.6290	3.6174	2.6580	3.2541
($\pm$ 1230–	h	0.8540	0.8390	0.9135	0.8219
1250$\pm$)	r, o	0.1460	0.1610	0.0865	0.1781
S^{-2}	H_{max}	4.2668	4.3223	2.5128	3.3836
	H	3.6364	3.6512	2.3313	3.0039
($\pm$ 1250–	h	0.8485	0.8468	0.9156	0.8716
1265$\pm$)	r, o	0.1515	0.1532	0.0844	0.1284
S^{-1}	H_{max}	4.3591	4.3993	2.8160	3.5627
	H	3.6183	3.6248	2.5796	3.0787
($\pm$ 1265–	h	0.8264	0.8259	0.9028	0.8450
1285$\pm$)	r, o	0.1736	0.1741	0.0972	0.1550
S^{0}	H_{max}	4.2504	4.3107	2.6356	3.2702
	H	3.5604	3.5800	2.4657	2.9058
($\pm$ 1285–	h	0.8313	0.8295	0.9198	0.8687
1320$\pm$)	r, o	0.1617	0.1705	0.0802	0.1313

[a] Summary average of the values of all six variables.

Minute changes in amounts of information listed in Table 3 conceal large-scale shifts in object numbers and sizes of value sets among the inventory variables due to the stability characteristic of the logarithm in the information measures. These information values, then, are extremely sensitive. Interpretation is based on a partial rather than a complete solution of the problem. It will be apparent that only the surface behavior of this system is examined in terms of grand mean information values. A rigorous solution would require a separate examination of the state-transition structure of each of the inventory variables (object use-state, size, etc.).

The microstructure of state transitions is initially mapped in terms of column vectors in Table 4, and re-mapped as flow diagrams in Figure 4 to permit easier reading.

We are concerned with interpreting the composition of the behavior of maximum (H_{max}) and actual (H) information which have common discrete values of the inventory variables. This structure permits insight into the instantaneous aspect of prehistoric inventory management during

TABLE 4

State-transition structure of the system program[a]

	Groundstone tools											
	Floor alone						Floor and level above					
	S^{-5}	S^{-4}	S^{-3}	S^{-2}	S^{-1}	S^0	S^{-5}	S^{-4}	S^{-3}	S^{-2}	S^{-1}	S^0
H_{max}	0	1	1	1	0		0	1	0	1	0	
H	0	1	1	1	0		0	1	1	0	0	
r, o	0	1	1	1	0		0	1	0	1	0	

	Bone tools											
	Floor alone						Floor and level above					
	S^{-5}	S^{-4}	S^{-3}	S^{-2}	S^{-1}	S^0	S^{-5}	S^{-4}	S^{-3}	S^{-2}	S^{-1}	S^0
H_{max}	0	1	0	1	0		0	1	0	1	0	
H	0	1	0	1	0		0	1	0	1	0	
r, o	0	1	0	1	0		0	1	0	1	0	

[a] Key:

    0 = relative decrease from a prior to a subsequent state (Table 3).

    1 = relative increase from a prior to a subsequent state (Table 3).

H_{max} = maximum average stimulus for chaos in potential task performance.

    H = actual average selection or response to the stimulus.

    r, o = amount of self-organization or control in potential task performance.

    0/0/0 = $H_{max}/H/r, o$.

Groundstone tools floor	0/0/0	1/1/1	1/1/1	1/0/1	0/0/0
(S^{-5})——(S^{-4})——(S^{-3})——(S^{-2})——(S^{-1})——(S^0)

Groundstone tools floor and level	0/0/0	1/1/1	0/1/0	1/0/1	0/0/0
(S^{-5})——(S^{-4})——(S^{-3})——(S^{-2})——(S^{-1})——(S^0)

Bone tools floor	0/0/0	1/1/1	0/0/0	1/1/1	0/0/0
(S^{-5})——(S^{-4})——(S^{-3})——(S^{-2})——(S^{-1})——(S^0)

Bone tools floor and level	0/0/0	1/1/1	0/0/0	1/1/1	0/0/0
(S^{-5})——(S^{-4})——(S^{-3})——(S^{-2})——(S^{-1})——(S^0)

FIGURE 4   State-transition diagrams. Key: 0, relative decrease from a prior to a subsequent state (Table 3); 1, relative increase from a prior to a subsequent state (Table 3); $\overline{H}_{max}$ maximum average stimulus for chaos in potential task performance; $\overline{H}$, actual average selection or response to the stimulus; r, o, amount of self-organization or control in potential task performance; $0/0/0 H_{max}|0/H/0r,o$.

any state of the system. It is appropriate to recall that maximum and actual information may in theory vary independently of each other to determine changes in the amount of organization (r, o) in any state transition. The structural mechanics of these independent behaviors in natural system trends and their inventory management analogues were presented in the first four hypotheses in the section of Trends in Physical, Biological and Cultural Systems above. The fact that H_{max}, H, and r, o *vary together* between most activity intervals at the Joint site to produce a simple composition of behavior in both stratigraphic partitions seems remarkable. *This finding permits strong suspicion that homeostats were operative in the prehistoric management of the groundstone and bone tool inventories, and that the process is analogous to the thermodynamics of organismic systems outlined in the hypothesis that deals with open biological systems, thermodynamics and homeostasis.* A prescribed internal environment of the inventory management system may have been homeostatically maintained in spite of fluctuations in management activity at the Joint site and change in the system's external natural environment. Evaluation of this possibility in terms of statistical inference entails prior definition of the microstructure of prehistoric management activity and homeostats below.

Inspection of state-transitions in the information values of inventory management in Table 3 shows that the regularity of composition noted above is caused by the fact that change in cost (H) of inconvenience incurred when demanded kinds of items are differentially available is a lag–response to the stimulus of change in cost (H_{max}) of storing various kinds of items in equal availability situations.[1] This dependency is best understood at present in terms of the adaptive reorganization of technological inventories to achieve a better fit with their effective environment. The concept has been formalized as a trial-and-error model (Campbell, 1960) which relates the stimulus of "blind variation" process in technological innovation to a "selective survival" response as technological imitation. In this view, "successful innovations were as blind in origin as those which failed, and the difference between them is due to the nature of the environment" (Campbell, 1960: 207). The shortcomings of this particular model are reflected in criticisms of "Neo-Darwinist" theory at the general system level (von Bertalanffy, 1969) in which assumptions concerning the operation of (a) behavioral mechanisms for introducing variation, (b) consistent selective process, and (c) mechanisms which preserve and reproduce selected variations prove to be intractible to rigorous investigation. Plog (1973: 658) has attempted to evaluate adaptive variation in technology in terms of such mechanisms, but the study of functional origins of inventory reorganization must be distinguished from my cost analyses of reorganization which do not rely directly on these principles for explanation.

Homeostats may control lag–response interaction in the following manner. Fluctuation in the ratio of storage (H_{max}) and demand (H) costs from one system state to the next directly determines change in the cost of procuring items from inventory (h), where amounts of task potential (r, o) in storage policy are residual. Consequently, we may speak of task potential as the "homeostatic mechanism of proportional control" (Goldman, 1960: 120). In a linear feedback control system such as this, the same mechanism (r, o) which corrects positive error (increase) in the cost of item procurement (h) also corrects negative error (decrease). Two sharply contrastive microstructures which contain each type of error define the regular fluctuations in management activity in Table 4. Each disturbs the stability of the management system's internal environment in an opposite manner.

The first of these is composed of a decrease in the cost of storage (H_{max}) that is associated with a disproportionately smaller decrease in the cost of demand (H). The result is positive error in cost of item procurement (h) and decline in task potential (r, o) given by (S^{-5}, S^{-4}) = 0,0,0 in Table 4, for example.

The second microstructure is the direct opposite of the first. This composition exhibits transitional increase in the cost of storage (H_{max}) which is associated with a disproportionately smaller increase in the cost of demand (H). The result is negative error in cost of item procurement (h) and rise in task potential (r, o) given by (S^{-4}, S^{-3}) = 1,1,1 in Table 4, for example. It is possible that sequential alternation of these microstructures in the system program reflect "undershoot" and "overshoot" in error control.

Inspection of Table 4 also reveals the existence of irregular compositions in the microstructure of the third (S^{-3}, S^{-2}) and fourth (S^{-2}, S^{-1}) state transitions in the management of the groundstone tool inventory. While certain of these nonconformities such as the cost of storage (H_{max}) and task potential (r, o) may reflect differential stratigraphic partitioning of the object population (floor alone vs. floor and fill) in the earlier problematic transition, it does not also explain the uniform irregularity in the later transition. We are left with the inference that management of the groundstone technological inventory exhibits perturbation during the period A.D. ±1230–1285±. The basis of inference is the uniform but irregular behavior of the cost of demand (H) as stimulus–response in both of these transitions which span fifty years of activity. The cost of demand (H) increases in the prior transition (S^{-3}, S^{-2}) when it should decrease and it decreases in the subsequent transition (S^{-2}, S^{-1}) when it should increase in a manner compatible with the overall program of the system. The sources of perturbation are not directly apparent. Inspection of Table 1 shows that most of an entire wing of rooms (R06, 07, 08, 09, 10, 31, 32) were constructed, occupied and abandoned between A.D. ±1230–1285±. Hevly, Ward, and Van de Graff (n.d.) have combined different lines of palynological and archaeological evidence from studies of various sites in the Hay Hollow Valley to infer regional changes in vegetation, climate and human demography during the period A.D. 1230–1270. Their analysis of ecofactal materials at the Joint site indicates that a shift from primary reliance upon cultigens toward increasing usage of noncultivated plants and small game animals occurred during this time interval, and was concomitant with the initial phase of human abandonment of the Hay Hollow Valley. Hanson (1975) has profitably investigated adaptive variation in other inventories as prehistoric cultural response to environmental stress at the Joint site during this period.

If the magnitude of these disturbances has no statistical significance, then homeostatic maintenance of a prescribed internal environment of the inventory management system can be inferred. Since the stability of the proportional control mechanism, i.e., task potential (r, o), depends on the stability of the ratio of storage (H_{max}) and demand (H) costs, an evaluation of the strength of the relationship between these two variables is the basis of inference. Measures of the spread of storage (H_{max}) and demand (H) costs for each inventory listed in Table 3 about the linear least-squares equation were derived from computer applications of the product–moment correlation (r) subroutine in the SPSS package (Nie, Bentley and Hull, 1970). The lowest correlation coefficient obtained was $r = .95$ with a corresponding level of significance $p = .002$. Since the measure (r) involves variance and covariance, it is highly affected by extreme costs of either storage (H_{max}) or demand (H). This may be the case where the effect of one extreme values (S^{-4} in Table 3) for the bone tool inventory (floor alone) is to produce a high correlation ($r = .99$) where none may exist in the remainder. Extreme values are not evident in the other inventories. Within the limits of both of these costs the relationship is approximately linear, and the inference is made that task potential (r, o) operates as a stable homeostat in regulating the cost of procuring items (h) from tool inventories.

The discovery of stable homeostats in the management of technological inventories at the Joint site permits us to narrow the analogy between the thermodynamics of organismic systems and this aspect of culture process even further. With respect to the hypothesis that deals with open biological systems, thermodynamics and homeostasis, the evidence suggests that variants (1) and (3) may be analogues where sequential values of task-potential are homeostatic. Whether these values are equal to or less than the amount of organization in the subsistence storage policy remains to be determined: this is the question of choosing reversible or irreversible thermodynamics as analogues to the dynamic management of linked inventories.

CONCLUSIONS

It is apparent that the concepts of *adaptive variation* in complex adaptive systems and *adaptive reorganization* in homeostatic systems differ profoundly in terms of alternative definitions of the effective environment of human technological behavior. The effective environment of either type of cultural system specifies its source of energy which is of critical importance in the study of technology when the dynamics of innovation and imitation are of interest. That the effective natural environment is clearly the source of energy for complex adaptive systems is evident in the concern with technology as the "limiting factor upon the production of goods and services" (Zubrow, 1975: 33). Innovation and imitation, the mechanics of adaptive variation in technological inventories are systematically related to the extent that either increases the production output (see Zubrow, 1975: 33). In the complex adaptive system model the concept of abundant free natural energy is fundamental to archaeological explanations of production increase that is measured in terms of change in a sequence of actual or specific tool configurations.

It is equally clear that the effective environment of homeostatic cultural systems is culture itself, in the sense that human information processing of stimuli from the natural environment involves cultural restraints of a fixed or probable nature (see von Bertalanffy, 1969; Clarke, 1968, and Rapoport,

1972). Innovation and imitation are the mechanisms for the reorganization of technological inventories here too, but the adaptive significance of either depends on its systematic relationship to the other. The cybernetic concept of energy which is implied by the homeostatic model assumes that a pre-historic cultural system was characterized by abundant free energy and asks why shifts in the occurrence and frequency of inventory items should result in specific configurations, rather than in alternative ones when the same occurrence and frequency data are considered independently. Here the problem is one of understanding the process by which a technological system is "organized and controlled into its restrictions" (Ashby, 1956: 3) as a trajectory of change to achieve a better fit with its effective environment. The homeostatic model implies that the adaptability of a cultural system itself depends on the maintenance of a viable balance between the management costs of technological innovation and imitation regardless of the level of "progress" involved. One conclusion drawn from this investigation is that the equilibrium of inventory management costs maintained by the task potential homeostat prevents "extra-systematic input overloads" which are claimed (Wood and Matson, 1973: 681) to be the source of change in homeostatic systems. Changes in the absolute costs of inventory management reflect changes in the complexity of technological inventories (Table 3), but the amount of task potential in the storage policy remains stable. The desirable "as-if-thinking" quality (Klejn, 1973: 706) is expressed in the reasonably stable control of item procurement costs in the homeostatic model. The stability of task potential has an additional interpretative consequence. The hypothesis has been advanced that in situations

where well-defined management objectives exist, the primary aim may be to manipulate the system to improve or even optimize its efficiency. (Munton, 1973: 686).

If we consider task potential to be the measure of the efficiency of the inventory storage policy, then we may infer that the "as-if-thinking" function does not support the hypothesis in terms of improving this aspect of management.

The major conclusion of this investigation is that a dynamic metaphor may exist between the trend of the technological inventory system and certain trends toward entropy that are possible in organismic systems. (A more definitive evaluation depends on completion of the analysis of the subsistence inventories at the Joint site.) This metaphor contains a paradox in that a "relatively closed" mechanical system of inventory management in its effective cultural environment is analogous to the thermodynamics of a "relatively open" organismic system in its effective natural environment.

If we are to view a cultural system in the same way that an organism is viewed, as a "purposeful machine" where inventory operations reflect the "choice of an organism to grapple with its environment in terms of rewards or penalties" (Churchman, 1971: 215), then the nature of the effective cultural environment must be redefined to include the effective natural environment. We may assume that cultural inventory systems were embedded in a much larger system that included the effective natural environment. This is possible because the self-organizing system of inventory operations in its effective cultural environment is meaningless unless it is in

close contact with an environment (nature) which possesses available energy and order and within which the self-organizing system is in a state of perpetual interaction (von Foerster, 1960: 33).

We can derive insight into the form of this interaction at the Joint site, if we assume the effective natural environment of this prehistoric culture to behave in a self-organizing manner, specifically in terms of the "progressive similarity" trend or the "progressive differentiation" trend discussed above under "Closed" and "Open Biological Systems" respectively. Since the length of time involved in either natural process is not specified, we may imagine that the short-term shifts in variety (H_{max}) and restraint (H), which define the community structure of the cultural subsistence species, reflect alternate trends. Here we wish to know whether the effective cultural environment can be defined as a map of the variety and restraint which exists in the cultural system's effective natural environment. In this situation, floral and faunal species are extracted and stored in direct porportion to their diversity (H_{max}) and availability (H) which corresponds to the structural mechanics of inventory management.

We know immediately that both natural variety and restraint cannot be encoded simultaneously by the cultural system in a one-to-one mapping situation such as this, because the trend of technological inventory operations at the Joint site does not correspond to either natural system trend. A cultural system may map (in an isomorphic manner) *either* variety *or* restraint contained in its effective natural environment. Here the shift from one natural system trend to the other permits rewards or imposes penalties which must be accepted by the cultural system if its technological inventory operations are to remain stable.

Regardless of whether natural variety (H_{max}) or restraint (H) is separately mapped directly into technological inventories, "progressive differentiation" trends in the community of subsistence species imposes a penalty on stable management by forcing either the cost of storage (H_{max})

or the cost of demand (H) upward. This may have happened at the Joint site during the period of environmental disturbance (A.D. 1230–1270) in which the cost of demand (H) from the groundstone artifact inventory behaves irregularly $(S^{-3}, S^{-2}, S^{-1},$ in Table 4).

Alternatively, short term "progressive similarity" trends in the community of subsistence species which compose the effective natural environment offers a reward (in terms of isomorphic mapping) to the cultural management system by permitting either the cost of inventory storage (H_{max}) or the cost of demand (H) to decline. If the amount of self-organization in the subsistence environment declines to a value which is less than the amount of task potential in the technological management policy then (in theory) the effective cultural environment becomes dysfunctional in the one-to-one mapping situation.

It is possible that no mapping correspondence exists between effective cultural and natural environments. In such a situation where the constraints of one environment fluctuate independently of constraints in the other, we can imagine technological inventories functioning in the human extraction of all rare economic species and few of the common ones in the effective natural environment. This is neither intuitively appealing nor likely for obvious reasons.

In sum, inventory operations research may be the framework for general system models of prehistoric cultural behavior.

NOTE

1) Except in cases where confusion might arise, these costs are abbreviated as "cost of demand (H)" and "cost of storage (H_{max})."

ACKNOWLEDGMENTS

I am particularly indebted to the late Paul S. Martin for his encouragement and support of this research through National Science Foundation Grants (GS 2381 and GY 4602) to the Field Museum of Natural History. I also wish to acknowledge D. Gregory, J. Hanson and M. Schiffer whose participation in the Joint Site Project as fellow staff members of the South-western Archaeological Expedition made the development of this analytic perspective possible. W. Odom kindly designed the ALGOL and FORTRAN algorithms for the CDC 6400 digital computer applications to data and J. Kelley made the taxonomic identifications of faunal remains. I am grateful to T. P. Culbert, W. L. Rathje and R. H. Thompson for their patient support of this research which was undertaken at The University of Arizona. Special thanks are extended to J. Justeson whose mathematical sophistication served as inspiration in my attempts to explore the strengths and weaknesses of this approach to archaeological interpretation.

REFERENCES

Ashby, W. R. (1956) *An Introduction to Cybernetics.* John Wiley, New York.

Ashby, W. R. (1968a) Variety, constraint and the law of requisite variety. In *Modern Systems Research for the Behavioral Scientist,* edited by W. Buckley, pp. 129–36. Aldine, Chicago.

Ashby, W. R. (1968b) Principles of the self-organizing system. In *Modern Systems Research for the Behavioral Scientist,* edited by W. Buckley, pp. 108–118. Aldine, Chicago.

Ashby, W. R. (1972) Systems and their informational measures. In *Trends in General Systems Theory,* edited by G. Klir, pp. 78–97. John Wiley, New York.

Bertalanffy, L. von (1969) Chance or law. In *Beyond Reductionism,* edited by A. Koestler and J. R. Smythies, pp. 56–84. Hutchinson, New York.

Buckley, W. (1968) Society as a complex adaptive system. In *Modern Systems Research for the Behavioral Scientist,* edited by W. Buckley, pp. 490–513. Aldine, Chicago.

Campbell, D. (1960) Blind variation and selective survival as general strategy in knowledge process. In *Self Organizing Systems,* edited by M. Yovits and S. Cameron, pp. 205–31. Pergamon, New York.

Churchman, C. (1971) *The Design of Enquiring Systems: Basic Concepts of Systems and Organization.* Basic Books, New York.

Clarke, D. (1968) *Analytic Archaeology.* Methuen, London.

DiPeso, C. C. (1956) The upper Pima of San Cayetano del Tumacacori. *The Amerind Foundation,* Inc. 7. Dragoon, Arizona.

DiPeso, C. C. and H. Cutler (1958) The Reeve ruin in southwestern Arizona: a study of prehistoric western pueblo migration into the middle San Pedro Valley. *Amerind Foundation,* Inc. 8. Dragoon, Arizona.

Edwards, E. (1964) *Information Transmission.* Chapman and Hall, London.

Foerster, H. von (1960) On self-organizing systems and their environments. In *Self-organizing Systems,* edited by M. Yovits and S. Cameron, pp. 31–50. Pergamon, New York.

Frick, F. C. (1968) The application of information theory in behavioral studies. In *Modern Systems Research for the Behavioral Scientist,* edited by W. Buckley, pp. 182–85. Aldine, Chicago.

Goldman, S. (1960) Further consideration of cybernetic aspects of homeostasis. In *Self-Organizing Systems,* edited by M. Yovits and C. Scott, pp. 109–21. Pergamon, New York.

Gorman, F. (1973) An investigation of degradation trends in natural and cultural systems. Paper presented at the 72nd Annual Meeting of the American Anthropological Association, New Orleans.

Hanson, J. and M. B. Schiffer (1975) The Joint site; a preliminary report. In Chapters in the prehistory of Eastern Arizona, IV. *Fieldiana: Anthropology* **65,** 47–87.

Hanson, J. (1975) Stress response in cultural systems: a prehistoric example from east-central Arizona. In Chapters in the Prehistory of Eastern Arizona, IV. *Fieldiana: Anthropology* **65,** 92–102.

Herdan, G. (1966) *The Advanced Theory of Language as Choice and Chance.* Springer-Verlag, New York.

Hevly, D., J. Ward and K. Van de Graff (n.d.) *Ecofact Inventory and Paleoecology of NS-605.* Manuscript, Department of Biological Sciences, Northern Arizona University, Flagstaff. Xerox.

Hill, J. (1970) Broken K Pueblo: prehistoric social organization in the American Southwest. *Anthropological Papers of The University of Arizona* 18.

Hill, J. N. and R. K. Evans (1972) A model for classification and typology. In *Models in Archaeology,* edited by D. Clarke, pp. 231–73. Methuen, London.

Justeson, J. (1973) Limitations of archaeological inference: an information-theoretic approach with applications in methodology. *American Antiquity* **38,** 131–49.

Klejn, L. (1973) Marxism, the systemic approach, and archaeology. In *The Explanation of Culture Change: Models in Prehistory*, edited by C. Renfrew, pp. 691–710. Duckworth, London.

Klir, G. (1969) *An Approach to General Systems Theory*. Van Nostrand Rheinhold, New York.

Legendre, P. and D. Robert (1972) Characters and clustering in taxonomy: a synthesis of two taximetric procedures. *Taxon* 21, 567–606.

Longacre, W. (1970) Archaeology as anthropology: a case study. *Anthropological Papers of The University of Arizona* 17.

Martin, P., J. Rinaldo and W. Longacre (1961) The Mineral Creek site and Hooper Ranch pueblo: Eastern Arizona. *Fieldiana: Anthropology* 52.

Miller, G. A. (1968) What is information measurement? In *Modern Systems Research for the Behavioral Scientist*, edited by W. Buckley, pp. 123–28. Aldine, Chicago.

Miller, J. (1971) The nature of living systems. *Behavioral Science* 16, 270–81.

Munton, R. J. C. (1973) Systems analysis: a comment. In *The Explanation of Culture Change: Models in Prehistory*, edited by C. Renfrew, pp. 685–90. Duckworth, London.

Nauta, D. (1972) *The Meaning of Information*. Mouton, The Hague.

Nie, N., D. Bentley and C. Hull (1970) *Statistical Package for the Social Sciences*. McGraw Hill, New York.

Odum, E. (1971) *Fundamentals of Ecology*. W. B. Saunders, Philadelphia.

Plog, F. (1973) Laws, systems of law, and the explanation of observed variation. In *The Explanation of Culture Change: Models in Prehistory*, edited by C. Renfrew, pp. 650–61. Duckworth, London.

Rapoport, A. (1968) The promise and pitfalls of information theory. In *Modern Systems Research for the Behavioral Scientist*, edited by W. Buckley, pp. 137–42. Aldine, Chicago.

Rapoport, A. (1972) The search for simplicity. In *The Relevance of General Systems Theory*, edited by E. Lazlo, pp. 15–30. George Braziller, New York.

Rosen, R. (1972) Some systems–theoretical problems in biology. In *The Relevance of General Systems Theory*, edited by E. Lazlo, pp. 45–66. George Braziller, New York.

Schiffer, M. B. (1972) Archaeological context and systemic context. *American Antiquity* 37, 156–65.

Schiffer, M. B. (1973) Cultural formation processes of the archaeological record: applications at the Joint site, east-central Arizona. Ph.D. Dissertation, The University of Arizona, Tucson.

Tracz, S. (1970) A formal analysis of the architecture at the Joint site pueblo. Manuscript, Field Museum of Natural History, Chicago.

Watson, P., S. LeBlanc and C. Redman (1971) *Explanation in Archaeology: An Explicitly Scientific Approach*. Columbia University Press, New York.

White, L. A. (1949) *The Science of Culture*. Farrar, Straus and Giroux, New York.

Wilcox, D. (1975) A strategy for perceiving social groups in puebloan sites. In Chapters in the prehistory of Eastern Arizona, IV. *Fieldiana: Anthropology* 65, 121–59.

Wood, J. and R. G. Matson (1973) Two models of sociocultural systems and their implications for the archaeological study of change. In *The Explanation of Culture Change: Models in Prehistory*, edited by C. Renfrew, pp. 673–83. Duckworth, London.

Zubrow, E. W. (1975) *Prehistoric Carrying Capacity: A Model*. Cummings, Menlo Park, California.

Response to Stress at Grasshopper Pueblo, Arizona

J. JEFFERSON REID

The University of Arizona

There is a nagging uneasiness these days that archaeologists everywhere, and especially in the Southwest, have been too quick to clutch at environmental variability as the causal agent responsible for variability in culture and behavior. As an antidote to seemingly facile explanations of the interaction of past human behavior and the natural environment, a general systems-ecological framework is employed in the ongoing quest for behavioral regularities. Proposed is a method by which human responses to conditions of environmental stress may be identified and understood. The regularity that diversity promotes stability is refined, formalized and applied to data from Grasshopper, a 14th century pueblo in east central Arizona. Though this specific analysis concludes appropriately in equivocation, it nevertheless serves well to illustrate the general theory and method for investigating human responses to environmental stress.

Environmental stress, in one or another of its many guises, has played a dominant, often bizarre role in forming interpretations of Southwestern prehistory. From unsightly drought to epidemics, rampaging arroyos to rambunctious nomads, stress has been particularly prominent in explaining away the seemingly erratic movements of Puebloan groups. In this regard, Dean (1969: 194) comments that

in trying to explain every known "migration" that took place in the northern Southwest after A.D. 1100, the "abandonment theories" become so general as to be meaningless.

This paper develops a method to answer the question of how people respond to environmental stress, not by first identifying changes in stress factors in the environment, as has been the case in much previous work in southwestern archaeology, but by isolating behavior associated with stress conditions and then scanning the prehistoric landscape for a reasonable set of causal factors. The priority is on human behavior, regardless of whether or not the environmental culprit is ultimately identified. Discussion begins with a consideration of stress and strain it produces in living systems. From these considerations a method of analysis is outlined and a measure offered for the identification of behavior under conditions of stress. These analytic tools are applied to data from the Grasshopper ruin.

STRESS AND STRAIN

The first systematic attempt to devise research for the archaeological investigation of responses to environmental stress is presented by Hill and Plog (1970; cf. Hanson, 1975). In formulating a research design they derive hypotheses and inspiration from Miller (1965a, 1965b, 1965c), whose ideas also form the framework for present considerations of environmental stress. Miller is quoted extensively as his ideas bear most directly upon this topic.

> There is a *range of stability* for each of numerous variables in all living systems. It is that range within which the rate of correction of deviations is minimal or zero, and beyond which correction occurs. An input or output of either matter–energy or information, which by lack or excess of some characteristic, forces the variables beyond the range of stability, constitutes a *stress* and produces a *strain* (or strains) within the system. Input lack and output excess both produce the same strain—diminished amounts in the system. Input excess and output lack both produce the opposite strain—increased amounts. Strains may or may not be capable of being reduced, depending upon their intensity and the resources of the system. . . .
>
> Stress may be anticipated. Information that a stress is imminent constitutes a threat to the system. A *threat* can create a strain. Recognition of the meaning of the information of such a threat must be based on previously stored (usually learned) information about such situations. A pattern of input information is a threat when—like the smell of the hunter on the wind; a change in the acidity of fluids around a cell; a whirling cloud approaching the city—it is capable of eliciting processes which can counteract the stress it presages. Processes—action or communications—occur in systems only when a stress or a threat has created strain which pushes a variable beyond its range of stability. A system is a constantly changing cameo and its environment is a similarly changing bas relief, and the two at all times fit each other. . . .That is, outside stress of [sic or] threats are mirrored by inside strains (Miller, 1965a: 224).

Several of Miller's points deserve emphasis. Stress, in drastically altering steady-state conditions, requires that a response be made in order to reestablish a steady state. This response can be viewed as an adaptive response. Thus, stress exists only as it produces a strain. Important in this regard is the notion that stress is system-specific. Stress to one system is not necessarily stress to another or to the same system at different times. Systems, therefore, possess different thresholds for coping with different stresses and for coping with the same stress at different times. Steila (1972) illustrates these points in a discussion of drought as stress and the different strains it produces. A concept of drought always implies negative moisture departures, yet the strain is contingent upon the nature of the system affected.

> To the forester, drought is thought of primarily in terms of the susceptibility of surface conditions to the threat of fire. To the agriculturalist, the concern of drought centers about his cultigen's water-needs and soil conditions, while to the hydrologist drought is evidenced by dropping water levels. However, basic to each of the previously mentioned physical definitions (e.g., as opposed to economic, etc.) is the fact that drought represents a negative departure from the expected moisture availability of an area (Steila, 1972: 3).

However, to define environmental stress is not to identify it in the archaeological record. The identification of environmental stress is fraught with
at least two major problems. First, there is currently no a priori basis for
asserting that specific changes in the environment will or will not force a
particular system beyond the range of stability, although it is possible to
isolate environmental factors that could reasonably produce stress for a
given system. Second, stress produces a strain on the system affected,
forcing the system beyond the range of stability. A response to stress is
the attempt to relieve this strain and restore the system to a steady-state
condition. Therefore, any method of identifying stress must first consider
the identification of behavior indicating strain.

Hill and Plog (1970) and Hanson (1975) present hypotheses adapted
from Miller (1965c) that emphasize experimentation and diversification in
behavior as generalized responses to subsistence-lack stress. Explicit in
their hypotheses and test implications is the notion that diversity is a
measurable indicator of strain. The behaviors exhibiting diversity should
be related directly to the system under strain and, therefore, by extension, to
the stress or threat producing that strain. For example, subsistence-lack
stress should create a strain on the subsistence system. This strain should be
manifest in diversity associated with subsistence-related behavior. It is here
proposed that strain can be identified by measuring behavioral diversity
represented in the archaeological record.

A related view of the interaction between environment and behavior is
presented by Clarke (1968: 126–7) in a simple expression:

$$E \rightleftharpoons (k)S$$

The "buffer" (k) in this expression would then represent the degree to which "S" [cultural
system] is "insulated" from changes in "E" [environment], and conversely "E" from "S".
Now, in an earlier section it was suggested that the regulatory or insulatory capacity of a
culture system is proportional to its variety and its capacity as a communication system—since
only variety in cultural activities can force down variety in outcomes in the environmental
"game".

Using Clarke's expression and incorporating thoughts on diversity
expressed by Hill, Plog and Clarke, it is argued that since (k) is specific to
S and insulates S from changes in E an increase in diversity of (k) should
insulate or correct for the effects of strain in S produced by a stress factor in
E. The identification of a relative increase in diversity of (k) should allow
identification of the presence of strain in S as well as the identification of E.
Put another way, since strain in S is manifest as an increase in diversity of
something designated (k), then the identification of this increase should
permit the identification of strain as well as the possible stress producing
factors in E.

Discovering Past Behavior

For example, strain in the subsistence system cannot be identified and measured directly. However, the subsistence system (S_1) interacts with the environment (E_1) through a series of "buffers" such as procurement tools (K_{11}) and facilities (K_{12}) as well as patterns of resource procurement behavior (K_{13}) and organization (K_{14}). A relative increase in diversity of subsistence related tools, facilities, and behavior should identify strain and its locus as somewhere within the subsistence system. This identification of subsistence strain is methodologically prior to and should assist in locating the source of environmental stress.

The reasoning behind the concept of diversity and its use to identify strain can be traced to ecology and general systems theory where one encounters the principle that diversity promotes stability (Odum, 1971: 143–54) or the diversity–stability rule (Wilson and Bossert, 1971: 138–46). Watt (1972: 75–6) maintains that:

There are only two basic elements in all theoretical arguments as to why diversity promotes stability. The first is the idea of spreading the risk. . . . The second idea is that a system functions more harmoniously if it has more elements because it then has more homeostatic feedback loops . . . the greater the variety of foods the human population has available for harvesting, hunting, or fishing, the less the likelihood of human catastrophe due to a disaster befalling a particular food species.

Miller (1965a: 220), Margalef (1968: 21), and Clarke, (1968: 126–7) make similar arguments concerning the inverse relationship between a system's diversity and its vulnerability to stress.

Others remark that variety can only destroy variety (Ashby, 1968: 135).

The "law of requisite variety" . . . states that the variety within a system must be at least as great as the environmental variety against which it is attempting to regulate itself (Buckley, 1968: 495).

It may be that what is discussed here as diversity articulates well with Ashby's general principle, yet, as Buckley (1968: 495) notes, ". . . such a general principle is a long way from informing more concrete analysis of particular cases. . ." To achieve insight into particular cases it is necessary to define diversity more precisely and to devise ways to measure it.

Margalef (1968: 18) defines diversity as the range of variation within a community or system and develops it into a comparative index (1968: 17–23; cf. Odum, 1971: 144; Wilson and Bossert, 1971: 144–5). Watt (1972: 74) defines the concept of general diversity in terms of what it measures:

Diversity measures two characteristics of any set of items: *evenness* in numbers of different items in the set; and *richness* in number of different items within the set.

Odum (1971: 148–54) discusses these two components of diversity in greater detail. The richness or variety component of diversity is expressed by ratios between total species and total numbers of importance values as expressed in several indices (Odum, 1971: 144). Evenness or equitability in the distribution of individuals among the species is the second major component of diversity (Odum, 1971: 149).

For example, two systems each containing 10 species and 100 individuals have the same S/N index richness, but these could have widely different evenness indices depending on the apportionment of the 100 individuals among the 10 species, for example, 91-1-1-1-1-1-1-1-1-1 at one extreme (minimum evenness) and 10 individuals per species (perfect evenness) at the other extreme.

Appeals to authority have been made to support the principle that diversity promotes stability. It is assumed that the greater the diversity, the greater will be the stability of a cultural–behavioral system and thus its capacity to withstand stress. All cultural–behavioral systems, as complex adaptive systems, must maintain a yet unspecified level of diversity in order to survive. The effects of stress, on the other hand, by producing strain and instability at points within the system, can only be regulated by returning the system to a near steady state. Since diversity, as a set of correction responses or a deviation counteracting mechanism (Clarke, 1968: 126–7; Margalef, 1968; Odum, 1971), promotes stability, it is proposed that under conditions of environmental stress diversification of behavior will increase. Diversification of behavior can also be a source of novelty, and, as such, can be seen as potentially amplifying in its long-term effect. Thus a post-stress steady state may not be identical with the pre-stress steady state.

The measure for diversity derives from information theory through Margalef, (1968: 19). Similar expressions are presented by Watt (1972: 74–5), Odum, (1971: 144), and Wilson and Bossert, (1971: 144–5). A restatement of Margalef's original expression is provided by Dr. Robert Laxton, Department of Mathematics, University of Nottingham (personal communication 1972)

$$DI = \left(\frac{N!}{N1!\,N2!\ldots Nn!}\right)1/N$$

where:
DI = diversity index
N = sum of all units within the set, total population
$N1, N2$, etc. = sum of all units within the subsets $N1, N2$, etc. so that $N = N1 + N2 \ldots Nn$
$N! = N \times (N-1) \times (N-2) \times \ldots 3 \times 2 \times 1$.

The computational form is also provided by Laxton to facilitate calculation of the factorials. Common logarithms are used.

$$DI = \frac{1}{N} [\log_{10} N! - (\log_{10} N1! + \log_{10} N2! + \ldots \log_{10} Nn!)]$$

The diversity index, as applied by Margalef and Watt, measures the diversity within a complete set in which all subsets and subset items are included. In contrast, archaeological context data rarely represent complete systemic context sets where all items are included (cf. Schiffer, 1972, 1973). The application of the index to only *one* partial set, whether the partial set is representative of the complete set or not, would be inappropriate. However, archaeologists are almost exclusively concerned with making comparisons between two or more partial sets, and it seems not inappropriate to utilize the index as a relative measure provided that the partial sets represent the complete sets. It is proposed that the diversity index provides a relative measure of diversity between two or more partial sets when it is assumed that they represent the complete sets.

Another problem centers on the isolation of meaningful sets (N) and subsets (N1, N2, . . . Nn) and making item assignments. Since there are no established rules for making these distinctions, especially on artifactual data, set inclusion rules must initially depend on arguments of reasonableness and ultimately on experimentation. Experimentation should include computing the index on different trial divisions of the same set as well as the sum of these different trial outcomes (Wilson and Bossert, 1971: 145–6).

Using the diversity index to identify the locus of strain, and thereby conditionally to monitor stress, is contingent upon the following assumptions:

1) Diversity is a manifestation of strain.
2) A relative measure of diversity provides a relative measure of strain.
3) The diversity index actually measures diversity in the archaeological record.
a) The partial sets measured in the archaeological context actually represent the total sets in the systemic context.
b) The partial sets measured actually reflect strain in the system.
4) Variations in diversity reflect variations in system strain. Only stress induced strains cause an increase in diversity.

The priority of identifying behavioral diversity associated with strain derives from the recognition that archaeologists are generally interested in behavior and in environmental factors only as they affect behavior. Previous studies of response to stress have emphasized identification of the environmental stress factor even when the techniques of palaeoenvironmental reconstruction are insufficient for a thorough reconstruction. By focusing on behavior under stress we are not only nearer that which we seek to explain, but we also allow for the possibility that all critical environmental factors cannot be examined. If strain can be isolated, then it may be possible to estimate the environmental factor responsible when that factor cannot be measured and examined directly. In many cases it may be sufficient to know only that strain was present regardless of the specific stress factor producing that strain.

THE TEST AT GRASSHOPPER RUIN

A theoretical framework and major methodological operations for the archaeological investigation of relationship between environmental stress and human behavior have been presented. What remains is to specify the concepts and operations that permit examination of the problem at Grasshopper ruin.

Today Grasshopper is a large pueblo ruin of approximately 500 rooms situated in an open meadow along Salt River Draw, ten miles northwest of Cibecue on the Fort Apache Indian Reservation (Thompson and Longacre, 1966; Longacre and Reid, 1974). Beginning around A.D. 1275 Grasshopper became an active pueblo growing quickly into one of the largest communities in what is now east central Arizona. After a relatively brief occupancy ending around A.D. 1400 the pueblo was abandoned forever. What conditions prompted people to aggregate then abandon Grasshopper? These questions have intrigued investigators at Grasshopper and at other prominent Southwestern ruins.

The specific problem to be investigated at Grasshopper is the effect of climatic variation (E) on the processes of pueblo aggregation and abandonment. If these processes are a response to stress, then stress should be manifested in strain during the period of aggregation, the period of abandonment or both. Subsistence strain is examined by looking at components (k_1) of the subsistence system (S_1) during the period of aggregation and abandonment. Subsistence strain during these periods is compared since the identification of strain is contingent upon a relative measure. This means that without an absolute standard for comparison, both aggregation and abandonment could have been responses to stress (see Grebinger and Adam, 1974, for a related discussion).

To simplify and make more explicit this examination of Grasshopper data, the research design is briefly outlined. The research design is more than processual chic, it duplicates both by intent and coincidence the actual conduct of the research.

1) *The Behavioral Regularity (Law)*
Diversity promotes stability. Under conditions of subsistence stress, stability of a cultural–behavioral system is restored by an increase in diversity of subsistence related procurement and processing tools, and behavior.

2) *The Hypothesis*
At Grasshopper aggregation occurred in response to local conditions of environmental stress. The null hypothesis of no association needs no formal statement.

3) *Acceptance–Rejection Criteria*
   3.1) If the hypothesis is to be *retained,* then the subsistence strain for the period of aggregation should be greater than or equal to the subsistence strain for the abandonment period.
   3.2) If the hypothesis is to be *rejected,* then the subsistence strain for the period of aggregation should be less than the subsistence strain for the abandonment period.

4) *Correlating Events: Aggregation, Abandonment and Subsistence Behavior*
It is necessary to isolate two contrasting sets of behavioral data, one representing procurement behavior and artifacts of the aggregation period, the other representing those of the abandonment period. A room abandonment measure was constructed to impose relative temporal control over the mass of data from excavated rooms at Grasshopper. The derivation of this measure is presented elsewhere (Reid, 1973; Reid, Schiffer and Neff, 1975). Four Room Abandonment Classes (RAC) are equated with the period of aggregation and abandonment as follows:
   4.1) *Aggregation = RAC 4 (early)*[1]. Remains in the secondary refuse (fill) of rooms within early abandonment class (RAC 4) represent food resources, procurement and processing tools of the aggregation period.
   4.2) *Abandonment = RAC 1 (late).* Remains in the secondary refuse (fill) of rooms within late abandonment class (RAC 1) represent food resources, procurement and processing tools of the abandonment period.
   4.3) *Abandonment = RAC 1 (late) and RAC 2 (probably late).*

Remains in the secondary refuse (fill) of rooms within the late abandonment class (RAC 2) represent food resources, procurement and processing tools of the abandonment period.

No simple application of the room abandonment measure is possible with plant resources since floated ethnobotanical remains come from floor or subfloor features, proveniences not explicitly ordered by the room abandonment measure. These proveniences must be considered in order to have a reasonable quantity of plant remains for analysis. The room abandonment measure provides the framework from which additional criteria are derived for assigning seed remains to aggregation and abandonment periods (Reid, 1973: 145–8).

5) *Systemic Transformations (Test Implications)*
Systemic transformations relate systemic context variables and information to specific units of analysis (Reid, 1973; Schiffer, 1973). Quantitative and qualitative measures of subsistence strain are applied to subsistence related behavior and tools as indicated in the following systemic transformations adapted from Hill and Plog (1970: 3). During periods of subsistence strain an increase is expected in:

5.1) the diversity of animals procured for food.
5.2) the diversity of plants procured for food.
5.3) the use of normally unused domestic animals as food resources.
5.4) the use for food of "scrubby" animals, those with a lower ratio of usable meat to total biomass.
5.5) the diversity of implements and facilities used in food procurement and processing.

6) *Identification Transformations (Analytic Units Operationalized)*
Identification transformations relate or operationalize units of analysis within the systemic context to units of observation within the archaeological context (Reid, 1973; Schiffer, 1973). Units of observation are the units of space and material remains recognizable in the archaeological record from their formal, spatial, quantitative and relational attributes.

6.1) *Diversity* is what the diversity index measures.
6.2) *Animals* are identified from osseous material according to identification procedures developed by zoologists and zooarchaeologists.
6.3) *Food-animals* include all edible animals minus unreasonable inclusions (modern fauna) and burrowing animals with nearly complete skeletons indicating death by natural rather than human agents (cf. Thomas, 1971).
6.4) *Plants* are identified from pollen, seeds and assorted plant parts

according to identification procedures developed by botanists and ethnobotanists (Bohrer, n.d.).

6.5) *Food-plants* include all edible plants. Cultivated and wild species are separated according to botanical criteria.

6.6) The use of *domestic animals as food* is identified by the occurrence of butchering and skinning marks on the bones of domestic animals (dog).

6.7) *"Scrubby" food-animals* are identified as those with a lower ratio of usable meat to total biomass.

6.8) The identification of *food procurement and processing tools* is a worrisome problem that is solved here in the most expedient manner possible. Since projectile points are the only tools used in this analysis, I will rely upon the reasonableness of the assertion that projectile points were used as parts of implements for hunting animals without documenting how one identifies projectile points and associates them with animal procurement.

7) *Assumptions*

The investigation of subsistence strain during the period of aggregation at Grasshopper incorporates the following assumptions:

7.1) The data sets and subsets isolated for the periods of aggregation and abandonment are representative and equivalent.

7.2) These data sets maintain the potential for reflecting subsistence strain.

7.3) Only stress induced strains cause an increase in diversity.

7.4) The diversity index provides a relative measure of strain.

TESTS FOR SUBSISTENCE STRAIN AT GRASSHOPPER RUIN

ANIMAL PROCUREMENT

This test uses data (excluding bird remains) collected through room excavation from 1963 to 1970. The specimens were analyzed and identified by Mathews and Greene (1972) of the National Park Service. They recorded specimens by provenience and identified each specimen to the species level when possible. A count of individual animals or minimum faunal count (MFC) was provided for each provenience. The MFC is used in computing the diversity index.

The data cards are grouped by room provenience, and the rooms are further grouped into Room Abandonment Classes (RAC 1 to 4). Only faunal remains in the secondary refuse (fill) above the last occupied floor are used. Specimens found in contact with a room floor and those below a floor are not used. Summary tabulations of animal remains from secondary refuse of excavated rooms are grouped according to Room Abandonment Class (Reid, 1973: Table 2).

The diversity index for the four faunal data sets as well as for RAC 2 and RAC 3 are presented in Table 1.

TABLE 1
Faunal Diversity by Room Abandonment Class (RAC)

Room Abandonment Class	Diversity index
1	4.04
2	4.886
4	4.41
1 and 2	4.96

The diversity index is computed using the minimum faunal count (MFC) within the secondary refuse of room abandonment classes as the total set (N). Subsets ($N1$, $N2$, ... Nn) are formed by genera. Minimum faunal counts for each genus provide the raw numbers entered into the equation. The results of the animal procurement test are ambiguous and do not support the hypothesis since:

$$\text{RAC 4 (Aggregation)} > \text{RAC 1 (Abandonment)}$$
$$4.41 \qquad\qquad 4.04$$

$$\text{RAC 4 (Aggregation)} < \text{RAC 1 and RAC 2 (Abandonment)}$$
$$4.41 \qquad\qquad 4.96$$

PLANT PROCUREMENT

This test for the presence of subsistence strain utilizes plant remains collected from flotation of room proveniences excavated in 1969, 1970, and 1971. The flotation samples are identified and discussed by Bohrer (n.d.). Although Bohrer has conducted extensive research and analysis on seed remains, pollen, and the modern plant communities, only the seed remains are utilized in this test. Qualitative features of these and other plant data presented by Bohrer (n.d.) are discussed later.

Bohrer (n.d.: Table 1) identified seed remains according to room and intra-room provenience. These data have been grouped into an early period and late period (Reid, 1973: Tables 4 and 5).

These data sets are divided into subsets according to cultivated and wild plants, and are further divided into genera. Only the presence of a genus is noted. The number of different genera within the cultivated and wild subsets are the counts used in computing the diversity index.

The diversity index for the aggregation period is greater than the index for the later period, thus indicating increased subsistence strain during the period of aggregation. The hypothesis is supported since:
Early Plant Resources (Aggregation)—1.636/>1.258—Late Plant Resources (Abandonment).

"SCRUBBY" FOOD-ANIMAL PROCUREMENT

Qualitative evidence for strain lies primarily within the faunal data. Perhaps the most interesting distribution in faunal remains is in deer (*Odocoileus* sp.), rabbits (*Sylvilagus* sp. and *Lepus* sp.), and squirrels (*Citellus* sp. and *Sciurus aberti*). Frequencies are calculated against total MFC in each Room Abandonment Class (Reid, 1973: Table 5). Through time the frequency of deer increases, while that of rabbit and squirrel decreases. Even though rabbit and squirrel are definitely smaller than deer (*Odocoileus* sp.), they are not for that reason necessarily "scrubbier." If one takes the ratio of usable meat to biomass as a measure of "scrubbiness," there is no difference between rabbit and deer since both provide 50% usable meat (White, 1953: 396–8). Squirrels (*Citellus* only) are less "scrubby" than either deer or rabbit in providing 70% usable meat (White, 1953: 398). Consequently, the implication of increased procurement of "scrubby" animals as an indicator of subsistence strain is not convincingly met during the early period when a ratio of usable meat to biomass is used as a measure of "scrubbiness." I feel, however, that the "scrubby" index is a poor measure. In order to approximate the amount of usable meat in one deer one would have to rustle 100 squirrels or 33 rabbits (*Lepus*). A meaningful measure must take into account energy output in procurement activities. In this regard if procurement of smaller animals indicates a decrease in energy return for energy expended and, thus, subsistence strain, then the higher frequency of rabbit and squirrel procurement during the early period supports the hypothesis of subsistence strain during aggregation (see Smith, 1974).

The increase in the frequency of deer through time is noted by Mathews and Greene (1972) in their presentation of faunal remains from different levels of the corridor south of Plaza I. Their discussion of mule deer (*Odocoileus hemionus*) centers on the age-classes represented in the total sample. Seventy-one percent of the deer in the Grasshopper sample are subadult, around 18 months old, in contrast to the average life-span for mule deer which is eight to nine years. Mathews and Greene (1972) interpret this distribution to mean that the mule deer population in the Grasshopper region was maintained under conditions of severe stress through heavy exploitation.

A brief test was made to determine if the frequency of age-classes in deer changed through time. Remains of deer (*Odocoileus* sp.) in secondary refuse room proveniences within RAC 1 (late) and RAC 4 (early) were tabulated according to age-class and size. The minimum faunal count was utilized when possible, yet with many large provenience units this was impossible. In the latter case, each identified specimen was tabulated, and this may have introduced an error increasing the adult age-class. The results are presented in Reid (1973: Table 6).

The 71% immature deer noted by Mathews and Greene (1972) in the total collection is not duplicated in either of the RAC samples representing early and late deer procurement. There is, however, a shift from 49% immature deer early to 36.2% immature deer late. This trend possibly indicates that the exploitation stress on the deer population noted by Mathews and Greene was more pronounced during the early period than during the late period. From this perspective, the presence of subsistence strain during the early period is again supported. However, one must note that when the young adult age-class is combined with the immature age-class, there is absolutely no difference in age-class frequencies between the early and the late periods.

PROCUREMENT AND PROCESSING TOOLS

It was originally thought that artifacts could be examined for evidence of diversity in behavior leading to the identification of subsistence strain. However, the abandonment measure indicated that comparable sets of artifacts representing early and late manufacture, use and discard could not be derived easily from the collections at hand (see Ciolek-Torrello and Reid, 1974). Research by Richard Ciolek-Torrello with metates indicates that the bulk (81.8%) of the metates in the available collection represent late discard and probably late manufacture and use from late room floors. Comparable sets of metates are not found on early room floors.

In 1974 Patricia Beirne, a student at The University of Arizona Archaeological Field School at Grasshopper, designed a project to test the hypothesis that an increase in the diversity of diet is directly correlated with an increase in the diversity of procurement tools. Using projectile points and working with data records, she tabulated all whole points from secondary refuse (fill) of excavated rooms noting five attributes—length, width, blade outline, base outline and notching. Dividing these data into

early and late sets according to the room abandonment measure, she
computed a diversity index using the formula presented here as well as one
of her own derivation. Both formulas resulted in consistent values showing
a greater diversity for the early projectile points, those associated with the
aggregation period. Her results support the hypothesis of subsistence
strain during aggregation.

EVALUATION

The quantitative tests did not produce consistent results showing a greater
diversity during the aggregation period. The tests on plant procurement
and on procurement tools support the hypothesis while the test on animal
procurement is equivocal. The qualitative test results are also ambiguous
and hardly compelling in their weak support of the hypothesis. Therefore,
the hypothesis that aggregation occurred in response to local conditions of
environmental stress is not retained.

SOURCES OF ERROR AND ALTERNATIVE INTERPRETATIONS

I approach this section with the belief that "truth will sooner out from error
than from confusion" (Francis Bacon quoted in Platt, 1964: 350). The
discussion of possible error will center on problems of correlating events in
time, the diversity index and the adequacy of data.

   A central concern is the correlation of room abandonment classes with
the periods of aggregation and abandonment. I am confident that RAC 1
and RAC 2 represent abandonment and fill of rooms as the site was undergoing abandonment. This confidence does not apply to the correlation of
RAC 4 with the period of aggregation. This correlation has not been
demonstrated, nor is it likely to be so demonstrated, until a reliable
construction sequence is formulated and combined with the room
abandonment measure and tree-ring dates. The room abandonment
measure was formulated to avoid the common assumption of a constant
use-life for pueblo rooms. In effect, this assumption is retained since the
application of the measure in this analysis must assume regular and
constant abandonment of rooms. The problem of absolutely correlating
RAC 4 with the period of aggregation cannot be resolved at this time.

   Another problem is the applicability of the diversity index. I do not
question that the index actually measures diversity and, although I
intuitively feel it to be a fragile measure when applied to archaeologically
derived sets of data, I think that this condition is a product of constructing

data sets and subsets and not of the argument behind the application of the measure.

The major concern in applying the measure is in forming subsets so that items can be assigned and counted. In the faunal analysis this was not a problem since biological taxa were employed. In tests on floral remains this concern is a possible source of error since the subset divisions—cultivated, semi-cultivated, and wild plants—are the simplest and most accessible but only one of many possible divisions. The subdivision of artifactual materials remains a problem for which there is no easy resolution.

The problem of data adequacy involves two related questions: (1) do the partial sets in the archaeological context, measured for diversity, represent the total sets in the systemic context? and, (2) do the partial sets measured actually reflect subsistence strain in the systemic context? There is no immediate answer to the first question at this time, although the assumption is necessary to the application of the measure. It is anticipated that further concern with sampling will provide more reliable estimates of systemic context parameters (Reid, Schiffer and Neff, 1975).

The second question is more important to the identification of subsistence strain, for it addresses the problem of whether variations in diversity actually reflect variations in human behavioral responses to stress. It has been assumed that frequency differences in animals and plants through time reflect differences in procurement choices and that changes in diversity, therefore, reflect changes in procurement behavior. This may not be the case with plants and animals in a changing environment, and it cannot be demonstrated that the differences in diversity do not represent differences in availability. Under these conditions, the diversity index would be an incomplete measure of community (plant and animal) diversity and not reflect behavioral diversity. This possibility underscores the investigation of artifactual remains in identifying strain. As the specialist investigating environmental change must take into account the effects of human behavior (Bohrer, n.d.; also Lytle-Webb, this volume), so must the archaeologist interested in behavioral change consider the possibility of intervening environmental variables.

I am not entirely satisfied with the outcome of the analysis in that some quantitative measures are not fully supported by the qualitative appearance of some of the data. Diversity in plant remains is highest during the early period assumed to be associated with aggregation, yet the frequency trends indicate that during the late or abandonment period there is a slight increase in different wild plant genera, a slight decrease in cultivated plant genera, and an increase in the procurement of deer. It is not certain to what extent the plant remains are representative of plant procurement behavior during these two periods.

If qualitative trends tend to indicate an increased emphasis upon hunting and collecting during the late period, does this change of emphasis represent a response to environmental stress? The palaeoclimatic reconstruction (Dean and Robinson, n.d.) indicates a return to normal moisture conditions after A.D. 1320, but the reconstruction ends shortly after A.D. 1350. There is no evidence from which to infer the possibility of environmental stress. Furthermore, the presence of maize throughout the sequence and the presence of *Cucurbita* sp. pollen in late rooms both indicate that agriculture is not necessarily decreasing and is perhaps not under stress. If there is no evidence that some environmental factor produced stress and no significant decrease in agriculture, then why was Grasshopper abandoned? This is an unsettling question. Several possible answers deserve consideration.

There may have been climatic stress as yet undetected. The lack of palaeoclimatic data prohibits a reconstruction from A.D. 1350 to 1400, the projected terminal date for complete abandonment of the pueblo. In addition, there may have been an environmental stress factor, as yet undiscovered, that would not show up in a palaeoclimatic reconstruction and would not register using the diversity index on a limited number of data sets. In such a case, the term "environmental stress" would be inappropriate as the condition may have been fostered by the prehistoric inhabitants themselves. For example, if construction of the Grasshopper pueblo consumed 12,000 to 14,000 trees (Dean and Robinson, n.d.), it is not improbable that the immediate area could have been stripped bare of usable wood for construction, heating and cooking. Wood choppers and gatherers would have to go increasingly farther away from the pueblo to gather wood until returns diminished to the point that it may have been simply more efficient to live elsewhere. The decrease through time of Abert's squirrel, *Sciurus aberti,* may indicate thinning of the ponderosa pine. This possibility, among many others, should lead to a consideration of a system's tolerance threshold in terms similar to Leibig's law of the minimum. According to Odum (1971: 106):

To occur and thrive in a given situation, an organism must have essential materials which are necessary for growth and reproduction. These basic requirements vary with the species and with the situation. Under steady-state conditions the essential material available in amounts most closely approaching the critical minimum needed will tend to be the limiting one.

It is possible that a minimum in one or more critical resources was reached with no available option left to the prehistoric inhabitants except to move to a new area where these resources could be secured within tolerance limits. Identifying fluctuations in these critical resources is not an easy task using only environmental data. Nonetheless, it is precisely in situations like this that the identification of strain by the method derived here permits one to monitor the effects of these critical resources through time.

The increase in deer procurement through time may not reflect agricultural failure as much as increased hunting. What may be indicated is the postulated seasonal occupation of canyon sites during a dispersion phase (Reid, 1973). It is suggested that hunting deer during the late fall and winter in the lower canyon elevations would have been an efficient exploitation strategy. Whether or not this is actually the case remains to be demonstrated. The significant point is this: if Grasshopper were occupied seasonally prior to complete abandonment, then the identification of strain at Grasshopper would only partially represent the total system strain during this period. That is, if the late period at Grasshopper represents a seasonal manifestation of the total system, then the identification of strain during the late period would also be a partial reflection of the total and, therefore, would not be equivalent to the early period. This possibility underscores the need for a regional perspective in investigating response to environmental stress.

The investigation of stress factors in the social environment should also be considered. The excessive attention of archaeologists to the treatment of the environment as an independent variable has recently been replaced by considerations of population growth. In a definitely non-Malthusian view of man–resource relationships, Boserup (1965) maintains that population varies independently of resources and determines the limits of the resources. She argues that agricultural intensification need not be accompanied by technological change but by an increase in labor input by more frequent cropping, weeding, irrigation, and terracing. Population-induced stress is an intriguing possibility for the stress culprit (Longacre, 1975), but one that cannot be handled within the framework of the hypothesis test here.

This discussion has emphasized the development of a more rigorous theory for modeling the interaction of human behavior under stress conditions and a more precise method for achieving explanations of responses to stress. The focus of this theory and method has been human behavior and its priority in the investigation of responses to stress. And though the test at Grasshopper produced inconclusive results, it serves well to illustrate application of the method to particular cases. That particular cases will someday be illuminated is not only the traditional benediction of archaeological research, but also a confident appraisal of our ability to give form and substance to the events of prehistory when attention focuses on human behavior.

NOTE

1) Room Abandonment Class 3 has been deleted from the present analysis because of functional differences in the rooms that render them nonequivalent to rooms in the other classes.

ACKNOWLEDGMENTS

The thoughts expressed here were originally aired in a dissertation with a similar title and the same author. That the aroma has substantially improved is in large part due to comments and criticisms by Richard S. Ciolek-Torrello, Jeffrey S. Dean, Paul Grebinger, William A. Longacre, Michael B. Schiffer, Raymond H. Thompson and R. Gwinn Vivian. The research upon which the example is based was sponsored by the Department of Anthropology and the Arizona State Museum with the consent and cooperation of the White Mountain Apache Tribal Council and supported by the National Science Foundation as part of The University of Arizona Archaeological Field School. I am solely responsible for any noxious vapors that may remain.

REFERENCES

Ashby, W. R. (1968) Variety, constraint and the law of requisite variety. In *Modern Systems Research for the Behavioral Scientist*, edited by W. Buckley, pp. 129–36. Aldine, Chicago.

Bohrer, V. (n.d.) Plant remains from rooms at Arizona P:14:1. In Multidisciplinary research at the Grasshopper ruin, edited by W. A. Longacre. *Anthropological Papers of The University of Arizona* (In press, ms. 1972).

Boserup, E. (1965) *The Conditions of Agricultural Growth*. Aldine, Chicago.

Buckley, W. (1968) Society as a complex adaptive system. In *Modern Systems Research for the Behavioral Scientist*, edited by W. Buckley, pp. 490–513. Aldine, Chicago.

Ciolek-Torrello, R. and J. J. Reid (1975) Change in household size at Grasshopper. *The Kiva* 40, 39–47.

Clarke, D. L. (1968) *Analytical Archaeology*. Methuen, London.

Dean, J. S. (1969) Chronological analysis of Tsegi phase sites in northeastern Arizona. *Papers of the Laboratory of Tree-Ring Research* 3. The University of Arizona Press, Tucson.

Dean, J. S. and W. Robinson (n.d.) Dendrochronology of Grasshopper pueblo. In Multi-disciplinary research at the Grasshopper ruin, edited by W. A. Longacre. *Anthropological Papers of The University of Arizona* (In press, ms. 1972).

Grebinger, P. and D. P. Adam (1974) Hard times?: Classic period Hohokam cultural development in the Tucson Basin, Arizona. *World Archaeology* 6, 226–41.

Hanson, J. A. (1975) Stress response in cultural systems: a prehistoric example from east-central Arizona. In Chapters in the Prehistory of Eastern Arizona, IV. *Fieldiana: Anthropology* 65.

Hill, J. N. and F. T. Plog (1970) Research design for 12th Southwestern Ceramic Conference. Manuscript, Department of Anthropology, University of California, Los Angeles. Mimeograph.

Longacre, W. A. (1975) Population dynamics at the Grasshopper pueblo, Arizona. In Population studies in archaeology and biological anthropology: a symposium, edited by A. C. Swedlund, pp. 71–4. *Society for American Archaeology, Memoir* 30.

Longacre, W. A. and J. J. Reid (1974) The University of Arizona Archaeological Field School at Grasshopper: eleven years of multidisciplinary research and teaching. *The Kiva* 40, 3–38.

Margalef, R. (1968) *Perspectives in Ecological Theory.* University of Chicago Press, Chicago.

Mathews, T. W. and J. L. Greene (1972) The mammalian fauna of Grasshopper ruin, Navajo County, Arizona. Paper presented at the 1972 Meeting of the Society for American Archaeology, Bal Harbor.

Miller, J. G. (1965a) Living systems: basic concepts. *Behavioral Science* **10,** 193–237.

Miller, J. G. (1965b) Living systems: structure and process. *Behavioral Science* **10,** 337–79.

Miller, J. G. (1965c) Living systems: cross-level hypotheses. *Behavioral Science* **10,** 380–411.

Odum, E. P. (1971) *Fundamentals of Ecology.* W. B. Saunders, Philadelphia.

Platt, J. (1964) Strong inference. *Science* **146,** 347–53.

Reid, J. J. (1973) Growth and response to stress at Grasshopper pueblo, Arizona. Ph.D. dissertation, The University of Arizona, Tucson.

Reid, J. J., M. B. Schiffer and J. M. Neff (1975) Archaeological considerations of intrasite sampling. In *Sampling in Archaeology,* edited by J. W. Mueller, pp. 209–24. The University of Arizona Press, Tucson.

Schiffer, M. B. (1972) Archaeological context and systemic context. *American Antiquity* **37,** 156–65.

Schiffer, M. B. (1973) Cultural formation processes of the archaeological record: applications at the Joint Site, east-central Arizona. Ph.D. dissertation, The University of Arizona, Tucson.

Smith, B. D. (1974) Middle Mississippi exploitation of animal populations: a predictive model. *American Antiquity* **39,** 274–91.

Steila, D. (1972) *Drought in Arizona.* Division of Economic and Business Research, The University of Arizona, Tucson.

Thomas, D. H. (1971) On distinguishing natural from cultural bone in archaeological sites. *American Antiquity* **36,** 366–71.

Thompson, R. H. and W. A. Longacre (1966) The University of Arizona Archaeological Field School at Grasshopper, east-central Arizona. *The Kiva* **31,** 255–75.

Watt, K. E. F. (1972) Man's efficient rush toward deadly dullness. *Natural History* February: 74–82.

White, T. E. (1953) A method of calculating the dietary percentage of various food animals utilized by aboriginal peoples. *American Antiquity* **18,** 396–8.

Wilson, E. O. and W. H. Bossert (1971) *A Primer of Population Biology.* Sinauer, Stamford, Connecticut.

Santa Cruz Valley Hohokam: Cultural Development in the Classic Period

PAUL GREBINGER

Eisenhower College

and

DAVID P. ADAM

The University of Arizona*

We present a new basis for understanding Classic period Hohokam cultural development in the Santa Cruz Valley, Arizona, using cluster and principal component analyses in the study of grave goods at Paloparado ruin, and discriminant and canonical variate analysis in the study of design attributes on Tanque Verde Red-on-brown ceramics from five sites in the Tucson Basin. We find patterns of variability among burial groups in the placement of grave goods and account for them as effects of the aggregation of people from physically and socially distant communities. The analysis of ceramic design reveals patterns that are ascribed to change in design style through time, to the existence of local design traditions and to the effects of the relocation of people in the late Classic period. The patterns and their interpretations form the basis for a model of Hohokam cultural development in which we postulate the operation of negative feedback processes in the Classic period. Attempts by others to test implications of the model neither confirm nor disprove it, but have produced information of considerable importance in structuring future research.

Archaeological investigation in the Santa Cruz Valley, Arizona has been conducted with many purposes guiding the collection of material culture. Not the least of these was a desire to know more about the social and cultural behavior of the occupants of the valley. Nonetheless, archaeological research generally consisted in the definition of local chronology and in "trait" distribution studies which gave little insight into the behavior of people or changes in that behavior through time. In 1969 and 1970 one of us (P.G.) felt that a new look at some old data might lead to a model of cultural process for the Classic period. Two kinds of reanalysis studies were undertaken. A model was developed from these studies and from the evaluation of existing data. Test implications were generated and this has led to further research along lines developed in the model.

---

*Present address: United States Geological Survey, Menlo Park, California 94025.

We use multivariate statistical methods in this study in order to describe and evaluate our data. Cluster and principal component analyses are used in the study of burial groups from the Paloparado ruin (Figure 1), and canonical variate and discriminant analysis are used in the study of Tanque Verde Red-on-brown ceramics from the Tucson Basin (Figure 2).

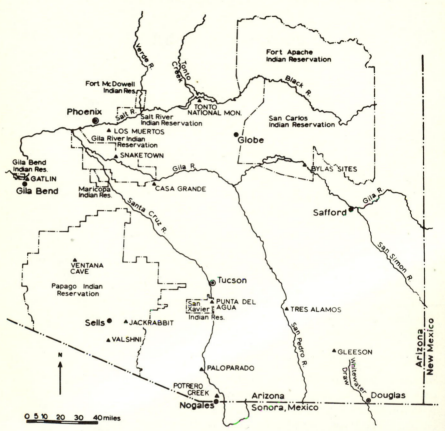

FIGURE 1   Archaeological sites in southeastern Arizona. Solid triangles mark the locations of the sites.

Results of these analyses lead us to postulate relationships between prehistoric communities that have not been evident in previous descriptions and evaluations of data from Classic period Hohokam sites in the Santa Cruz Valley. The model developed here is based on an evaluation of *all* of the analytical results, and the analyses in turn used *all* of the data that we felt were relevant. We think that we would have committed serious methodological errors by either presenting the results of our analyses as

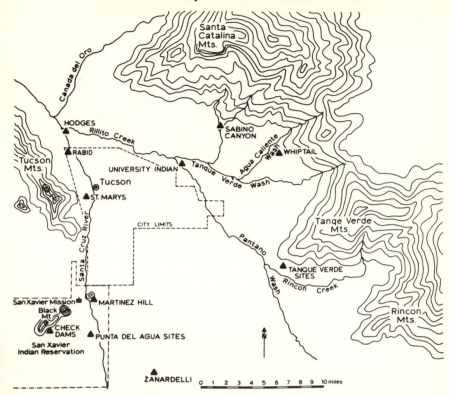

FIGURE 2   Archaeological sites in the Tucson Basin. Solid triangles mark the locations of
the sites. Contours are schematic.

though one part had a clearly logical priority over the other, or by using
one half of our data to test hypotheses derived from the other half. The
process of discovery was not as systematic as the presentation of the analysis
and its interpretation might lead the reader to believe (cf. Meehan, 1968).

VARIABILITY WITHIN A SITE: ANALYSIS OF BURIALS AT PALOPARADO RUIN

Of the ten burial areas defined by excavation in the "Upper Pima"
component (late Classic period) at Paloparado ruin (Arizona DD:8:1
Amerind), six are used in this analysis. A total of 194 burials were found
distributed among these six burial groups, which contained from 17 to 46
burial units each. The burials occurred in spatially delimited clusters
within compounds, each of which consisted of a cluster of noncontiguous

house structures, often enclosed by a wall or banquette. Five of the burial groups were located on the second terrace above the Santa Cruz River and are described by DiPeso (1956). They represent the burial populations from five of twelve compounds which he defined (1956: Figure 83). The remainder of the compounds were either insufficiently excavated to provide an adequate burial sample, or their status as compounds is questionable. Immediately below the second terrace, on the first terrace above the Santa Cruz River, were perhaps two or three other compounds. The sixth burial group (Burial Area 10) was within one of these compounds, and was excavated as a project of the Arizona Highway Salvage Program and reported in Brown (1966), Grebinger (1967) and Brown and Grebinger (1969).

DATA

The attributes or variables used in the cluster and principal component analyses consist of artifact types found in burial context. DiPeso has devised a typological scheme for his artifacts that takes advantage of traditional artifact categories in Southwestern archaeology. However, he further subdivides traditional types into subtypes based on use, form, size and material composition. Use is inferred through reference to archaeological context, through a combination of careful metric analysis and a body of unstated general principles of the relationships between items of material culture and behavior, and through analogy with the uses of material culture among recent Pima and Papago Indians. We make use of these types in this study knowing that they may be unsuitable for the techniques of analysis employed here.

Variables were organized according to two different systems of categorization that enables us to examine the effect of varying classification on computer output. In one system, most artifact types and their subtypes, as defined by DiPeso, were used each as a variable. Those types represented by fewer than five occurrences were eliminated from the analysis, leaving 44 variables.

In a second system, individual types and their subtypes were combined into 12 use categories. The types and subtypes included within the 12 use variables are defined at length in various sections of DiPeso's monograph (1956). Some of the 12 use variables may be directly attributed to DiPeso, and others are our own. DiPeso (1956: 274-9) defined storage and water carrier jars, here combined as storage-transportation vessels: family cooking vessels—stew bowls (1956: 280-1), here designated family stew vessels; personal vessels—cooking (1956: 282-9), here termed cooking vessels; personal vessels—eating (1956: 289-91), here termed eating vessels;

spindle whorls (1956: 387–401); personal ornamentation, here divided into head and neck ornaments, and appendage ornaments; body paint pigments (1956: 78–80), here pigments; and socio-religious objects (1956: 421–32), here socio-religious items. Cutting tools, grinding and abrading tools, and weaving tools are our own categories and combine several distinct categories in DiPeso's classification system. They seem valid, however, on the basis of the functional relatedness of the items within the categories. (For further description see Grebinger, 1971.)

The results of the cluster and principal component analyses based on 12 use variables and on 44 variables taken from among artifact types as defined by DiPeso are similar. Only the results of the analysis of 12 use variables are presented in this paper.

ANALYSIS

For each burial, the 12 variables were recorded as being present, absent or unobservable. The percentage of the burials within each burial area that contained a given attribute was then computed as

$$\% \text{ present} = \frac{\# \text{ present}}{(\# \text{ present} + \# \text{ absent})} \times 100.$$

The unobservable variables within each burial thus did not contribute to the value of the data element for the burial area.

Once the proportions of the attributes present in the various burial areas were calculated, they were subjected to a centering transformation (Orloci, 1967; Adam, 1970). Each data element was expressed as the departure of the observed proportion from the average or expected proportion taken over all groups. Data subjected to the centering transformation are referred to here as "standardized data." "Raw data" are data that have not been subjected to the centering transformation.

Both kinds of data were subjected to a principal component analysis which compared burial areas to each other, using the program BMDO3M of the UCLA Biomedical Computer Programs series (Dixon, 1968), and to a mean-linkage cluster analysis using a program written for the CDC 6400 computer at The University of Arizona Computer Center (Adam, 1970; Sokal and Sneath, 1963).

The principal component analysis of the burial areas is similar to running a canonical variate analysis on the individual burials, but no program capable of accounting for missing data (unobservables) was available for canonical variate analysis. Further discussion of these methods may be found in Adam (1970), as well as in standard multivariate statistical texts.

Raw data

Figure 3 summarizes an analysis in which data are not standardized. These data have not been manipulated to reduce the swamping effect that frequently occurring variables have on the expression of those occurring infrequently. The cluster tree on the left indicates the degree of similarity between burial areas.

Burial Areas 1 and 2 are similar, but not strongly so, as are Burial Areas 5 and 6. The cluster tree further indicates that variables in Burial Area 10 act in a manner unrelated to those in Burial Areas 1 and 2 and, likewise, the Burial Area 4 variables operate in a manner unrelated to those of Burial Areas 5 and 6. Finally, variables in Burial Areas 1, 2 and 10 taken as a group act in opposition to Burial Areas 5, 6 and 4 taken as a group. There are four distinct burial clusters represented in the cluster tree. They are Burial Areas 1 and 2, 5 and 6, 10, and, finally, 4. The latter two are not actually clusters but Burial Areas that are not similar to any others in the sample, including each other.

One question that immediately arises is, which variables are responsible for these relationships? The cluster analysis is no help here, but the principal component analysis is useful. The right side of Figure 3 is a schematic representation of three principal components or factors that account for 79% of the total variance of variables in the data.

Factor I. Burial Areas 1 and 2 have high positive loadings on Factor I. Certain variables account for the similarity between these areas, which have been singled out by their similar high loadings. The variables that account for similarity or difference between burial areas are indicated by the size and the sign of the factor scores (located below the factor loadings). Positive factor scores relate to positive factor loadings. For instance, family stew vessels, cutting tools, grinding or abrading tools and socio-religious items occur in higher than expected frequency in Burial Areas 1 and 2. Conversely, eating vessels and cooking vessels occur in less than expected frequency in those two burial areas. In other words, family stew vessels have the highest positive factor scores (and occur frequently), and eating vessels have the highest negative factor scores (and occur infrequently) in those groups with high positive loadings on Factor I. The opposition in the behavior of opposite signed factor scores is represented in Figure 3 by the High A_1, Low B_1, etc.

Using the same procedure to interpret the correlation between Burial Areas 5 and 6, we find that High B_1 and Low A_1, the reverse of the above, account for the similarity between them. Burial Areas 1 and 2 are negatively correlated with Burial Areas 5 and 6 on the cluster tree. These differences are due to greater than expected frequency of family stew vessels, cutting

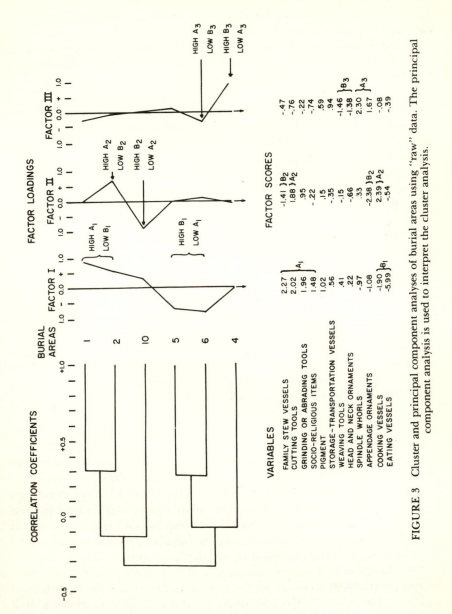

FIGURE 3   Cluster and principal component analyses of burial areas using "raw" data. The principal component analysis is used to interpret the cluster analysis.

tools, grinding and abrading tools and socio-religious items coupled with less than expected frequencies of cooking and eating vessels in Burial Areas 1 and 2, and to a greater than expected frequency of cooking vessels and eating vessels together with low frequencies of family stew vessels, cutting tools, grinding or abrading tools and socio-religious items in Burial Areas 5 and 6.

The other factors may be used in the same way and in combination with Factor I in order to describe what variables account for the similarities and differences expressed in the cluster tree.

Factor II. The cluster tree (Figure 3) indicates that variables act in an opposite manner between Burial Areas 1 and 2, and 10. There is a high positive loading on Factor II for Burial Area 2 and a high negative loading for Burial Area 10. The former is accounted for by High A_2 and Low B_2 among factor scores, the latter by High B_2 and Low A_2. There is a tendency in Burial Areas 2 and 10 for cooking vessels and cutting tools to act in an opposite manner to appendage ornaments and family stew vessels. Cooking vessels and cutting tools occur in greater than expected frequency in Burial Area 2. Appendage ornaments and family stew vessels occur in greater than expected frequency in Burial Area 10.

Factor III. The cluster tree (Figure 3) indicates that variables act in an unrelated manner between Burial Areas 5 and 6, and 4. There is a high positive loading on Factor III for Burial Area 4 and a negative, although not high, loading for Burial Area 6. The latter is accounted for by High A_3 and Low B_3, the former by High B_3 and Low A_3. Spindle whorls and appendage ornaments occur in greater than expected frequencies in Burial Area 6. Storage–transportation vessels and weaving tools occur in greater than expected frequencies in Burial Area 4.

Standardized data

Figure 4 presents the results of the analysis of the data again organized into use categories. However, these data have been standardized by subtracting the expected frequency of a variable from the observed frequency and then dividing by the expected frequency. Standardization should tend to raise the level of correlation by reducing the swamping effect of common variables on the variance. Those variables that occur less commonly have a better chance of being expressed in standardized form.

The cluster tree (Figure 4) shows that Burial Areas 4 and 5 are fairly highly positively correlated. Burial Areas 2 and 6 are positively correlated with one another and 10 is positively, but not strongly, correlated with 2 and 6. Burial Areas 2, 6 and 10 as a group are negatively correlated with Burial Areas 4, 5 and 1 as a group. There are actually three groups shown on the cluster tree, Burial Areas 2, 6 and 10, Burial Areas 4 and 5, and Burial

Area 1. The factors in Figure 4 may be interpreted by the same method
described in the section on nonstandardized data.

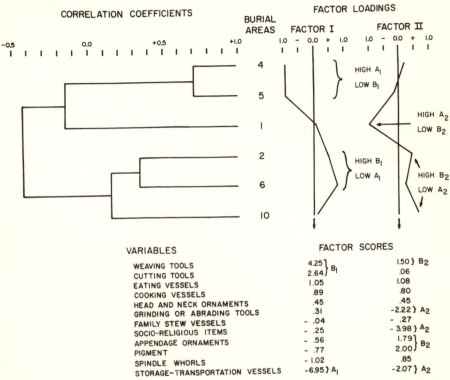

FIGURE 4   Cluster and principal component analyses of burial areas using standardized
data. The principal component analysis is used to interpret the cluster analysis.

Factor I. Burial Areas 4 and 5 have a correlation of .72, the highest
coefficient between burial areas in either the raw data or standardized data
analyses. This correlation is due in part to the higher than expected
frequency of weaving tools and cutting tools in both areas. Both types of
tools occur infrequently among the burials.

Burial Areas 2 and 6 correlate with one another because they both have
greater than expected frequencies of weaving and cutting tools and lower
than expected frequencies of storage–transportation vessels.

Factor II. Burial Area 1 is negatively correlated with Burial Areas 4 and 5
taken as a group. It stands alone. Socio-religious items, grinding or
abrading tools and storage–transportation vessels occur in greater than

expected frequencies in Burial Area 1. Burial Areas 2 and 10 are related. Pigment, appendage ornaments and weaving tools occur in greater than expected frequency in these areas. Socio-religious items, grinding or abrading tools and storage–transportation vessels occur in less than expected frequency.

Comparison of raw data and standardized data analysis results

Figure 5 provides a comparison of the cluster trees in Figures 3 and 4. The cluster analyses using raw data and standardized data differ considerably. The analysis of standardized data produces higher correlations between burial areas than the analysis of raw data. However, the correlations are still low, and negative correlations occur as well. This reflects the lack of similarity between burial areas apparent in the raw percentages. Certain kinds of grave goods always accompany several burials within each area, for example, eating vessels. But there are numerous differences in specific subtypes, or in the kind and quantity of other accompanying artifact types. Low correlation, or low similarity, and negative correlation can be accepted as useful measures of the material results of a particular pattern of behavior.

ASSUMPTIONS

In order to attempt an interpretation of analysis results it is necessary to make certain assumptions about relationships between material culture and behavior. We have organized the data in terms of burial areas, each of which is located within a compound. We assume that the compound in which these burial areas are located represents the residence of a distinct social group. Further, we assume that the burial area within the compound is the cemetery of the social group that occupied the compound. Since the burial population within each compound probably represents interments over several generations, we must assume also that the compound was occupied by the same social group over time. It should be possible to test this assumption of correlation between social group, compound and burial area through the study of stylistic similarities or differences among artifacts in burial and domestic context.

Another assumption fundamental to our interpretation is that the selection of artifacts for interment was nonrandom. In light of the analysis results described above, it seems advisable to state that interactions with the dead as with the living are controlled by compelling socio-cultural rules. Funerary ritual is not capricious behavior. Therefore, if the primary social ties of the deceased were with other members of the compound, then

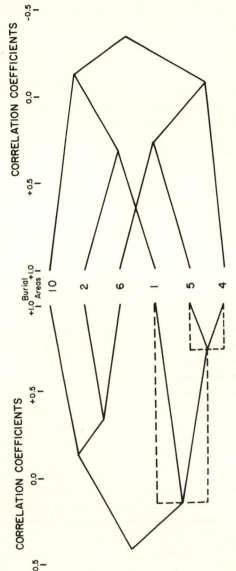

FIGURE 5 A comparison of burial area cluster diagrams that result from standardized data (on the left) and "raw" data (on the right) analyses. Dashed lines are added to show how this diagram relates to the cluster diagrams of Figures 3 and 4.

the status position of the individual within that group will be reflected in the treatment afforded him at death (cf. Binford, 1971). This is the social dimension. Also, we may view the question of random vs. nonrandom behavior in the placement of artifact types in graves through the cultural dimension. The choice of funerary offerings, their quality, quantity, and combinations may reflect distinctive preferences of the groups resident in the compound.

Finally, we assume that funerary ritual is conservative behavior. Among the many subsystems of culture, this one would not be expected to undergo rapid change. The choice of artifact types for inclusion with the deceased is subject to well-established conventions. Alterations in this subsystem only occur in tandem with significant transformations of the total cultural system (cf. Binford, 1971: 14–15).

INFERENCES

In this section we attempt to account for the results of the analysis presented above.

Time dimension

DiPeso was able to establish that the Upper Pima occupation, or late Classic period village, grew from west to east, or toward the edge of the second terrace. His intrasite seriation is based on the following evidence: (1) village wall alterations (the western segment remained stationary while segments were added toward the east); (2) trash heaps (those in the west were larger than those in the east); (3) abandoned houses (there were nearly three times as many abandoned houses in the west as in the east); (4) house feature changes (adobe rim or base boards decrease, raised floors increase replacing the base board, and there is a change in preference from large fire pits to remodeled adobe-lined hearths from west to east at the site); and, (5) Spanish material (the only items recovered come from the vicinity of Compound A along the edge of the second terrace) (DiPeso, 1956: 120–3). The compound on the lower terrace that contains Burial Area 10 exhibits late features and is located on the easternmost extremity of the site (Grebinger, 1967; Brown and Grebinger, 1969: 186–7). Given the above information, the burial areas can be divided into an early and a late group. Burial Areas 1, 5 and 6 are earlier than 2, 4 and 10. The burial areas cannot be further subdivided in time.

The similarities that do exist between Burial Areas 1 and 2, and between 5 and 6 using raw data cannot be interpreted as a function of time. Burial Area 1 is probably earlier than 2, but the same relationship does not hold between Burial Areas 5 and 6. If the correlation between 1 and 2 were higher, it might be explained as a relationship between them through time. The absence of other such continuities might stem from the inadequate sample.

The higher correlations that result from the use of standardized data are more amenable to interpretation in terms of time. Similarities exist between Burial Areas 4 and 5, and among Burial Areas 6, 2 and 10, but at very low levels. These relationships might be explained as being due to time with each branch of the tree representing an earlier and later component of a single local tradition. Burial Area 5 is earlier, Burial Area 4 later; Burial Area 6 is earlier, Burial Areas 2 and 10 later. A third group represented by Burial Area 1 is also indicated.

The preceding results must be carefully evaluated. In order to accept the interpretation based on time, the effect of infrequently occurring items must be evaluated. For example, the correlation between Burial Areas 6, 2 and 10 is based on greater than expected frequencies of weaving and cutting tools, pigment and appendage ornaments, and less than expected frequencies of storage–transportation vessels, socio-religious items and grinding or abrading tools. Only appendage ornaments occur in quantity in all burial areas. The two most highly correlated Burial Areas 2 and 6 are related by the presence in each of relatively rare items. To give an example, five weaving and cutting tools occurred within Burial Area 2 which had only 17 burials. However, since the method of recording data was its presence or absence within a burial, weaving and cutting tools were recorded only three times within the burial area. In other words, three presences in Burial Area 2 are the basis for comparison with Burial Area 6. While this relationship is, therefore, tenuous, it may reflect a significant preference of a particular social group. Few or no other groups used the items in funerary context.

In Burial Area 4 with 36 burials (twice the number in Burial Area 2), there are only two occurrences of weaving and cutting tools. One occurrence was an awl fragment, possibly nothing more than an item of trash fill in the grave. The other was of lithic flakes, perhaps of the same derivation. In short, social groups may have shared a common pattern in the funerary use of a few items, but they did not share a common pattern in the use of most items.

A second point regarding the interpretation of the results of standardized data analysis is that, in spite of the greater similarities between areas there are still three separate groups: Burial Areas 4 and 5, Burial Areas 6, 2 and 10, and Burial Area 1. Burial areas did not cluster into an earlier and a later group. Instead, earlier and later burial areas occurred in the same cluster.

Social dimension

Archaeological analysis of burial populations can throw light on two aspects of past social life, the "social persona" of the deceased and the "composition and size of the social units recognizing status responsibilities to the deceased" (Binford, 1971: 17). Individuals are treated differently according to age, sex, social rank within their group, affiliations with larger order groups to the boundary of the society itself and, finally, peculiar circumstances surrounding death (death in war, death in disgrace, death at a distance).

Our analysis was designed to compare burial areas rather than to discover types of burials. Therefore, it is not very helpful in further defining the status structure of the Paloparado community or of individual social groups within the community. On one hand, the lack of similarity among burial areas described by the cluster analysis, and the high degree of variability in preference for grave goods described by the principal components analysis may indicate differential treatment according to a variety of social components. DiPeso (1956: 515–30) has already satisfactorily demonstrated that males are differentiated from females in that the former were normally accompanied in death by quantities of "personal" ornaments while the latter were not. Also, infants and subadults were differentiated from adults by burial without grave goods. Furthermore, some individuals were buried with tool kits, possibly an indication of an occupation or skill for which they were well-known in life. On the other hand, given multiple status there still should be greater similarity in the treatment of each category between compounds than is indicated by the results of the analysis. This assumes, of course, that compounds may be equated with social groups (see ASSUMPTIONS above).

Our analysis was not designed to define the

composition and size of the social unit recognizing status responsibilities to the deceased.

This aspect of variability is held constant as we assume that the compound was the maximum social boundary in terms of death ritual for the individuals buried within its confines. If social ties beyond the compound are important elements in the structure of mortuary ritual, then differential participation of individuals buried in the compound burial area may well account for the fact that there is no strong pattern of grave goods placement between burial areas.

We have found what seems to be a pattern of heterogeneity among burial areas at the Paloparado ruin. It may be that this pattern can be accounted for in terms of the social dimensions discussed here. However, further analysis along different lines than those here will be necessary (e.g., Brown, 1971; Tainter, 1975).

Cultural dimension

There is yet a third approach to interpreting the results of our analysis. Binford (1963) has presented the model of cultural drift upon which this interpretation is based. We propose that population convergence would account for the lack of similarity in funerary ritual among burial areas. It is possible that social groups, such as those occupying a compound, were dispersed in smaller, more numerous sites prior to their incorporation into the Paloparado community. During this period we would expect social distance between communities to have been great and divergence through cultural drift probably an on-going process. Later amalgamation without accompanying breakdown of the separate traditions for doing things would have produced a pattern of several burial clusters indicating variation in funerary ritual. This alternative seems feasible in terms of what we know about the chronology of the Classic period at the Paloparado ruin, the size of the earlier Colonial and Sedentary period occupations at Paloparado ruin and elsewhere, and the settlement pattern in the Santa Cruz Valley and its tributaries prior to the Classic period (Grebinger, 1971).

EVALUATION

DiPeso's monograph on the Paloparado ruin is an extraordinary achievement in data recording and reporting. Except for some documents in the ill-fated Archives of Archaeology, there are few total site reports in which data are presented in a form that can be used by later investigators with different theoretical and methodological backgrounds. The typological method that DiPeso has used in ordering the vast material collections from the Paloparado ruin must be evaluated, however, as it may be a fundamental source of distortion in the analysis we have attempted.

Although some may quarrel, we think there are methodological similarities in excavation technique, analysis and particularly in presentation of analysis results between DiPeso's work and what has been termed the "conjunctive approach" (Taylor, 1948: 152–202). The over-all impression is that DiPeso was concerned with establishing the Paloparado ruin within its cultural context, that is, the relationships and affinities of all cultural items from the site in order to arrive at

a picture of the site and the life of its people that is historiography (Taylor, 1948: 180).

One way to arrive at this kind of reconstruction without coming to grips with basic epistemological questions about the relationships of material objects and real behavior is to borrow descriptions of the systemic context of the objects from the ethnographic literature. This ignores the fact that the systemic context is 200 (more probably 300 or 400) years removed from the archaeological context (Fontana, 1965; Schroeder, 1957), a period of profound change in native Southwestern cultural systems. The ethnographic literature contains many descriptions about specific episodes of manufacture and use of material objects, but does not describe how these relate to other subsystems of the total culture. As a consequence DiPeso's description of "life" at the Paloparado site emphasizes processes of artifact manufacture and the specific activities (primarily subsistence) in which artifacts were used. Social, political and religious behavior are reconstructed through unstated assumptions and pure speculation. Some of the effect of this approach is mitigated by reference to archaeological context.

Functional typologies derived from a combination of ethnographic analogy, archaeological context and unstated principles of the relationship between material culture and behavior dominate the classification scheme. For example, Tanque Verde Red-on-brown pottery, a type defined in terms of design style, is further divided into seven subtypes: Type 1B—seed jars; Type 2A—water carrying jars; Type 3A—stew bowls; Type 4B-1—single handled jars; Type 7A—shallow bowls; Type 7B—deep bowls; Type 8—personal miniature vessels. We have had to use data in the form presented to us. In short, some of the difficulty in interpreting factors may stem from noise introduced through artifact typologies that do not reflect the systemic context.

We encountered further difficulties related to the fact that the structure of our analysis did not seem particularly well suited to developing inferences about the extinct social system at Paloparado ruin. This is especially unfortunate as the variability that exists may be interpreted differently in the social and cultural dimensions. And, our hunch is that the variability is more likely to stem from the kind of social, political and socio-economic involvements the deceased maintained as a participant in the social life of the Paloparado community as a whole. A promising possibility for further analysis of the social dimension is a recent study by Tainter (1975) in which the information statistic is used to isolate behaviorally meaningful burial types.

In short, our organization of the data tends to isolate the compound with its associated burial area from the larger community. We then compare burial areas in terms of their similarities and differences. We find that the differences are great. But, is this fact a function of variation in normative behavior of the residents of the compound or is it a function of differential involvement in the social life of the larger community?

VARIABILITY AMONG SITES: ANALYSIS OF CERAMIC DESIGN IN THE TUCSON BASIN

While we were developing the alternative interpretations of variability in the treatment of the dead at Paloparado ruin, but before they had taken the above form, we decided that chances of discovering the meaning of variability among burial areas within a site might be improved if we could get some idea of the nature of variability among sites. We entered this analysis without clearly formulated hypotheses. In no sense can this study be considered a test of the interpretations presented above.

Ideally, this analysis would have included sites in the vicinity of Paloparado ruin, sites that bracket it in time, and data that pertain to funerary ritual at these sites. However, none of these requirements could be met. Only in the Tucson Basin (Figure 2), 40 miles downstream, could we find a sample of sites large enough, and a category of material culture sufficiently numerous, to attempt multivariate analysis. Hodges site (Arizona AA:12:18), Rabid (Arizona AA:12:46) and Whiptail (Arizona BB:10:3) ruins of the early Classic period (A.D. 1200–1350), and Martinez Hill (Arizona BB:13:3) and University Indian (Arizona BB:9:33) ruins of the late Classic period (A.D. 1350–1500) were chosen for study. The data we chose were design and form attributes of 159 Tanque Verde Red-on-brown pots. For full presentation of this study see Grebinger and Adam (1974) and Grebinger (1971).

DATA AND ANALYSIS

Canonical variate and discriminant analysis were used in this study in order to describe and evaluate data. The data are attributes of design at three levels of design execution (single elements, element sets and motifs). Each was given the same weight in the analysis. Each was recorded as either present (1) or absent (0). It is assumed in discriminant analysis that data for each group (pots) are multivariate normal with equal variance–covariance matrices. In our study these assumptions could not be met since presence/absence data were used. Nonetheless, we have found that groups of vessels can be successfully separated using this technique. Palaeo-ecological studies (Buzas, 1972), in which the same technique has been used successfully, support this conclusion.

Groups of vessels were adequately separated by using three canonical variates as the axes of a three-dimensional space (Grebinger and Adam, 1974: Table 4). The location of each vessel as well as the site means for 159 Tanque Verde Red-on-brown vessels were projected into this space. Information about the separation of groups of vessels was obtained by observing the dispersal of the symbols that represent vessels in the canonical axis space (Figures 6 and 7). The effectiveness of the separation of the groups was good as indicated by a classification matrix (Table 1). Each row in the matrix corresponds to one of the original vessel groups and each column represents the group to which the individual vessels were assigned by the discriminant analysis. In a completely effective classification only zeros should appear off the principal diagonal of the matrix since each vessel then has been assigned to the group or site from which it came. Not all vessels were assigned to their group of origin. This imperfect classification may be ascribed to the behavior of the pottery makers and to errors in classification.

TABLE 1

Classification matrix of Tanque Verde Red-on-brown vessels according to the discriminant analysis

| Vessel provenience | Number of vessels classified into each site | | | | | |
	Hodges	Martinez Hill	University Indian	Whiptail	Rabid	Total
Hodges	46	3	0	4	4	57
Martinez Hill	3	25	0	3	0	31
University Indian	1	0	10	0	0	11
Whiptail	1	0	0	34	1	36
Rabid	1	0	0	0	23	24

The results of the canonical variate analysis are presented in Figures 6 and 7.

The vessels in Figure 6 (positioned by the first and second canonical variates) may be subdivided into three groups (shown by dashed line) based on the clustering of the groups of vessels about the group mean (indicated by the encircled symbol). The vessels of the Hodges site and Rabid ruin (both of the early Classic period Tanque Verde phase) are grouped together on the diagram. Vessels of Martinez Hill and University Indian ruins (both of the late Classic period Tucson phase) are grouped together. The vessels from Whiptail ruin (Tanque Verde phase) are separated from those of any other site. If the positioning of vessels is considered also in terms of the third canonical variate, a further pattern in the data emerges (Figure 7).

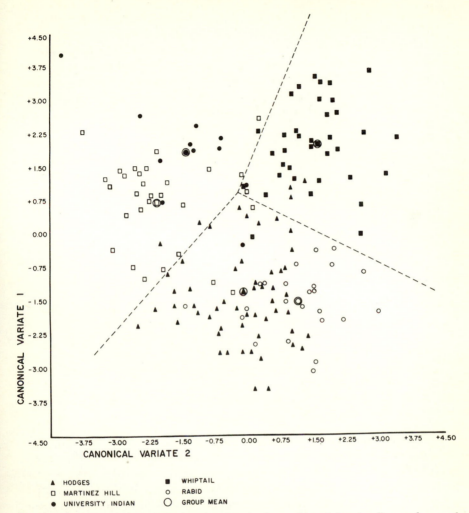

FIGURE 6 Tanque Verde Red-on-brown vessels positioned by the first and second canonical variates.

On Canonical Variate 3 the Hodges site and University Indian ruin tend to have negative values and Rabid and Martinez Hill ruins positive values. Hodges site, University Indian ruin and Whiptail ruin can be grouped together, while Rabid and Martinez Hill ruins can be combined into another group. This information modifies the previous simple configuration in which site groupings appear to reflect periods of cultural development either Tanque Verde or Tucson phase. This new pattern links sites downstream and upstream along the Rillito Creek and the Santa Cruz River.

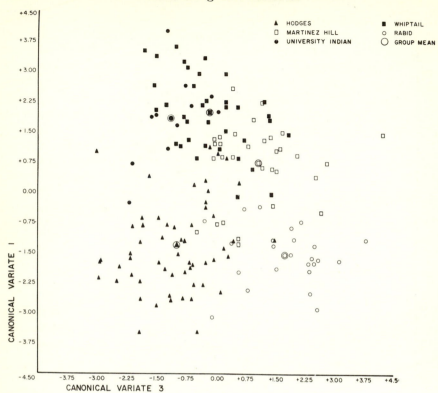

FIGURE 7   Tanque Verde Red-on-brown vessels positioned by the first and third canonical variates.

The discriminant analysis shows that, in general, Tanque Verde Red-on-brown vessels from each site tend to resemble one another more than they do vessels from other sites. Few vessels were cross-classified. Of these four (two under Martinez Hill and two under Whiptail ruins) can be accounted for as misclassified items (bad data), and are not taken into consideration below. The distribution of the remainder represents patterning in the data that requires interpretation.

Four Hodges site vessels cross-classified as more similar to Rabid ruin vessels follow the pattern graphically described by the canonical variate analysis (Figure 6). The same applies to University Indian, Rabid and one of two Whiptail ruin vessels cross-classified as more similar to those from other sites. There are two results of the discriminant analysis that do not conform with those we have already discussed. First, one Whiptail ruin vessel is cross-classified as more similar to Rabid ruin vessels and two Hodges site vessels as more similar to Whiptail ruin vessels even though in canonical variate terms Whiptail vessels as a group are distinct from all others (Figure 6). Second, one Hodges site vessel cross-classified as more similar to Martinez Hill ruin vessels cross-cuts the pattern (in canonical variate terms) that seems to link sites downstream and upstream along the Rillito Creek and the Santa Cruz River. Note, however, that Hodges site is located on the point of land where Rillito Creek joins the Santa Cruz River (Figure 2). Also, six Martinez Hill ruin vessels three of which were cross-classified as more similar to Hodges site vessels, and three more similar to Whiptail ruin vessels, cross-cut the pattern that seems to link sites downstream and upstream along the Rillito Creek and Santa Cruz River.

INFERENCES

In this section we attempt to account for the results of the analysis presented above.

Time dimension

The results of the analysis illustrated in Figure 6 may be interpreted in part as a function of time. On a subjective level Hohokam archaeologists have been aware of differences in the style of Tanque Verde Red-on-brown design between the early and late Classic periods (Tanque Verde and Tucson phases respectively). The first two canonical variates objectively demonstrate this difference. Whiptail ruin is a Tanque Verde phase site and stands apart from Rabid ruin and Hodges site for reasons that are ascribed to the cultural dimension.

Cultural dimension

The group means of Hodges site and Rabid ruin ceramics occur close together in Figure 6. These sites are located within approximately two miles of one another along the Santa Cruz River (Figure 2). Both are Tanque Verde phase sites. The potters of these sites apparently shared in a local tradition of pottery design. Whiptail ruin is located in the northeast corner of the Tucson Basin, approximately 18 miles from Hodges site and Rabid ruin. Whiptail ruin potters must have shared in another distinct local tradition of pottery design. This confirms via objective means still another subjective impression of archaeologists interested in the Santa Cruz Valley.

There is subjective confirmation of the existence of localized stylistic traditions. A Tanque Verde Red-on-brown vessel excavated at Whiptail ruin after our analysis and, therefore, not one of the vessels included within the Whiptail group, has the distinctive attributes of the Hodges site–Rabid ruin ceramics. It happens that this bowl was found nested with others including nonlocal redwares and plainwares. There undoubtedly was interaction between Tanque Verde phase communities throughout the Tucson Basin. The discriminant analysis has produced cross-classifications of Whiptail ruin and Hodges site vessels as more similar to those from other sites of the same phase. This pattern also can be accounted for by interaction. At the moment, however, no priority can be given to any particular mechanism of interaction such as economic exchange or intermarriage.

As a further result of our analysis we find that ceramics from Hodges site (downstream), Whiptail ruin (in the upper bajada), and University Indian ruin (upstream) share similarities. Hodges site, Whiptail ruin and possibly Rabid ruin show no evidence of occupation in the Tucson phase. Among the five sites in our sample, only University Indian and Martinez Hill ruins were inhabited in the late Classic period. Therefore, the stylistic similarities among these communities cross-cut time. We interpret this as evidence of a population shift upstream and down from the bajada to the vicinity of the confluence of Pantano Wash and Rillito Creek during the Classic period. The stylistic similarities between Rabid ruin located down-stream and Martinez Hill ruin upstream may also be attributed to population movements.

The movement of entire village populations may have been involved in the relocation of human settlement. However, sites of the Tucson phase became more densely settled and the number of sites decreased. One result of the discriminant analysis can best be understood in terms of population aggregation. There were vessels in Martinez Hill ruin that are stylistically more similar to vessels from the earlier Hodges and Whiptail ruins. This pattern would be accounted for if population relocation involved the dispersal of some Tanque Verde phase communities into several Tucson phase settlements. In sum, we are postulating two kinds of population movement, one in which an entire community moves as a group to a new locality, and the other, a relocation of segments of a population among communities with whom they had had no previous co-residence.

Social dimension

In order to postulate population movement on the basis of pottery design style similarities we have had to make certain assumptions about the relationships between this form of material culture and the social behavior of the Classic period Hohokam. Following Deetz (1967) we suggest that the stylistic attributes we have used in this analysis relate to the behavior of individual potters. A design repertoire was learned in the context of some social group and perhaps modified through participation in another. The structure and organization of the group or groups is of no concern here. When the group relocates this is expressed as dislocations in space and time of the designs produced by the individual potter members of the group involved. In other words, it is logical and in accordance with general understandings of human behavior to postulate the movement of groups of people to account for the patterns in the data we have discovered. Nonetheless, the material culture on which the inferences are based are the products of individuals.

We have not attempted to discover the nature of the social structure of Tanque Verde or Tucson phase communities. In light of our interpretations of the Paloparado burial analysis and the possibility of population relocation in the Tucson Basin, we feel that a clearer understanding of the social system is now necessary. We think we have established the possibility that the Classic period Hohokam in the Santa Cruz Valley were involved in a dynamic situation that required major redistribution of population. We now wish to explore the means for confirming this possibility.

CLASSIC PERIOD CULTURAL DEVELOPMENT IN THE SANTA CRUZ VALLEY: A MODEL

We think we have detected in two different sets of archaeological data, indications of stress and the nature of the Hohokam population's response. Like Reid (this volume), we are looking at changes through their effects. In this section we propose a model of the events that would account for the patterns we have described in the data. Some implications of this model have been tested since it was first developed and will be presented in the concluding section.

The Tanque Verde phase (A.D. 1200–1350) of the Classic period (A.D. 1200–1500) was a period of population stability in the Santa Cruz Valley. This was the end of a period of range expansion and eventual range budding of Gila-Salt Basin Hohokam populations into the Santa Cruz Valley during the Colonial period (A.D. 500–900) (see Grebinger 1971 for full development of this aspect of the model). By the end of the Sedentary period (A.D. 900–1200) prehistoric communities had become established in two main environmental zones in the Tucson Basin, the riparian zones (Hodges site and Rabid ruin) and the upper bajada (Whiptail ruin). From meager indications this was the pattern throughout the middle Santa Cruz Valley. In the Sedentary period and the Tanque Verde phase of the Classic period there developed a pattern of interaction among communities in which ties were strongest where the least time and space separated their original divergence. Local traditions of pottery decoration, as well as other variations in cultural behavior, might be expected to develop under these conditions (cultural drift).

Between A.D. 1250 and 1350 this pattern was disrupted. The early Classic period sites such as Hodges site, Whiptail ruin, and perhaps Rabid ruin, were abandoned. Fewer, more densely settled sites, located primarily upstream in the riparian zone, became characteristic of the settlement pattern in the Santa Cruz Valley during the Tucson phase. University Indian and Martinez Hill ruins are examples of late Classic period settlements (A.D. 1350–1500). The dating of Paloparado ruin is not well enough controlled for us to know whether it was occupied throughout the Classic period. We think it should be assigned to the Tucson phase (A.D. 1350–1500) (cf. DiPeso, 1956: 264–8). We suggest that the transition from the Tanque Verde to the Tucson phase involved a shift in population from the earlier sites downstream to the later sites located upstream and a shift down from the upper bajada into the riparian zone. The streams were a natural avenue of population movement and focus of population concentration for people dependent upon agriculture for subsistence.

These developments might best be accounted for in terms of negative feedback or deviation-counteracting processes (Maruyama, 1963; Tustin, 1955). Objects in related systems interact with one another in such a way as to counterbalance the effects of an initial deviation in one of the systems. Population movement and aggregation are two responses that human groups can make to a variety of deviations emanating from either cultural or environmental subsystems.

We have explored a variety of possible causal agents (Grebinger and Adam, 1974: 235–7). There are two that seem most probable, only one of which is easily checked. In other areas of the Southwest between A.D. 1100 and 1350 there is a correlation between deteriorating environmental conditions and changes in the distribution of the prehistoric population (Hill, 1970: 82–6; Lytle-Webb, this volume). Deterioration of the environment is attributed to a shift from even distribution of annual rainfall to a pattern in which rainfall became concentrated in torrential summer thundershowers. Heavy summer rainfall brings about headward cutting of streams, heavy alluviation downstream and a lowering of water table below levels suitable for agriculture on the floodplain.

A change in rainfall periodicity is detected in the pollen record by a shift to greater proportions of nonarboreal pollen, especially cheno-ams, relative to arboreal (tree) pollen. Changes in the ratio of arboreal to non-arboreal pollen types, primarily from archaeological contexts, are commonly used to reconstruct the past environment in the Southwest (e.g., Schoenwetter, 1962; Schoenwetter and Eddy, 1964; Hevly, 1964). There is some palynological evidence that similar changes took place in south-eastern Arizona during the thirteenth century (Martin, 1963). None of the existing reconstruction applies directly to the Santa Cruz Valley, however. There are important topographic and climatological differences between parts of the Santa Cruz Valley (especially the Tucson Basin) and areas in which pollen studies have been carried out. We hesitate to extrapolate analysis results too freely, as the effects of environmental deterioration may be somewhat different than reported elsewhere.

The areas that would have been most suitable for cultivation during times of summer dominant rainfall and stream head-cutting were those either downstream (north of the Tucson Basin) beyond the effects of heavy alluviation, or upstream (south and east within the Basin) above the entrenched stream channels and lowered water tables. Both Hodges site and Rabid ruin were located at likely points of alluviation. Swift flowing flood waters and alluviation would have damaged agricultural facilities of all kinds, whether floodwater fields or canals. We have earlier noted that both were abandoned in the Tanque Verde phase, and the pattern described by canonical variate analysis (Figure 7) may be interpreted as the result of movement of Hodges site and Rabid ruin populations upstream. Also, it may be possible to attribute the heterogeneity of burial practices at Paloparado ruin to aggregation of groups with no previous experience of co-residence.

The abandonment of Whiptail ruin under these conditions is not easily accounted for. One causal agent that is not easily checked would be the possibility of population pressure at the eastern periphery of the Santa Cruz Valley. Population movements were common in response to environmental stress in the thirteenth century Southwest. Groups from east central Arizona or west central New Mexico did move south, as is documented at Reeve ruin the the San Pedro Valley, due east of the Tucson Basin (DiPeso, 1958). We are unable to document any such pressure in the archaeological record, although its effects may be present, confounded by the larger effects of change in the natural environment.

In summary, we have developed a model that attempts to account for similar patterns in two sets of archaeological data from the Santa Cruz Valley in terms of adjustments that the Classic period Hohokam population developed in response to changes in their total environment, natural and cultural. Two causal agents are postulated. The usefulness of this model depends upon how well it stands up under attempts to test its various implications.

TESTING THE MODEL

In the final section of this paper we present the results of two recent studies that were designed, in part, as tests of the model. The test implication is first stated, followed by a presentation of research that bears on it.

1) If suitable deposits can be found, there should be palynological evidence of environmental deterioration between A.D. 1200–1350. There should be high frequencies of cheno-am pollen and low pine pollen counts, an indication of a cycle of erosion, headward cutting of streams, alluviation and lowered water tables, all a consequence of a change to a pattern of summer dominant thundershowers.

1A) At the Cienega Creek locality in the Empire Valley *c.* 60 miles southeast of Tucson, Martin has found evidence of a shift from dominant Compositae to cheno-ams. He suggests that

this may represent a change in vegetation induced by cutting in the thirteenth century. Conspicuous channels were cut and filled into beds of late Hohokam age (Martin 1963: 34).

Did similar conditions exist along the Santa Cruz River and Rillito Creek? There is considerable local variation in the headward cutting of streams. As Martin himself points out (1963: 34) with reference to a location along Matty Wash within one-half mile of the Cienega Creek locality:

Schoenwetter encountered a similar shift from Compositae to cheno-ams at a position much higher in the section, within historic time. If the dating is reliable for both sites, an overall climatic control of the composite/cheno-am shift is ruled out and some other factor, perhaps differences in cutting at different points, may explain the change.

We expect that variation in cutting was characteristic of the Santa Cruz Valley as well, with important consequences for interaction of prehistoric communities there.

1B) A study has been made of pollen collected at Whiptail ruin (Lytle, 1971; Lytle-Webb, this volume) in an attempt to reconstruct the palaeoenvironment of the site. The percentages of cheno-ams (weeds) in the samples from Whiptail ruin (30–80%) are larger than in samples from the Sonoran Desert at present and pine pollen counts (0–1%) are as low as counts in surface samples from the site. The Southwest is presently experiencing a cycle of erosion similar to the one that has been postulated for the thirteenth century. One might be tempted to regard these findings as a favorable test for a shift to a summer dominant rainfall pattern during the early Classic period. However, Lytle-Webb interprets them as probably reflecting cultural activities at the site. An archaeological site is an environment produced by man in which nonarboreal pollen producers (weeds) find a favorable habitat while the relative amount of pollen from the natural vegetation is reduced (Lytle 1971: 53). Research at Whiptail ruin has led Lytle-Webb to investigate the effect of human activity on the pollen rain in archaeological sites. Her work (this volume), especially the study of a living Papago village, has led her to caution against the use of pollen collected in archaeological context for the interpretation of past environments.

We have not yet succeeded in establishing environmental change as the causal agent leading to hard times in the Santa Cruz Valley. However, we are a step ahead in knowing that the palaeoenvironment cannot be reliably reconstructed from pollen samples collected in archaeological context. Pollen profiles from localities outside a site (especially along existing and previous water courses) should be studied.

2) A further test implication of the model concerns population response to changing environment. Torrential summer thundershowers would produce headward erosion along streams, as well as downcutting and lateral erosion. Lowered water tables and a reduction of land available for floodwater farming would result. A possible response to a reduction in land available for crops is an increase in the concentration of existing population in the vicinity of the remaining arable land. It is worth noting that interregional conflicts between adjoining populations at the peripheries of the Santa Cruz and San Pedro Valleys could lead to abandonment of sites like Whiptail and aggregation of people in the vicinity of arable land in the riparian zone to the West (e.g., at University Indian ruin). Nevertheless, this phenomenon would not account for the abandonment of communities such as Hodges site and Rabid ruin located in the heart of the Valley.

2A) A recent survey of the Salt-Gila Aqueduct right-of-way (Grady, 1973) has provided support for this suggestion. The survey area is a transect that runs roughly northwest–southeast from two miles west of the Orme Dam site to the town of Marana, approximately 25 miles north of Tucson. The area of the survey is located at least in part in the lower Santa Cruz Valley.

Grady found that "long-term multiple use sites" are most frequently found in proximity to arable land. The survey east of the Picacho Mountains, the section closest to Tucson, revealed two of these sites close to large stream beds. Only one of the two can be dated to the Classic period with certainty, however. Also, of importance in this context is the extremely large Hohokam site along McClellans Wash (Arizona AA:7:4) west of the aqueduct right-of-way. It contains evidence of earlier Colonial and Sedentary period occupation. But, from Grebinger's observation of surface indications, the Classic period occupation was clearly more extensive than in earlier periods. Furthermore, there is evidence of a rainfall runoff control system (canals and possible reservoir) that appears to be associated with the Classic period occupation. Although final confirmation of this test implication will have to await a more systematic survey, we regard it as tentatively confirmed.

3) The model would be further supported if evidence could be found indicating decreasing success in agriculture. The resulting subsistence stress might manifest itself in one or more of the behavior patterns suggested by Reid (this volume). Also, any evidence of increase in dependence on hunted and gathered resources, including simple increase in the number of facilities devoted to getting subsistence from wild foods, could be regarded as a confirmation of the model.

3A) Grady (1973) has found a large number of what he terms "natural resource exploitation stations" along the Salt-Gila Aqueduct Right-of-way. Grady apparently ascribes most sites located along the survey transect to the Classic period. He states (1973: 45) that

> over half of the sites located are interpreted as natural resource exploitation stations, supporting the implication that Classic period subsistence leaned more heavily on wild resources than in previous times.

We have carefully reexamined the survey data and do not feel that they provide firm support for the implication. First, along the segment of the transect crucial to this study, Reach 6 (in the vicinity of the Picacho Mountains north of Marana), natural resource exploitation stations are not abundant nor do they clearly date from the Classic period. Most such stations are found flanking the Gila River, north and east of Florence. Also, we would like to point out that future research designed to test this implication will have to make a clear distinction between the early and late Classic periods, Tanque Verde and Tucson phases. Given the difficulty of accurately dating temporary resource exploitation stations, we think that the most successful checks can be made in conjunction with the excavation of large late Classic period sites.

We feel encouraged by these results in spite of the fact that attempts to test the model have been only partially successful. The work completed so far has pointed directions that future research must take. We are another step closer to a solidly based understanding of Classic period Hohokam cultural development in the Santa Cruz Valley.

ACKNOWLEDGMENTS

We wish to thank William A. Longacre, Emil W. Haury and Raymond H. Thompson for their assistance in guiding the research that led to the model as part of Grebinger's dissertation at The University of Arizona. This work was completed while Adam was a Research Associate at The University of Arizona. Computer time was provided by The University of Arizona Computer Center. The analysis was in part supported by NSF grant GB–7794 to Paul S. Martin.

Charles DiPeso generously offered his time and the collections of the Amerind Foundation, Inc. while analysis of the lower terrace compound artifacts from Paloparado ruin was in progress. Aileen Ayres and Richard Dannells offered valuable assistance in the analysis of Tanque Verde Red-on-brown pottery design. The staff of the Arizona State Museum has been most helpful in making collections available and in providing facilities for the study of Tanque Verde Red-on-brown ceramic design. We thank Dorothy Washburn, Charles DiPeso and anonymous reviewers for their helpful comments on various aspects of this study. We assume full responsibility for the analysis and its interpretation.

REFERENCES

Adam, D. P. (1970) Some palynological applications of multivariate statistics. Ph.D. dissertation, The University of Arizona, Tucson.

Binford, L. R. (1963) "Red ocher" caches from the Michigan area: a possible case of cultural drift. *Southwestern Journal of Anthropology* **19**, 89–108.

Binford, L. R. (1971) Mortuary practices: their study and their potential. In Approaches to the social dimension of mortuary practices, edited by J. A. Brown, pp. 6–29. *Society for American Archaeology. Memoir 25.*

Brown, J. A. (1971) The dimensions of status in the burials at Spiro. In Approaches to the social dimension of mortuary practices, edited by J. A. Brown, pp. 92–112. *Society for American Archaeology, Memoir 25.*

Brown, J. L. (1966) Lithic artifacts from a lower terrace compound at San Cayetano del Tumacacori. Manuscript, Arizona State Museum, Tucson. Typewritten.

Brown, J. L. and P. Grebinger (1969) A lower terrace compound at San Cayetano del Tumacacori. *The Kiva* **34**, 185–98.

Buzas, M. A. (1972) Biofacies analysis of presence or absence data through canonical variate analysis. *Journal of Paleontology* **46**, 55–7.

Deetz, J. (1967) *Invitation to Archaeology*. Natural History Press, New York.

DiPeso, C. C. (1956) The Upper Pima of San Cayetano del Tumacacori: an archeohistorical reconstruction of the Ootam of Pimeria Alta. *The Amerind Foundation, Inc.* 7.

DiPeso, C. C. (1958) The Reeve ruin, southeastern Arizona. *The Amerind Foundation, Inc.* 8.

Dixon, W. J. (1968) BMD biomedical computer programs. *University of California Publications in Automatic Computation* 2.

Fontana, B. L. (1965) On the meaning of historic sites archaeology. *American Antiquity* **31**, 61–5.

Grady, M., S. Kemrer, S. Schultz, and W. Dodge (1973) An archaeological survey of the Salt-Gila aqueduct. *Arizona State Museum Archaeological Series* 23.

Grebinger, P. (1967) A lower terrace compound at San Cayetano del Tumacacori. Manuscript, Arizona State Museum, Tucson. Typewritten.

Grebinger, P. (1971) Hohokam cultural development in the middle Santa Cruz Valley, Arizona. Ph.D. dissertation, The University of Arizona, Tucson.

Grebinger, P. and D. P. Adam (1974) Hard times?: Classic period Hohokam cultural development in the Tucson Basin, Arizona. *World Archaeology* **6**, 226–41.

Hevly, R. H. (1964) Pollen analysis of Quaternary archaeological and lacustrine sediments from the Colorado Plateau. Ph.D. dissertation, The University of Arizona, Tucson.

Hill, J. N. (1970) Broken K pueblo. *Anthropological Papers of The University of Arizona* 18.

Lytle, J. L. (1971) A microenvironmental study of an archaeological site, Arizona BB:10:3, Whiptail ruin. M.A. thesis, The University of Arizona, Tucson.

Martin, P. S. (1963) *The Last 10,000 Years*. The University of Arizona Press, Tucson.

Maruyama, M. (1963) The second cybernetics: deviation-amplifying mutual causal processes. *American Scientist* **51**, 164–79.

Meehan, E. J. (1968) *Explanation in Social Science: A System Paradigm*. Dorsey, Homewood.

Orloci, L. (1967) Data centering: a review and evaluation with regard to component analysis. *Systematic Zoology* **16**, 208–12.

Schoenwetter, J. (1962) The pollen analysis of eighteen archaeological sites in Arizona and New Mexico. In Chapters in the prehistory of eastern Arizona, I., P. S. Martin, J. D. Rinaldo, W. A. Longacre, C. Cronin, L. G. Freeman, Jr. and J. Schoenwetter. *Fieldiana: Anthropology* **53**, 168–209

Schoenwetter, J. and F. W. Eddy (1964) Alluvial and palynological reconstruction of environments, Navajo Reservoir district. *Museum of New Mexico Papers in Anthropology* 13.

Schroeder, A. H. (1957) Comments on *San Cayetano de Tumacacori*. Manuscript.

Sokal, R. R. and P. H. A. Sneath (1963) *Principles of Numerical Taxonomy*. W. H. Freeman, San Francisco.

Tainter, J. A. (1975) Social inference and mortuary practices: an experiment in numerical classification. *World Archaeology* **7**, 1–15.

Taylor, W. W. (1948) A study of archeology. *American Anthropologist, Memoir* 69.

Tustin, A. (1955) Feedback. In *Automatic Control*, A Scientific American Book, pp. 10–23. Simon and Schuster, New York.

Hohokam use of Nonriverine Resources

WILLIAM HARPER DOELLE

Arizona State Museum, The University of Arizona

Recent research has shown that subsistence strategies other than the cultivation of domesticates by canal irrigation were of importance to the prehistoric Hohokam. The goal of archaeological studies within the CONOCO Florence Project area, an area which was not amenable to canal irrigation prehistorically, was to document patterns of Hohokam land use within a nonriverine setting. The subsistence potential of this area is considered, and evidence for the utilization of four wild plant species as well as the use of runoff farming methods is presented. The distribution of decorated ceramics and redwares provides the only control of time, and it indicates that agricultural activities in the study area occurred predominantly in the Santa Cruz and Sacaton phases (A.D. 700–1100). Since there is presently insufficient information to adequately explain the observed patterns of land use, several areas of future research are suggested.

Father Kino and Captain Manje, the first Spaniards to visit the Gila River, commented on the large irrigation canals which had once brought water to the households and fields around the Casa Grande (Burrus, 1971: 371). The first archaeologists to work along the Lower Salt and Middle Gila Rivers were also impressed by the size and extent of Hohokam irrigation canals (Fewkes, 1912; Gladwin and others, 1937: 50–8; Haury, 1945; Turney, 1924, 1929). Understandably, the emphasis on Hohokam canal irrigation has continued into the present (Haury, 1976: 120–51; Herskovits, n.d.; Masse, 1976; Woodbury, 1960, 1961), for there are still many unanswered questions. This study, however, seeks to explore an aspect of the Hohokam subsistence system which has received much less attention. A number of resources can be grown in or collected from nonriverine settings. Ethnographic accounts indicate that some of these resources were very important to the Indians of southern Arizona in historic times, and there is mounting evidence that nonriverine resources were important pre-historically as well. This discussion, then, focuses on the evidence for Hohokam use of nonriverine resources based on a recent study of the CONOCO Florence Project area within the Gila River basin.

STUDY AREA

The study area is located north of the Gila River, near Florence, Arizona (Figure 1). Two seasons of fieldwork have been carried out there by the

245

Arizona State Museum under contract with the Continental Oil Company (CONOCO) (Doelle, 1975, 1976). The CONOCO study area includes over 31 km² (12 mi²) and contains two distinct environmental divisions. Over half of the CONOCO area consists of gravel terraces which support a paloverde-saguaro community. The other major environmental unit is an area of deep alluvial soils vegetated by creosotebush and bursage. A major wash system runs through this creosotebush-bursage community and supports a dense growth of mesquite. Additional information on the archaeology of the nearby first terrace of the Gila River comes from survey and excavation in the Escalante ruin group (Ayres, 1971; Doyel, 1974; Windmiller, 1972) and from the Arizona State Museum site survey file. A linear survey (Grady and others, 1973) also passed through part of the study area.

Although the first terrace of the Gila River has not been intensively surveyed, Midvale (1965) has documented the existence of a prehistoric irrigation canal, the Poston Canal, which reached a maximum length of at least 11 km (7 mi). Nine permanent habitation sites are known to occur along this canal in the vicinity of the CONOCO study area (i.e., west of Florence). Ceramics from these sites suggest a continuous occupation of the first terrace from the late Pioneer or early Colonial period (about A.D. 550), through the end of the Classic period (A.D. 1450). The construction date of the Poston Canal is not known, but the site which is located at its terminus, the Lastwater Ruin (Arizona U:15:9 ASU), was occupied from the Gila Butte through the Sacaton phases (A.D. 550–1100). This suggests that the Poston Canal system reached its maximum extent at least by the Sacaton phase and possibly as early as the Gila Butte phase.

RESEARCH PROBLEM

Although the outlook for the future is promising, the day is not yet at hand when it can be said that archaeologists have an adequate understanding of Hohokam subsistence. The major components of the Hohokam subsistence base have been identified, but there is only an incomplete understanding of how these were integrated as a system. Even less is known about how this system changed through time. Nonetheless, progress is being made. For example, several studies related to Hohokam irrigation practices were cited above, and other recent work has focused on nonriverine resources. These latter studies have considered the prehistoric use of wild plants (Bohrer, 1970; Doelle, 1975, 1976; Goodyear, 1975; Gasser, 1976), as well as the use of agricultural systems dependent on intermittent surface runoff (Brooks, 1975; Wood, 1972, n.d.). Because attention has only recently turned to such problem areas, the mere identification of nonriverine resource use often presents a major task. For instance, the problems of developing appropriate data collection and data interpretation methods must usually be approached in new ways. As a result individual studies are likely to be somewhat limited in scope. The present study, for example, is concerned primarily with documenting patterns of Hohokam land use in the CONOCO area, an area which was not amenable to prehistoric canal irrigation. An attempt is also made to place the different types of prehistoric land use in a temporal perspective. It is hoped that eventually the results of studies such as this one can be integrated into models which consider the entire Hohokam settlement-subsistence system. For now, however, the goals are more limited.

RESEARCH METHODS

Three sources of data are utilized in this discussion. They include archaeological, environmental, and ethnographic data, each of which is discussed in greater detail below.

ARCHAEOLOGICAL DATA

In all discussion of the material remains recovered from the CONOCO area an important distinction is recognized between the archaeological and the systemic context. According to Schiffer (1972: 157)

Systemic context labels the condition of an element which is participating in a behavioral system. Archaeological context describes materials which have passed through a cultural system, and which are now the objects of investigation of archaeologists.

A prehistoric archaeologist can make direct observations only on objects in archaeological context; he must make inferences about their past systemic context.

Archaeological context data from the CONOCO area have been classified into two general categories. The first category includes sites. Nine sites were located during CONOCO I, and two additional sites were discovered during CONOCO II (Figure 1). Sites were defined in the field on the basis of the presence of features (e.g., rock alignments) and/or the presence of substantial concentrations of artifacts. The second data category is nonsites. Thomas (1975: 62) defines nonsite archaeology as an approach which takes

...the cultural item (the artifact, feature, manuport, individual flake, or whatever) as the minimal unit, and ignore(s) traditional sites altogether. . . .This is not to deny that artifacts generally occur in well-defined sites. . . .but rather to assert that in some instances, under special research circumstances, discrete clumpings of artifacts (a) either do not occur or (b) are not relevant to the problems immediately at hand.

The distinction between a large nonsite cluster of artifacts and a small site is not as arbitrary as it might first appear. In deciding whether or not to designate a set of material remains as a site, the information potential of those remains was an important consideration. Most remains from the nonsite study consist of a single class of artifacts (e.g., only sherds, or a core and associated waste flakes). Individual clusters of this sort generally have limited information potential, unless they are compared with a large sample of similar clusters from different spatial and environmental contexts. All sites from the CONOCO area, however, contain multiple artifact classes, thus making possible behavioral inferences based upon an intrasite analysis of artifact classes and their spatial relationships.

During CONOCO I the entire study area was surveyed. It was possible to cover such a large area because the primary goal of this survey was to locate archaeological *sites*. Since the nonsite study of CONOCO II focused on individual *artifacts*, more intensive methods of field coverage were necessary which could only be accomplished by employing a sampling strategy. Sample units 100 m on a side were randomly selected for intensive study, and field survey was completed in 193 sample units, or 8.7% of the study area (Figure 2).

In the field each sample unit was divided into four quadrants (area = 50 x 50 m) and one member of the four person field team was assigned to each. This area was walked over two or more times with the goal of locating, mapping, and collecting all artifacts. In addition detailed information on environmental conditions within and adjacent to each sample unit was recorded.

ENVIRONMENTAL DATA

The present discussion departs somewhat from Doelle (1976: 41–48) where five separate environmental zones were defined. Here only four zones are distinguished (Figure 2). The primary reason for the difference is a change in an earlier assumption. The original five zones were defined primarily on the basis of present day vegetation with secondary consideration given to soil type, substrate, and topography. For the purpose of correlating environmental and archaeological variables it was assumed that

...unless evidence of disturbance indicates otherwise, density of a present day (plant) species reflects relative density of that species in the past (Doelle, 1976: 41).

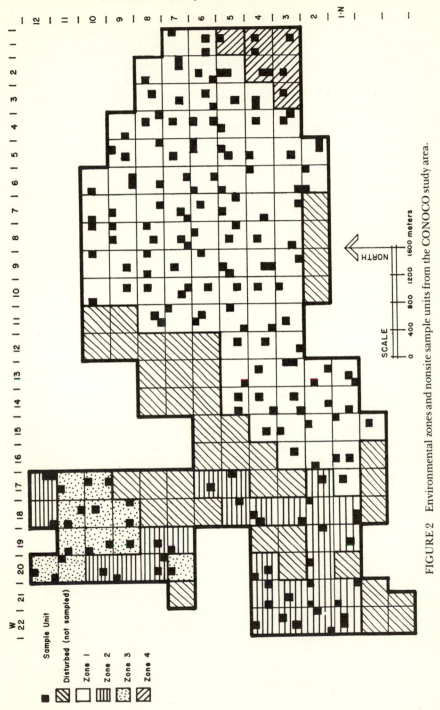

FIGURE 2 Environmental zones and nonsite sample units from the CONOCO study area.

This assumption was recognized as lacking firm support when it was first used (Doelle, 1976: 41). Therefore, it now seems preferable to employ a more conservative assumption. It will be assumed that the boundaries of plant communities within the study area have maintained relative stability over the last 2000 years. While there is evidence of climatic variability during this time period (Fritts, 1965; Schoenwetter, 1970), it is unlikely that climatic fluctuations (Martin, 1963) so severe as to displace the boundaries of the natural plant communities have occurred (Van Devender, 1973). This suggests that the four factors of present vegetation, topography, soil type, and substrate can be equally weighted so as to define environmental zones where present conditions are roughly equivalent to those of the pre-historic past. No assumptions are made about variation in density of individual species through time, however.

Zone 1

This area is a Pleistocene gravel terrace which is dissected by arroyos. A creosotebush-bursage association and a paloverde-saguaro association occur together in this zone. The surface is generally covered with gravels, and in many areas there are extensive caliche deposits just below the surface. Many of the larger cobbles found in this zone are suitable for lithic manufacture.

Zone 2

This zone is characterized by deep alluvial soils which support a creosotebush-bursage community. A large wash flows through Zone 2 and hosts a dense growth of mesquite. It cannot be established with certainty that this mesquite grove was present in the past, but the relatively large drainage basin of this wash would have maintained a consistently high water table which in turn would have been a favorable habitat for mesquite.

Zone 3

This is a large basalt outcrop in the northwest corner of the study area where creosotebush-bursage and paloverde-saguaro communities occur together. Soils are generally quite shallow and the surface is covered with basalt boulders.

Zone 4

This zone includes only a small area in the southeast corner of the study area. The soils are deep alluvial soils similar to, although containing more gravels than, those of Zone 2. Erosional processes have removed an unknown quantity of finer grained particles from this surface, leaving an abundance of exposed gravels. Zone 4 supports a creosotebush-bursage community.

ETHNOGRAPHIC DATA

Published ethnographic sources have aided in the formulation of a general research approach for the CONOCO project. In addition, they have provided detailed information on the kinds of material culture utilized in many kinds of subsistence related behavior. These sources generally do not contain data on the subsistence potential of wild and cultivated resources, however. Therefore, additional research on the yield of mesquite, saguaro, cholla, and Papago corn was carried out. This was accomplished by actual observation and through interviews with Papago informants. Since these data are based on observations from a single year, and since comparative data from more than one household are not available, they must be considered as preliminary. Nonetheless, such ethnographic data can provide an important supplement to the environmental and archae-ological data if they are used with caution.

THE SUBSISTENCE POTENTIAL OF NONRIVERINE RESOURCES

To the untutored eye the natural bounty of the Sonoran Desert is concealed by a "deceptive barrenness" (Felger and Nabhan, 1976). The aboriginal inhabitants of the desert learned to utilize a wide variety of wild plants. Felger and Nabhan (1976: 34) state that:

In e Sonoran Desert of southwestern North America, there are more than 375 species of wild foo plants. About 40 of these species were utilized as major staples by the native peoples of the region.

In addition to using wild plants these native peoples were able to raise domesticated crops utilizing surface runoff from seasonal rains. Thus, while the importance of the riverine environment to aboriginal groups has usually been stressed in past research, the nonriverine environment was of an importance not yet fully realized. A brief description of the major ethnographically documented uses of cholla, saguaro, and mesquite, and a consideration of their season of availability serves as an introduction to these important wild resources. The potential of runoff agriculture is also considered.

It was the cholla buds, rather than the developed fruits, which were of primary importance aboriginally (Bohrer, 1969; Castetter and Underhill, 1935: 20). These buds generally developed in May and were one of the earliest wild plant foods available. Thus if stored foods had run short over the winter, cholla buds would have served as a welcome food supply. Even if stored foods were sufficient, cholla buds would add diversity to the diet, and after processing and drying the buds can be stored for later use.

The fruit of the saguaro, or giant cactus, are available during a three to five week season from late June through mid-July. The fruit can be processed into a number of useful products. A sweet syrup, which can be fermented into a mildly alcoholic wine, has long been important among the Pima and Papago. In addition the seed is a nutritious, high calorie food which was heavily used in the past (Russell, 1908). Saguaro syrup was stored in ceramic containers, and the seed and even the dried fruit could be kept for long periods.

The time of maturation of the fruit of the mesquite tree varies from place to place. For the last three years the mesquite pods in the CONOCO area have ripened by late July to early August. When fully ripe the pods fall to the ground making gathering relatively easy. The season of availability of ripe pods is approximately two to three weeks. Judging from the ethnographic literature (Bell and Castetter, 1937; Bean and Saubel, 1972; Felger and Moser, 1971) it was the sweet flour of the pod, or mesocarp, which was of primary importance aboriginally, rather than the seeds which are very hard and small. Felger and Moser (1971) and Doelle (1976: 53–60) describe the processing of mesquite pods into flour. This flour can be made into compact cakes which require no cooking and can be stored. The dried pods can also be stored for later processing and use.

Felger and Nabhan (1976: 35) state that

Certain drought-evading perennials, such as the mesquite tree with its very deep taproots, and cacti with their succulent water storage tissue, produce fruit even during drought years, although yield may be reduced.

The characteristics that have allowed these unfailing resources to adapt to the harsh conditions of the desert have often served to ameliorate that harshness for man. The relatively dense stands, consistently high yields, palatability, and ability to be stored make mesquite, saguaro, and cholla especially important resources. While archaeologists have tended to consider wild plant use by the Hohokam as a response to stress (Bohrer, 1970), recent researchers (Doelle, 1976; Gasser, 1976) have considered the possibility that these unfailing resources were incorporated into the

subsistence system as staples. Table 1 presents some preliminary date on gross rates of energy yield for mesquite, saguaro, and cholla in order to illustrate the potential contribution of these wild resources to a desert subsistence system.

TABLE 1
Preliminary estimates of the yield of three wild plant species

Wild plant species	Observed range of yield of fresh fruit per hour (kg)	Dry weight of edible portion	Kilocalories per kilogram (kcal)	Gross energy yield from one hour of work (Ross, 1941)
Cholla	2.1–5.3 (buds)	0.30–0.77 (buds)	3440	1032–2649
Saguaro	3.0–4.6 (pulp)	1.16–1.88 (seeds)	5280	6125–9926
Mesquite	3.0 (estimated dry weight of pods)	0.9 (mesocarp)	3500	3150

While Hohokam use of agricultural techniques other than canal irrigation was recognized as early as the late nineteenth century (Matthews, Wortman, and Billings, 1893: 148), detailed studies of the use of surface runoff by desert cultivators in southwestern North America have not been carried out. Limited descriptive studies are available, however. Castetter and Bell (1942: 54) even present information on the yield of Pima and Papago crops:

Under early conditions Piman native corn yielded on the average only 10–12 bushels of shelled corn per acre, although as grown by the U.S. Field Station on the Reservation at Sacaton the same corn yields 20–25 bushels; teparies under native conditions, 500–800 pounds per acre—under Field Station cultivation, as high as 1500 pounds. . . .

The yields documented by Castetter and Bell are apparently for canal irrigated fields along the Gila River. Estimation by the author of the yield obtained from fields along Sells Wash on the Papago Reservation, however, suggests that maize yields of 10–12 bushels per acre can be obtained even though the only water source is an intermittently flowing wash. Likewise, Nabhan and Felger (n.d.) indicate that tepary yields in the range specified by Castetter and Bell can be achieved using runoff farming methods.

Direct comparison of the yields of wild and cultivated plants is not possible with presently available data, but there are several points about the yield and seasonality of the particular species under discussion that need to be emphasized. First is the fact that wild resources require much less labor input than do cultivated crops. The tasks of field clearing, construction and

maintenance of water control devices, planting, and weeding are all avoided by utilizing wild resources. Second, the species under consideration are all complementary as to their seasons of availability. This means that cholla, saguaro, and mesquite could all have been gathered and fields of maize and teparies planted without serious conflicts in labor demands.

HOHOKAM LAND USE IN THE CONOCO STUDY AREA

An important assumption is employed about the spatial distribution of archaeological remains for the purpose of making behavioral inferences. This assumption states that if a particular resource was exploited within the study area then at least some archaeological evidence of that activity will occur within the present day distribution of that resource. Several factors provide support for this assumption. First, since an argument has already been made that the boundaries of past and present plant communities are roughly equivalent, the use of present day boundaries is justifiable. Second, the two major environmental zones (Zones 1 and 2) are very large. This increases the probability of the assumption being true, for materials could enter the archaeological record not only at the particular point of resource use, but enroute and returning from that location as well.

Presentation of the archaeological data and the derivation of behavioral inferences from these data are carried out separately for each environmental zone. Then land use evidence from the different zones is compared.

ZONE 1

The primary wild economic species of Zone 1 are paloverde, saguaro, and cholla. Goodyear (1975) has documented the occurrence of large seasonal camps where these resources were processed by the prehistoric inhabitants of the Papagueria. No such large sites were encountered in Zone 1, however, suggesting that if these resources were collected in the study area prehistorically they were processed elsewhere. Permanent habitation sites on the nearby first terrace of the Gila River would have been likely places for such processing activities. Thus, only artifacts associated with gathering would be expected to occur in Zone 1.

Ethnographic observations

Most archaeological and ethnographic discussions of wild plant use focus on the kinds of processing activities that render the resource edible. Since wild plant gathering was likely an important activity in Zone 1, the ethnographic literature is reviewed with an emphasis on the following: (1) Group composition during gathering; (2) the kinds of activities performed; and, (3) the kinds of material remains that might be encountered in the archaeological record.

Group composition during gathering activities probably varied greatly, but ethnographic sources suggest that gathering was *primarily* the responsibility of women—especially when gathering occurred relatively close to the home village (Castetter and Underhill, 1935; Russell, 1908; Shaw, 1974). Castetter and Underhill (1935: 13–14) provide a good description of the roles of the participants in Papago gathering activities.

When a crop was reported ripe the village organized its food gathering expedition. If the expedition were only for a day the women went alone; if it were a longer trip, whole families went. The younger women and boys fetched water daily, the men hunted and at times helped in the picking.

Pima men often accompanied gathering expeditions to protect them from attack by Apaches as well (Russell, 1908: 42). Since the CONOCO study area is so close to the permanent habitation sites of the first terrace, it might be expected that women would have gone there alone or in small groups to gather wild foods. While men might be expected to occasionally help the gatherers, it is more likely that the role of men would be to hunt or to provide protection from enemies.

Saguaro and cholla. Castetter and Underhill (1935) provide descriptions of both the activities and tools used in gathering saguaro (1935: 20) and cholla (1935: 15).

The fruit of the saguaro grows at the extreme top of the shaft, which is sometimes twenty-five feet high, or at the tips of the branches, and is hooked down with a long pole made of two giant cactus ribs spliced together.... Each [gatherer] carries a bowl-shaped, water-tight basket (more recently a lard pail is used) to receive the pulp. One large basket, used as a general receptacle, is propped in an ocotillo bush (*Fouquieria splendens*) at some central point.

... the flower buds [of cholla] which develop at the tips of the branches are gathered as they come out in May.... Women go out in parties to gather the crop, this being done with wooden tongs made of a length of the giant cactus rib (*Carnegiea gigantea*), split in two. The buds or joints are collected in coiled basket bowls and brought to a central point where an old woman directs the baking.

None of the tools described above would be preserved at an open site. Raab (1973) and Goodyear (1975) have argued that small circular arrangements of rocks or "rock rings" may have functioned to support large baskets into which saguaro pulp was deposited. Thus, the rock rings would have performed the function of an ocotillo as specified in the above quote by Castetter and Underhill. It is at least possible that rock rings may be indicators of cholla gathering as well.

Paloverde. The edible portion of the paloverde fruit is the seed, which is encased within a pod. When dry this pod breaks open easily, releasing the seed. Spier (1933: 53–4) describes the gathering of ironwood pods by the Maricopa, a description which could also apply to paloverde (paloverde matures in July, however).

By the end of the season, October, they (ironwood pods) are said to lie thickly under the trees. Gathered in piles, they were beaten until broken, winnowed in baskets, and the meats taken home.

Again, no durable artifacts are noted.

There are at least two means by which durable items could have entered the archaeological record which are not considered above. One would result from the substitution of ceramic vessels to perform the functions ascribed to baskets in the above descriptions. It is unlikely that this would have occurred with regularity, however, due to the added weight which would result from using a ceramic vessel rather than a basket. The second derives from the need for a ceramic vessel to carry drinking water to be consumed by the gatherer(s). Since saguaro and paloverde mature during the hottest season of the year, and since surface water probably was not available in the CONOCO area, it is likely that gatherers would have carried at least some drinking water with them. Russell (1908: 128–9) provides an especially interesting description of Pima water carrying practices while gathering:

Canteens were formerly made of pottery. . . . They were globular in form and not provided with projections or loops for the attachment of straps. In fact, they were intended to be carried in the woman's kiaha [burden basket]; men on the warpath or traveling far from water must learn to endure thirst, but the women when compelled to go far for wood or cactus fruit were accustomed to carry water in these canteens. The vessels were sometimes broken, and Sala Hina told us of such an experience in which she nearly perished of thirst before she reached the river, though she had gone but a few miles from home.

Table 2 summarizes the kinds of ceramic vessels which might have been used during the gathering activities described above.

TABLE 2

Wild plants and possible ceramic vessel forms used in collecting them[a]

Wild plant species	Collection container		
	Bowl	Storage jar	Water jar
Cholla	x	x	*X*
Saguaro	x	x	*X*
Paloverde	x		*X*

[a] Key: x—Expected infrequently; *X*—Expected frequently.

Test implications

The following test implications are derived from the above discussion of ethnographic data and are used to evaluate the hypothesis that gathering of cholla, paloverde, and saguaro occurred in Zone 1.

1) Since gathering was usually done by individuals or by small groups of individuals working at individual plants, and since a gatherer was unlikely to be carrying more than one ceramic vessel while gathering, it is expected that ceramic indications of plant collecting would consist primarily of isolated clusters of broken pottery. Clusters of several vessels might indicate either breakage associated with some other activity, or breakage that occurred at different times.

2) The ceramic assemblage should be predominantly jars (Table 2). Bowls are expected, but at a much lower frequency than jars.

3) Rock rings would be expected as indicators of cholla and/or saguaro gathering. They should occur primarily in Zone 1, though a few might be found in Zone 3. No rock rings should be found in Zones 2 and 4.

Archaeological observations

Test implication 1 specifies that ceramic indicators of gathering would consist of isolated clusters of broken pottery and most of the clusters should contain sherds from a single vessel. Since artifacts which occurred in well-defined clusters were collected as a unit, there is a good basis for evaluating this test implication. A total of 101 ceramic loci were defined in Zone 1, and of these 78 included only one vessel. Eighteen loci contained sherds from two vessels, four contained three vessels, and a single locus included six vessels. These data demonstrate that the overwhelming majority of loci contained only one vessel, thus test implication 1 is supported by the nonsite data.

Test implication 2 specifies that jars should greatly outnumber bowls in Zone 1 as gathering was the primary activity there. Because most of the ceramics recovered were body sherds, ceramic data were divided into three categories: definite jars/bowls, possible jars/bowls, and indeterminate (Doelle, 1976: 177–94). The jar to bowl ratio for the 53 vessels in the definite category was 3.1 : 1, while the ratio for the possible jar/bowl category was 3.7 : 1 with a total of 56 vessels. Since both sets of data indicate a clear predominance of jars in the ceramic assemblage of Zone 1, these results are judged to support test implication 2.

The third test implication specifies that rock rings should be encountered in Zone 1, and possibly in Zone 3, both areas where saguaro and cholla occur. Rock rings should not be encountered in the other zones. Table 3 lists the location and descriptive data on all rock rings encountered during both CONOCO I and II. These data illustrate that rock rings were only encountered in Zones 1 and 3. While rock ring number 10 would appear to be too large to have supported a container for cactus fruit, all other rock rings appear to be of appropriate size and location to have served such a function. Therefore, test implication 3 is also supported.

TABLE 3
Rock rings recorded in the CONOCO area

Environmental zone	Rock ring field number[a]	Dimension diameter (m)
Zone 1	1	0.7
	2	0.7
	3	1.0
	10	2.0
	11	1.0
	12	1.0
Zone 3	8	0.75
	9	0.8

[a] Missing numbers were assigned to other kinds of rock features (Doelle, 1976 : 96).

The evidence presented above is too indirect to be considered as conclusive support for the hypothesis that saguaro, cholla, and paloverde were gathered within the study area. The available evidence did not disconfirm any of the three test implications of this hypothesis, however. Since it is doubtful whether any direct evidence to support this hypothesis is preserved in the study area, failure of the present evidence to disconfirm the hypothesis will be considered as preliminary confirmation.

ZONE 2

A single wild resource, mesquite, predominates in Zone 2, but the occurrence there of deep alluvial soils and a large wash system suggests the potential for agriculture in this zone as well. Ethnographic observations on mesquite utilization and on agricultural systems using intermittent washes as water sources are reviewed in order to develop an understanding of the range of material indicators of these activities.

Ethnographic observations

Mesquite. When fully mature, mesquite pods fall to the ground making gathering relatively easy. Alternatively, Bean and Saubel (1972: 109) note that the pods can be picked before reaching full maturity, and that these pods can be processed after being sun dried. Bean and Saubel (1972: 109) provide a description of mesquite gathering among the Cahuilla of southern California.

The green and dried pods were picked by all members of a family. Children were able to crawl among the branches more easily than adults, however, and pick pods from the center of each tree. . . .Since the gathering period spanned several weeks, people usually remained at the gathering site for the duration of the pod-gathering season if groves were any distance from their village site. If the groves were nearby, the people gathered the green beans, carried them home, and returned several weeks later for the naturally dried pods.

Two major food uses for the mesquite fruit have been identified ethnographically. First, the pod, or mesocarp, can be reduced to a sweet flour through processing with a mortar and pestle (Felger and Moser, 1971; Doelle, 1976: 53–60). Second, by pounding the residue of the above process again with mortar and pestle (Felger and Moser, 1971), or by processing fresh pods with a gyratory crusher (Felger, n.d.; Felger and Nabhan, 1976; Hayden, 1969) the mesquite seeds are freed. The seeds can then be ground with a mano amd metate. Hayden (1969) also notes that some groups obtained a finer flour by grinding the mesocarp flour with a mano and metate.

The above discussion suggests that a mortar and pestle and/or a mano and metate might be expected as archaeological indicators of mesquite processing. If the seeds were parched, shallow bowls or large flat sherds might have been utilized and therefore might occur in the archaeological record. If a mesquite processing camp was occupied throughout the season of availability of this resource, it is likely that a much wider variety of material items might be encountered archaeologically. Such items could include the full range of material culture related to food preparation, as well as evidence of additional activities (e.g., hunting) engaged in by persons living at the camp. The evidence for temporary camps in Zone 2 is reviewed below after consideration of the possibility that runoff agricultural systems functioned along the wash system of this zone.

Runoff agriculture. Archaeologists have yet to adequately document the temporal and spatial distribution of prehistoric techniques of managing runoff for agricultural purposes. Their understanding of the role such systems may have played in past subsistence systems is even less complete. To date all documented runoff systems within the Middle Gila Basin include surficial rock features of three major types: (1) Check dams (Wood, n.d.); (2) grid pattern field systems (Russell, 1908: 88–9; Wood, 1972, n.d.; Brooks, 1975); and, (3) rock piles (Brooks, 1975; Doelle, 1976; Wood, 1972).

Castetter and Bell (1942) provide additional information about systems of water control employed by the Papago which would leave little enduring evidence for the archaeologist. An extended quotation (1942: 168) serves to summarize their observations.

In their [Papago] country the run-off of the mountain areas collected in streams with well-defined channels, which, on reaching the large undissected alluvial basins, lost their momentum and spread out in broad sheets over the level land for a square mile or more. . . .These were favorite locations for flood-water fields. . . .In many cases shallow ditches and dykes, or wings, were constructed starting a mile or more from the fields in order to collect the surface run-off for the few acres on which they converged. Low embankments, small brush dikes and short shallow ditches were used where necessary to control, divert, distribute and retain water. At times embankments were disposed as levees, somewhat after the manner of borders around a field, to retain water until it could soak into the soil, but this was not common. For some fields water was led out from the arroyo by ditches, a deliberate effort thus being made to conduct the flood water to the fields.

Unfortunately, more detailed descriptions of these features are not provided. It is apparent that such features may be very difficult to recognize in the field. Therefore, even when no direct physical evidence of such subtle features can be identified, the archaeologist should pay attention to the agricultural potential of localities where fertile soils and a water source occur together.

At present there is no direct evidence that runoff carried by the major wash system of Zone 2 was used to water agricultural fields. A complicating factor in identifying runoff control features—if indeed they did exist—is the degree of recent disturbance along the major wash. Several large areas were cultivated in the recent past and four cattle tanks have been constructed in the wash. Since there are still limited areas of relatively undisturbed land along this wash system that have not been surveyed (as they are outside the CONOCO project area), it may be possible to identify such water control features through additional survey.

Test implications

Since direct evidence of runoff farming has not been documented for Zone 2, possible indirect evidence is considered. For example, the presence of small, temporary camps may provide indirect evidence for runoff farming, mesquite processing, or both. Therefore, two sites from Zone 2 are considered in greater detail in order to determine whether they may have been temporary camps. Discussion of specialized activities carried out at camps is postponed until additional data from Zones 3 and 4 have been considered.

A temporary camp is defined as a location which was the residence of one or more persons on a short-term or seasonal basis. Reference to residence in this definition is meant to indicate that a temporary camp is more than a place where a traveler, for example, spent a single night. Specialized activities may have occurred at or near a temporary camp, but all such camps should exhibit evidence of everyday activities like food preparation, eating, and sleeping. Based upon the above definition the following general indicators of a temporary camp can be deduced.

1) The quantity of trash and the inferred conditions of deposition of that trash are important factors in identifying a temporary camp. Secondary refuse, which consists of materials discarded at other than their location of use (Schiffer, 1972: 161), would serve as a reliable indicator of a temporary camp. This is based on the assumption that establishment of specialized areas for trash disposal is unlikely to occur unless length of residence in a place is of sufficient duration for large quantities of waste items to accumulate. Primary refuse, which consists of materials discarded at their location of use (Schiffer, 1972: 161), is a much less reliable indicator of a temporary camp. If only primary refuse is present at a site, then strong supportive evidence would be necessary to establish that the site was a temporary camp, for it would be possible that the site represented an activity area where residence had not taken place.

2) Temporary shelter. A temporary shelter would have been needed primarily for protection from the intense heat of the summer sun. Many activities such as food preparation, food consumption, or resting would

likely occur at or near such a shelter. Water, food, and tools not in use were likely stored at such a location.

3) Hearth. Most of the prehistoric food staples required cooking to render them edible, therefore evidence of a cooking hearth would be expected. A hearth may not be detectable from surface evidence.

Archaeological observations

From Zone 2 intensive surface collections have been carried out only at Arizona U:15:51. This site consists of a surface scatter of sherds and lithics. The painted pottery recovered indicates that the site was occupied during the Santa Cruz phase (A.D. 700–900). Figure 3 is a map of ceramic density at Arizona U:15:51. It also shows the location of the major lithic artifacts. Almost all artifacts occur within a very restricted area. Two clusters (Figure 3, Areas A and B) can be defined within the artifact scatter on the basis of differences in ceramic density. The distribution of several artifact classes suggests that Area A was being cleaned on a regular basis, and that Area B was receiving the wastes discarded from Area A. Therefore, it is hypothesized that Area A represents a prehistoric activity area, while Area B represents a trash disposal area.

The first line of evidence in support of this hypothesis is the difference in ceramic density between the two areas (Figure 3). The distribution of lithics provides additional support. For example, Area A contains only seven flakes but five (71%) of these flakes show edge damage, suggesting that they were utilized. In Area B 26 flakes were found, but only seven (27%) were utilized. Nonflakes (any piece of stone removed from a larger nodule that does not possess a platform or proximal bulb of percussion (Bayham, 1976: 197), also show an unequal distribution. Area A contains only two nonflakes, one of which shows use wear, while Area B contains 14 unutilized nonflakes. Finally, a schist "knife" with such extensive edge damage that it is unlikely that it could have been used further was found in Area B along with six small tabular schist fragments, most of which could have once been part of a schist "knife." No such materials were found in Area A. In summary, Area A contains a lower artifact density, and a high percentage of the artifacts which do occur there show evidence of having been used. Area B, on the other hand, contains a greater number of artifacts and those classes of artifacts present tend to be items that were never suitable for use. While this evidence suggests that Area A may have been an activity area excavation will be necessary to establish this with certainty. Evidence of a temporary shelter (most likely indicated by postholes) or a hearth might be identifiable through excavation. The evidence that Area B

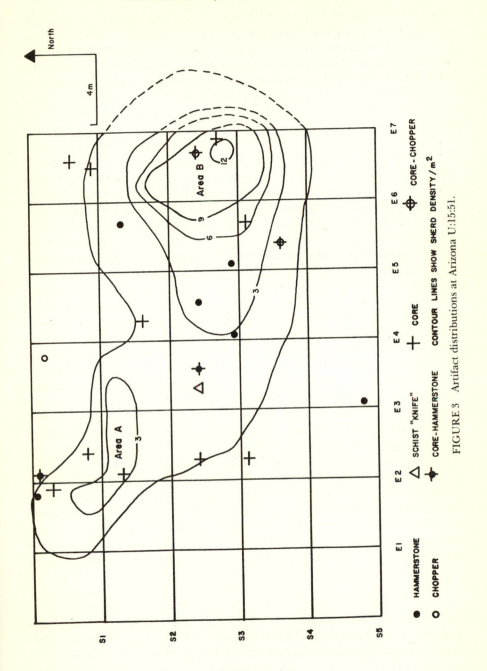

FIGURE 3   Artifact distributions at Arizona U:15:51.

is comprised of secondary refuse is more convincing, however. In addition to the data presented above, the predominance of exhausted cores, the low frequency of cores and flakes of the same material type, and the generally heterogeneous nature of the artifact assemblage all suggest that this was a specialized area for trash disposal. Thus Arizona U:15:51 contains the primary indicator of a temporary camp, secondary refuse, and there is reason to believe it may contain evidence of a hearth and temporary shelter as well.

A second site, Arizona U:15:18, was also discovered in Zone 2. This site is a low density sherd and lithic scatter located near a small wash which flows into the main wash of Zone 2. Pottery at the site is predominantly Gila Plain, but several pieces of Santa Cruz Red-on-buff and a single sherd of Gila Butte Red-on-buff were collected. Lithic artifacts include several cores, flakes, nonflakes, and a large cobble hammerstone. The artifacts are distributed in two distinct clusters, indicating that this site, too, may contain evidence of both an activity area and a trash area. At present, however, there is insufficient data to test this hypothesis as controlled surface collections have not yet been carried out.

The two known sites from Zone 2 share similarities in location, artifact assemblage, artifact distribution, and approximate temporal placement. In addition, both sites lack grinding implements, at least in surface contexts. This might be interpreted as evidence that foodstuffs were not processed at these locations and that, therefore, these sites do not represent temporary camps. There are a number of factors which suggest that such reasoning is invalid. First, in comparison to ceramic vessels and chipped stone tools, grinding tools have a long use life. This, and the greater energy expenditure required for their manufacture increase the likelihood that grinding tools would be removed by the original occupants when a temporary camp was abandoned. Finally, usable grinding tools which did enter the archaeological context may have been collected and reused elsewhere by subsequent prehistoric or historic visitors to a site. And modern artifact collectors are often not selective, finding even fragments of grinding tools worthy of collection. Consequently, while grinding stones may have been present in the past systemic context, many factors could account for their absence from the present archaeological context.

ZONE 3

The wild resources present in Zone 3 include cholla, saguaro, and paloverde. The limited area of this zone would have meant that only a few gatherers could have collected here during a single season. The nonsite data provide limited support for the hypothesis that some collecting of these resources did occur, for of the eight isolated vessels recovered from Zone 3, six were either jars (3), or possible jars (3), while the other two were possible bowls. In addition two rock rings were noted in Zone 3 (Table 3). The presence of two sites in Zone 3, neither of which can be demonstrated to have been related to resource gathering within this zone, indicates that gathering may not have been the primary activity carried out in Zone 3.

One site, Arizona U:15:36, is a rock alignment in the shape of an anthropomorph (Jernigan, 1976: 137–141). Since it cannot presently be integrated into a discussion of subsistence practices, it is not considered further.

The second site, Arizona U:15:35, merits further discussion. It is located at the base of the western slope of a butte which rises above the rest of the zone. A total of 32 room spaces, 27 of which occur in a 55 m x 55 m area, were mapped within the site. Most room spaces were constructed by arranging a single course of basalt cobbles into a roughly circular shape. Several room spaces had up to eight courses of stone, however. The precarious nature of these higher walls, the presence of burned cow bone within one of the high-walled room spaces, and the occurrence of other recent remains at the site, indicate that a small portion of the site was rebuilt in the recent past. The remainder of the site is definitely prehistoric, however, as is evidenced by the presence of Gila Plain, transitional Santa Cruz–Sacaton and Sacaton Red-on-buff ceramics, a hammerstone, several flakes, and two projectile points (possibly pre-Hohokam). Inspection of the site suggests that very little labor was expended in constructing these features. Almost all room spaces were constructed so as to incorporate large natural outcrops, and additional rock for construction was immediately available. If any superstructure ever existed it was perishable, perhaps brush. In sum, Arizona U:15:35 contains evidence of features that may have been shelters, but it lacks evidence of any accumulation of trash, which indicates that this site was not a residence area.

ZONE 4

Zone 4 is located on the upper portion of the first terrace. The soils of this zone are deep and support a creosotebush-bursage community. While the washes which cut through this zone do support several potential economic species, the species diversity is high. This means that Zone 4 does not contain any dense concentrations of wild economic resources. Prehistoric exploitation of wild resources probably was not an important activity in this zone. Extensive areas of rock piles are found here, however. Each individual rock pile is about one meter in diameter and less than one-half meter in height. They were formed by the intentional clearing of cobbles from the surrounding surface. While not well understood, these features are generally interpreted as being related to agriculture (Brooks, 1975; Canouts, 1975: 82–6; Debowski and others, 1976: 89–91; Masse, n.d.).

Several interpretations of these rock pile features are possible. Canouts (1975: 83) notes that while functional studies of such features have not been carried out in Arizona,

Similar rock piles and rock alignments have, however, been the subject of intensive study in the Negev Desert. . .(Evanari *et al.* 1970). . .It was found that clearing cobbles from the ground surface produces a significant increase in runoff.

This increased runoff is then led to field areas where it is allowed to soak into the ground and water the crops.

An alternative interpretation is that rock piles indicate dry farming systems. Two possible functions can be suggested for the rock piles. They may be the result of clearing of the surface so that the cleared land could be planted, or the rocks may have functioned as a mulch to conserve soil moisture, with planting taking place within the rock pile.

At present none of the above alternatives can be ruled out. A site, Arizona U:15:50 (Figure 4), located in Zone 4 helps shed some light on the purpose of these rock pile features in the CONOCO area. It is argued that Arizona U:15:50 was a temporary camp, most probably occupied during the summer while tending crops planted nearby.

Several features at Arizona U:15:50 support this hypothesis. As was the case at Arizona U:15:51, there is evidence of secondary refuse within a restricted area. Over 1000 sherds were collected from the area labeled in Figure 4 as a trash scatter. Lithics have been collected only from the transect (28 m x 4 m) shown in Figure 4, which yielded 122 artifacts. The spatial clustering of the refuse is indicated by the fact that sample squares 1 and 2 of the transect contained one and three lithic items respectively. Sample squares 4 and 5, however, contained 40 and 45 lithics respectively. The former sample squares were located just outside the trash scatter, while the latter were within it. The majority of the lithic items were unutilized flakes (55%) and nonflakes (27%), while the remaining 18% included utilized flakes, cores, and hammerstones. The ceramics were predominantly plainwares, but Santa Cruz Red-on-buff and transitional Santa Cruz–Sacaton Red-on-buff were also present. In summary, the great quantity of artifacts, their occurrence in a restricted area, and the general heterogeneity of the artifact classes present supports the interpretation that this deposit represents secondary refuse.

A cleared area (Figure 4) is visible immediately to the north of the trash deposit. This area measures approximately 12 m x 10 m and contrasts

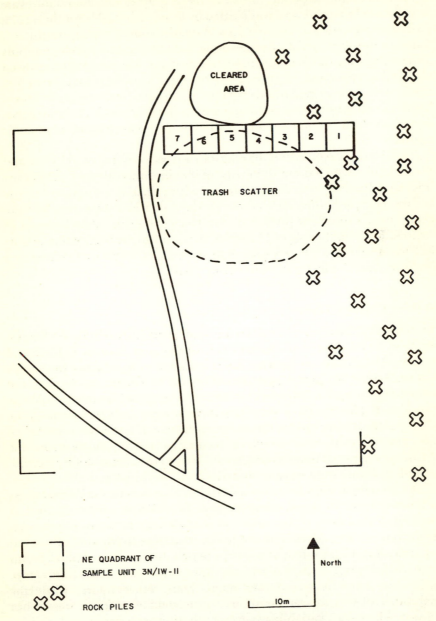

FIGURE 4   Map of Arizona U:15:50.

sharply with the adjacent surfaces where gravels are abundant. It is hypothesized that this area was cleared by those responsible for the nearby trash scatter for use as an activity area. A small grinding stone fragment was found in this area, which provides some support for this hypothesis. The area is otherwise almost devoid of surface artifacts. Another grinding tool, a two-handed mano that had been used in a trough metate prior to breaking, was found about 50 m to the west of the cleared area, further support for the hypothesized activity area in this general vicinity. Whether the cleared area represents such an activity area will require excavation to adequately resolve.

A final factor to consider is the relationship between Arizona U:15:50 and the rock piles which occur to the east of the site. Since the rock piles occur immediately adjacent to the site, but not within it, it would appear that the site was occupied either after or during the time when the rock piles were being used. If the rock piles were constructed after the abandonment of Arizona U:15:50, they should have occurred within the occupation area as well as outside of it. This indicates that at least some of the rock piles which occur in Zone 4 date to the Santa Cruz phase.

INTERZONE COMPARISON

The probable function of the temporary camps identified in Zone 2 has not yet been established. The artifact classes present at Arizona U:15:18 and Arizona U:15:51 do not provide direct evidence as to whether the camps were occupied by runoff agriculturalists or by persons gathering and processing mesquite. Therefore, an alternate approach to this problem is considered. The length of the occupation at a camp related to mesquite exploitation is compared to the occupation span at a seasonally occupied agricultural camp. Since length of occupation has implications for the quantity of material remains which would enter the archaeological record, an indirect evaluation of camp function will be possible.

The growing season for maize and beans, as grown by the Pima, ranges between 10 and 15 weeks (Castetter and Bell, 1942), while mesquite is available for about three weeks. During a single year the period of potential deposition of cultural remains would be about three to five times longer at an agricultural camp than at a mesquite processing camp. Therefore, an agricultural camp is likely to contain more refuse than a mesquite camp, unless the latter is reused over many years. Furthermore, while the magnitude of year to year variability in the yield of mesquite trees is not known, where such variability is great gathering and processing locations would have to shift frequently. Finally, it is possible that mesquite processing was done back at the home village, as there are permanent habitation sites in proximity to the CONOCO area. The data on gathering within Zone 1 would certainly support such a possibility, as no evidence of processing camps was recovered.

There are a number of reasons why an agricultural camp might be reoccupied over several seasons. First, runoff agriculture in which water from an intermittent wash is used involves a labor investment in land clearing and construction of diversion features. Second, the labor requirements of runoff farming, such as planting, weeding, maintaining diversion structures, protecting crops from pests, and harvesting, are spread over the entire season, making the establishment of temporary camps likely even though the farmers home village might be only an hour's walk away. On the basis of this reasoning, camps in Zone 2 were related to agricultural activities. Only data collected through excavation are likely to fully resolve this question, however.

The nature of the activities which took place at Arizona U:15:35 has not yet been considered. The close proximity of this site to the wash system of Zone 2 suggests that the site might have been used for storing crops harvested from fields along the wash. This hypothesis would account for the absence of refuse at Arizona U:15:35, and it relates activities at the site to activities occurring in the general vicinity. It merits testing against new archaeological data.

Further consideration should be given to the temporal setting of the archaeological remains from the CONOCO area. All four sites discussed above contain Santa Cruz, transitional Santa Cruz–Sacaton, or Sacaton Red-on-buff ceramic types. One problem in considering the time dimension is the infrequent occurrence of good ceramic time markers. Therefore, only two time periods will be examined here. The first period includes the Santa Cruz and Sacaton phases and the second includes both the Soho and Civano phases of the Classic period. Based on Haury (1976: 338) the first period dates between A.D. 700–1100 and the second between A.D. 1100–1450. For the earlier period Santa Cruz and Sacaton Red-on-buff are the diagnostic types, while for the later period Casa Grande Red-on-buff, Gila Polychrome, and redwares were used to indicate time. Zone 3 was deleted from this test since datable pottery occurred at only one locus. The data in Table 4 confirm different patterns of land use in the study area during these two time periods.

Before accepting this conclusion, the possible effects of the rather large amount of unidentified decorated wares recovered from the study area needs to be considered. Zone 1 contains 11 sample units with unidentified decorated wares, while Zone 2 and Zone 4 contain six and two such sample units respectively. Since all of these unidentified decorated wares are buff or red-on-buff, it is most likely that they date to the earlier of the two time

TABLE 4
Sample units and sites with temporarily diagnostic ceramics.
Figures in parentheses are expected values

Environmental zone	Time periods		
	Santa Cruz–Sacaton	Soho–Civano	Totals
Zone 1	4 (9.1)	16 (10.9)	20
Zone 2	8 (5.0)	3 (6.0)	11
Zone 4	4 (1.8)	0 (2.2)	4
Totals	16	19	35

Corrected $X^2 = 9.478$; $df = 2$; $p = 0.01$.

periods under consideration. The frequency of red-on-buff wares had declined greatly by the Soho phase and their production apparently had ceased by the Civano phase (Haury, 1976: 203). Consequently, if these materials were datable, the effect on the figures in Table 4 would be to decrease the contrast in intensity of use of Zone 1 over time, but it would only magnify the evidence of heavier use of Zone 2 and Zone 4 during the Santa Cruz–Sacaton period.

Based upon the archaeological evidence discussed above, it is probable that at least a major component of the Santa Cruz–Sacaton utilization of Zone 2 and Zone 4 is related to agriculture. There is reason to believe that the present evidence does not accurately reflect the magnitude of these activities. In Zone 2, for example, major sections of the wash system have been heavily modified by recent agricultural activities, and the nature of the study area boundaries resulted in the exclusion of another portion of the wash system. Likewise, Zone 4 is only minimally represented in the study area. The rock pile features have been observed to continue to the west, south, and east of the small area included in this study.

Agricultural systems of this nature are not without precedent in the Hohokam area. Nonirrigated agricultural systems are well documented near the junction of the Salt and Verde Rivers (Canouts, 1975), in the Buttes Reservoir area(Debowski and others, 1976), and along the Lower San Pedro River (Masse, n.d.). Runoff and rock pile agriculture in the CONOCO study area is one manifestation of a much broader phenomenon. Nevertheless, present evidence indicates that the relationship between irrigation, and runoff and rock pile agriculture was probably unique in each locality. In all of the above areas except the CONOCO, bottomlands suitable for irrigation agriculture are very limited. Near the CONOCO area extensive tracts of potentially irrigable land are available between the first terrace and the Gila River. Since we are still in a stage where the range of variability in

Hohokam subsistence practices is being defined, the nature of the relationship of these different kinds of agricultural systems should be given consideration in future research.

FUTURE RESEARCH

In regard to future work within the CONOCO area, several possibilities have been noted in the above discussion. Inferences made here about the function of temporary camps, such as Arizona U:15:50 and Arizona U:15:51, require further testing. Limited test excavations would be useful in further defining function and in providing important new information on dating. All inferences in which a time element was involved have been based upon limited quantities of decorated ceramics and redwares. Hearths and temporary shelters that are expected to occur in temporary camps could provide materials suitable for radiocarbon and archaeomagnetic methods of absolute dating. Improvement in our ability to place past behavior in a reliable time frame is essential if studies such as this one are to provide insight into the nature of, and changes in, Hohokam subsistence practices.

There is also a need for further work in areas adjacent to Zones 2 and 4. These areas were not studied previously because they lie outside the CONOCO project boundaries, but additional survey work here will allow a better evaluation of the extent of the expansion of Hohokam agricultural systems into these nonriverine settings.

The research problems noted above are oriented toward further documentation of the kinds of behavior that occurred in the CONOCO area. While an essential step in the process of explanation, such research will not explain why the observed behavior patterns occurred. In order to answer that question, the research framework will have to be expanded to consider the Hohokam settlement–subsistence system as a whole. A logical first step toward this end will of necessity include intensive survey of remaining undisturbed areas along the first terrace of the Gila River. It is essential that the size of permanent villages and their distribution in space and time be known if hypotheses accounting for prehistoric behavioral patterns are to be tested. Dating of the Poston Canal system is also critical. Clearly, there are abundant possibilities for future archaeological research. There are also some limitations inherent in the archaeological record requiring additional, complementary lines of research. One example is considered.

The archaeological record is a poor source of information about the yield of prehistoric subsistence strategies. Despite marked improvements in recovery methods, botanical remains from archaeological contexts only rarely are suitable for the quantitative reconstruction of past subsistence practices. Similarly, the effects of modern land use patterns have generally destroyed evidence of Hohokam fields where crops were grown under irrigation, thereby blocking this approach for assessing agricultural productivity. An alternative is to carry out research into the potential yield of the wild and cultivated resources known to have been utilized prehistorically. The preliminary results of such research on the yield of three species of wild resources presented earlier (Table 1), serve as an example. However, this is only a starting point. Many more species need to be considered, and the nature of variability in yield needs to be closely examined as well. The goal should be to secure adequate data so as to be able to model the amount of labor (energy) expenditure by humans and the subsequent yield of energy and nutrition to humans of various strategies of resource exploitation. Hypotheses developed from such work could then be tested against independent archaeological data.

In light of the above research possibilities, the preliminary nature of the present study hardly needs to be emphasized. However, the prospects of achieving an understanding of Hohokam subsistence are promising. Small areal studies, such as the CONOCO project, and much larger areal studies (Canouts, 1975; Debowski and others, 1976) are beginning to offset the longstanding focus of Hohokam archaeology on single sites. And slowly, studies directed toward the understanding of prehistoric behavior are being implemented. These trends are promising.

ACKNOWLEDGMENTS

Funding for this research was provided by the Continental Oil Company. Gordon L. Fritz, Michael B. Schiffer, and David R. Wilcox provided constructive comments on earlier drafts of this paper. Linda L. Mayro and Charles Sternberg drafted the figures.

REFERENCES

Ayres, J. E. (1971) Proposed archaeological excavations within CONOCO's Flor project area near Florence, Arizona. *Arizona State Museum Archaeological Series* 4.
Bayham, F. E. (1976) Appendix II: Lithics. In Desert resources and Hohokam subsistence: The CONOCO Florence project, by W. H. Doelle, pp. 195–218. *Arizona State Museum Archaeological Series* 103.
Bean, L. J. and K. S. Saubel (1972) *Temalpakh: Cahuilla Indian Knowledge and Usage of Plants.* Malki Museum Press, Banning, California.
Bell, W. H. and E. F. Castetter (1937) Ethnobiological studies in the American Southwest V: The utilization of mesquite and screwbean by the aborigines in the American Southwest. *University of New Mexico Bulletin* 5(2).
Bohrer, V. L. (1970) Ethnobotanical aspects of Snaketown, a Hohokam village in southern Arizona. *American Antiquity* **35**, 413–30.

Bohrer, V. L., H. C. Cutler, and J. D. Sauer (1969) Carbonized plant remains from two Hohokam sites, Arizona BB:13:41 and Arizona BB:13:50. *The Kiva* 35, 1-10.

Brooks, D. (1975) An archaeological investigation of the Queen Creek floodway project. *Arizona State Museum Archaeological Series* 66.

Burrus, E. J., S.J. (Editor) (1971) Kino and Manje: Explorers of Sonora and Arizona. *Sources and Studies for the History of the Americas* 10. Jesuit Historical Institute, Rome and St. Louis.

Canouts, V. (1975) An archaeological survey of the Orme Reservoir. *Arizona State Museum Archaeological Series* 92.

Castetter, E. F. and W. H. Bell (1942) *Pima and Papago Indian Agriculture.* University of New Mexico Press, Albuquerque.

Castetter, E. F. and R. M. Underhill (1935) Ethnobiological studies in the American Southwest: II. The ethnobiology of the Papago Indians. *University of New Mexico Bulletin* 4.

Debowski, S. S., A. George, R. Goddard, and D. Mullon (1976) An archaeological survey of the Buttes Reservoir. *Arizona State Museum Archaeological Series* 93.

Doelle, W. H. (1975) Prehistoric resource exploitation within the CONOCO Florence project. *Arizona State Museum Archaeological Series* 62.

Doelle, W. H. (1976) Desert resources and Hohokam subsistence: The CONOCO Florence project. *Arizona State Museum Archaeological Series* 103.

Doyel, D. E. (1974) Excavations in the Escalante ruin group, southern Arizona. *Arizona State Museum Archaeological Series* 37.

Evanari, M., L. Shana, and N. Tadmor (1970) *The Negev: The Challenge of a Desert.* Harvard University Press, Cambridge.

Felger, R. S. (n.d.) Mesquite in southwestern Indian cultures. In *A Tree in Perspective: Prosopis in Desert Shrub Ecosystems,* edited by B. Simpson. Dowden, Hutchinson, and Ross, Stroudsburg, Pennsylvania (In press).

Felger, R. S. and M. B. Moser (1971) Seri use of mesquite (*Prosopis Glandulosa var Torreyana*). *The Kiva* 37, 53-60.

Felger, R. S. and G. P. Nabhan (1976) Deceptive barrenness. *Ceres* 9, 34-9.

Fewkes, J. W. (1912) Casa Grande, Arizona. *Twenty-eighth Annual Report of the Bureau of American Ethnology,* pp. 25-179. Smithsonian Institution, Washington, D.C.

Fritts, H. (1965) Tree-ring evidence for climatic changes in western North America. *Monthly Weather Review* 93, 421-443.

Gasser, R. F. (1976) Hohokam subsistence: A 2000 year continuum in the indigenous exploitation of the lower Sonoran Desert. *Archaeological Report* 11, USDA Forest Service, Southwestern Region, Albuquerque.

Gladwin, H. S., E. W. Haury, E. B. Sayles, and N. Gladwin (1937) Excavations at Snaketown: I. Material culture. *Medallion Papers* 25.

Goodyear, A. C. (1975) Hecla II and III: An interpretive study of archaeological remains from the Lakeshore project, Papago Reservation, south central Arizona. *Arizona State University Anthropological Research Paper* 9.

Grady, M., S. Kemrer, S. Schultz, and W. Dodge (1973) An archaeological survey of the Salt-Gila aqueduct. *Arizona State Museum Archaeological Series* 23.

Haury, E. W. (1945) The excavation of Los Muertos and neighboring ruins in the Salt River Valley, southern Arizona. *Papers of the Peabody Museum of Archaeology and Ethnology* 24.

Haury, E. W. (1976) *The Hohokam. Desert farmers and craftsmen. Excavations at Snaketown, 1964-1965.* The University of Arizona Press, Tucson.

Hayden, J. D. (1969) Gyratory crushers of the Sierra Pinacate, Sonora. *American Antiquity* 34, 154-61.

Herskovits, R. M. (n.d.) Arizona U:9:46: A dual component Hohokam site in Tempe, Arizona. Manuscript, Arizona State Museum, Tucson.

Jernigan, E. W. (1976) Ariz. U:15:36—A possible rock alignment anthropomorph. In Desert resources and Hohokam subsistence: The CONOCO Florence project, by W. H. Doelle, pp. 137–41. *Arizona State Museum Archaeological Series* 103.

Martin, P. S. (1963) *The Last 10,000 Years.* The University of Arizona Press, Tucson.

Masse, W. B. (1976) The Hohokam expressway project: A study of prehistoric irrigation in the Salt River Valley, Arizona. Arizona State Museum, Tucson.

Masse, W. B. (n.d.) The Peppersauce Wash project: Excavations at three multicomponent sites in the San Pedro Valley, Arizona. Manuscript, Arizona State Museum, Tucson.

Matthews, W., J. L. Wortman, and J. S. Billings (1893) Human bones of the Hemenway collection in the United States Army Medical Museum. *The Miscellaneous Documents of the Senate of the United States for the First Session of the Fifty-second Congress* Vol. 6, Seventh Memoir.

Midvale, F. (1965) Prehistoric irrigation of the Casa Grande ruins area. *The Kiva* 30, 82–6.

Nabhan, G. P. and R. S. Felger (n.d.) The ecology and ethnohistory of Teparies *(Phaseolus acutifolius)* in southwestern North America. *Economic Botany* (In press).

Raab, M. L. (1973) AZ AA:5:2: A prehistoric cactus camp in Papagueria. *Journal of the Arizona Academy of Science* 8, 116–8.

Ross, W. (1941) Present day dietary habits of the Papago Indians. Unpublished M.A. Thesis, University of Arizona, Tucson.

Russell, F. (1908) The Pima Indians. *Twenty-sixth Annual Report of the Bureau of American Ethnology, 1904–1905*, pp 3–390. Smithsonian Institution, Washington, D.C.

Schiffer, M. B. (1972) Archaeological context and systemic context. *American Antiquity* 37, 156–65.

Schoenwetter, J. (1970) Archaeological pollen studies of the Colorado Plateau. *American Antiquity* 35, 35–48.

Shaw, A. M. (1974) *A Pima Past.* The University of Arizona Press, Tucson.

Spier, L. (1933) *Yuman Tribes of the Gila River.* University of Chicago Press, Chicago.

Thomas, D. H. (1975) Nonsite sampling in archaeology: Up the creek without a site? In *Sampling in Archaeology*, edited by J. W. Mueller, pp. 61–81. The University of Arizona Press, Tucson.

Turney, O. A. (1924) *The Land of the Stone Hoe.* Arizona Republican Print Shop, Phoenix.

Turney, O. A. (1929) *Prehistoric irrigation in Arizona.* Arizona State Historian, 1929, Phoenix.

Van Devender, T. H. (1973) Late Pleistocene plants and animals of the Sonoran Desert: A survey of ancient packrat middens in southwestern Arizona. Ph.D. dissertation, The University of Arizona, Tucson.

Windmiller, R. (1972) Archaeological salvage excavations at two drilling sites within CONOCO's Flor project area near Florence, Arizona. *Arizona State Museum Archaeological Series* 8.

Wood, D. (1972) Archaeological reconnaissance of the Gila River Indian Reservation: Second action year (phase III). *Arizona State Museum Archaeological Series* 16.

Wood, D. (n.d.) Introduction to Gila River Indian Reservation grid pattern field systems. Manuscript, Arizona State Museum Library, Tucson.

Woodbury, R. B. (1960) The Hohokam canals at Pueblo Grande, Arizona. *American Antiquity* 26, 267–70.

Woodbury, R. B. (1961) A reappraisal of Hohokam irrigation. *American Anthropologist* 63, 550–60.

Index